Trailing the Longhorns

TRAILING THE LONGHORNS

A CENTURY LATER

Text and photographs by
SUE FLANAGAN
Foreword by WAYNE GARD

MADRONA PRESS, INC. / AUSTIN, TEXAS

Frontispiece

RASCALITY OF THE RIO GRANDE. *On the devious river between Texas and Mexico, wild Longhorns grew and great cattle trails began, blending into regional romance and strife. Century-worn cow paths still lace both banks near the Rio Grande's mouth. After 1836, land north to the Nueces gave contentious birth to a raider called a "cowboy."*

To Catherine McDowell

whose interest in this work began with mine,
and whose immeasurable help in the roundup
continued until the last photo, line, and
Longhorn were bedded down.

Foreword

IN THE TEXT OF THIS BOOK, as in her *Sam Houston's Texas*, Sue Flanagan has not been content to rehash the works of earlier writers. Her historical research has been admirably thorough, and she has come up with many interesting details not readily found in accounts by others. Wisely, she has avoided being misled by any of the erroneous accounts and maps in this field. She has contributed substantially to new knowledge on the effect that the fever tick and Texas fever had on the cattle industry.

Yet the attention of most readers will be focused on her photographs. They are superb by any standard. In following the great cattle trails with her camera, she has known what to look for and has had the patience and perseverance to find surviving reminders of events that took place a century ago. Here are the rolling prairies, the river crossings, the mountain passes. Here are homes of frontier drovers, forts and rock formations that marked the trails, and glimpses of rowdy cow towns.

Those amateurs who pride themselves on the snapshots they take can appreciate Sue Flanagan's superior professional artistry. She knows where to place her camera and is expert in knowing what to include in a picture and what to leave out. She obtains the right lighting, makes use of clouds and evening glow, and captures the play of sun and shadow. She gives depth to her landscapes and enables the reader to imagine that he is there on the spot, viewing each scene.

Fortunately, there still are Longhorn cattle to be photographed. A number of present-day ranchmen raise a few Longhorns on the side to keep this historic breed alive.

Sue Flanagan gained much in 1966 by going along on the symbolic Longhorn drive to Dodge City, a year ahead of the centennial celebration of the opening of the Chisholm Trail. This trek, which called attention to the vast post-Civil War trailing movement, enabled her to obtain pictures of Longhorns in action.

If the horns of these present-day cattle do not look quite like those mounted in some Texas homes, museums, and places of business, that does not mean that the size and shape of the horns has changed much. Many of the horns now on display came not from Texas ranges but from Africa. They have been soaked and stretched to give them a wider span, and some have been expanded further by having the space between them broadened in the mounting.

Horns of the early Texas cattle varied in shape; but most of them, instead of going almost straight out, as in many of those now mounted, went out and then up, as in the pictures shown in this book. Thus they were more useful for defense, because, when the cow lowered her head, the horns pointed forward instead of to the sides.

The ground that the Longhorns trod is pictured here in its many faces. There are succulent grasses, sometimes with spring flowers. There are sage and chaparral, green prickly pear, and gnarled branches of mesquite with waving fronds. Rising higher in places are cedar brakes and live-oak mottes. Occasionally, the sameness of the prairies is broken by buttes, mountains, or canyons.

The rivers, with their shifting, perilous sands and their banks fringed with cottonwoods and other trees, are clearly depicted. Shown are the treacherous Pecos that drovers from Palo Pinto and the Concho encountered in trailing to New Mexico, and a succession of streams crossed by herds headed north. Even the Rio Grande had to be forded or swum by cattle bought or stolen in Mexico. Then came the usually manageable Nueces, the muddy Brazos, the Trinity, the big and often overflowing Red, the Washita, the Canadian, the Cimarron, and the Arkansas. For those who went beyond Kansas, there were the wide but shallow Powder and finally the scenic Yellowstone.

Sue Flanagan has pictured also the battered chuck wagon, the lonely graves of fallen trail hands, and the stone jails of the cow towns that helped the more ebullient to get over their Saturday night sprees. She depicts, too, the barbed wire that spelled the doom of trailing—even on those woodless Kansas prairies where fenceposts had to be cut from stone.

Some still assume that railroads ended the long-distance trailing of Texas cattle, yet the knockout blow came instead from barbed wire fences, with Texas fever a major contributing factor. From 1873 Texas had rail lines to St. Louis and Chicago, but heavy trailing continued until 1886. The railroads at first had equipment to handle only a fraction of the cattle. Too, their rates were so much higher than the cost of trailing that many drovers continued to take their herds afoot.

Only when fences of barbed wire were stretched across the old routes did the trailing cease and grass begin to cover the hoofprints. The barbs, which some cowmen called an invention of the devil, had ended a romantic era, whose sites, relics, and other vestiges Sue Flanagan has so faithfully pictured here.

WAYNE GARD
Dallas

Preface

THE SUSTAINED GLAMOR attached to the great cattle trails yet defies explanation. A century of voluminous writing, analysis, and portrayal has left the mirage largely intact, and as appealing to the mind today as it was to men who moved Texas Longhorns to Dodge City and beyond.

By their own admission, the word "freedom" came closest to defining the call heard by those who followed the trail. Because the rigors of the trade required youth, and because the period of cattle trailing was brief, participants had time to reflect. As old men they were pleased to read that history had credited them with the spread of ranching to the Great and High Plains, and with the economic recovery of post-Civil War Texas. But they hotly contested suggestions that the enforced routine of eighteen-to-twenty-four-hour days in the saddle and adamantly rigid rules of trail bosses had—in any way—limited their freedom.

It was understood that there would be no drinking on the trail. No gambling, said Charles Goodnight, outlawing even a casual game around the campfire. None of these and "no cursing in our presence," insisted the wide-ranging Snyder Brothers.

The trail drivers looked back on body lice, boots iced to the stirrups, and fever from sun and wind as conditions that tested their timbre. Pitting themselves against unruly cattle and the worst of nature's violence was sheer adventure in self-reliance, and few made money in the process. The trail was as much a spirit as a pathway.

Only two of the almost three hundred veteran hands who put their memoirs into a book in 1925 were disenchanted with their days on the trail. The overwhelming majority agreed with Sam Garner as he laid his finger on a major element of the magic. "Old as I am," he wrote at seventy-three, "I would undertake to go through it all again if I knew where there was a country like this was in those good old days."

Since white men first saw "country like this was," they have attempted to describe its effect upon them. Albert Pike's record of a journey to the prairie in 1832 is among the most eloquent examples:

—Its sublimity arises from its unbounded extent, its barren monotony and desolation, its still, unmoved, calm, stern, almost self-confident grandeur, its strange power of deception. its want of echo, in fine, its power of throwing a man back upon himself and giving him a feeling of lone helplessness, strangely mingled at the same time with a feeling of liberty and freedom from restraint.

To several generations of Americans now who never have known land without fences, enormous islands of the Western Plains devoted to grazing still impart this romance of distance. Spindly wired posts and silhouetted windmills are but relative measurements stressing the size of the land that dwarfs them. And a trip to the prairie by car, book, or television screen affords "freedom from restraint" in a therapeutic escape from the ravages of commuting and congested living.

Hopefully, this offering, which follows the country of the trails in contemporary photographs, captures something of the lasting spell cast by a land that is different from the drover days, and yet the same. Hopefully, too, it illustrates in some measure the forces of change that even then were at work to harness this land. It goes with the trail in touching almost every frontier process on the Plains and, in so doing, dwells more on the economic import of the movement and its problems than on cowboy celebrations at the trail's end.

The mistaken idea that any of the trails was a single highway is dispersed quickly when one takes even a cursory glance at information available on the subject. In the formidable mountains of related material, he finds that the course of a trail changed almost annually. New cattle markets developed, settlements and railheads advanced—and most of all —states in the path of the trails enforced increasingly stringent quarantines that banned from their borders the fever-bearing Texas herds.

One discovers also how seasons of extreme drouth, or heavy traffic on the trail, could move its course thirty to forty miles to either side in any given year. The whole theory of trailing revolved around the cow's capacity to make meat as she meandered to market—an impossible dream if the trail area was bare of grass.

Little of the early writing about the trails was done by actual drovers. Journalists and promoters were the authors, flocking to explore this new and novel way of life. Confusion of the role played by trader Jesse Chisholm with that of cattleman John Chisum is but one case of jumbled facts perpetuated by these writers.

In the main, many years had passed when the trail drivers themselves got around to penning their accounts. Then, saturated with previous stories, their recollections often were a blend of firsthand experience with the color of fiction and hearsay. Since the Chisholm Trail was the one most glorified by literature and song, a number of these old waddies decided that was the trail they drove, although the route they mentioned did not approximate the Chisholm course.

While such factors make cattle-trail research and retracing difficult, the effort is worthwhile to those who love the feel of pristine land and the lore of hoof and horn. The trails generally avoided settlements, and few large cities have grown up along the routes to cover them with concrete.

SUE FLANAGAN

Acknowledgments

THE IDEA FOR THIS BOOK was conceived in 1965, when rereading an old article on the cattle trails focused my attention on a date. The next year, 1966, would mark the centennial of the beginning of these famous Long-horn routes that gave birth to modern ranching and immortality to the cowboy.

With an itchy shutter finger caressing my camera, I wondered how the country traversed by the trails looked a century later. Would recording such a glimpse help tell the seldom-stressed story of the trails' national and international import? Would it add insight into the drover's work, which has taken a back seat to the smoke of his six-gun? Would it give another clue to the perennial popularity of the trail theme?

Houston attorney and author Dillon Anderson encouraged me to commit my wonderings to outline. With this written proposal in hand, he secured a generous grant for the project from Mrs. Jack Hutchins of Houston and the Raymond Dickson Foundation. Through the efforts of R. Henderson Shuffler, then director of The University of Texas Texana Program, this grant was administered by the university.

From that point, an army of interested persons in twelve states helped guide this effort. After more than twenty thousand miles of travel, I grate-fully remember each gift of time and knowledge from the two hundred persons listed in the bibliography under "Interviews and Correspondence." Unfortunately, space allows special mention of only a few.

The long months of research were shortened appreciably by Miss Catherine McDowell, librarian of the Daughters of the Republic of Texas Library at the Alamo, in San Antonio. Ranch-born and -oriented, she kept this project constantly in mind in her daily work, suggesting reliable standard sources and discovering choice bits of fresh fodder for this grist of the trails.

The leading authorities on the Goodnight and Chisholm Trails—authors J. Evetts Haley and Wayne Gard, respectively—shared unstintingly of their historical resources. Haley took me into Palo Duro Canyon and pointed out significant places in the genesis of Texas Panhandle ranch-ing—places that Charles Goodnight had shown him.

In far South Texas, A. A. Champion and Joe Vivier of Brownsville resur-rected early maps that indicated the storied cattle routes there near the mouth of the Rio Grande. The Vivier-Champion team, armed with inter-views of other lifetime residents on both sides of the river, led me to old crossings used by trail cattle coming in from Mexico.

Up near Laredo, Elvie Turner of the John Mecom Ranch helped me capture in pictures the only sizable herd of wild horses in Texas. For two days before they were sighted, he drove a pickup over the ranch while I peered through binoculars and balanced a Rolleiflex on my lap.

The patience of John Cypher at the King Ranch deserves singular attention. Without a drum of the fingers, he stood by for hours while I waited out the right clouds for photographic emphasis of that mammoth spread.

A dust-stormy day on the Pecos in West Texas with Charles Stroder, Fred Wilkinson, and Mrs. J. L. Dameron of Crane produced the pictures of Horsehead Crossing and Castle Gap. Historian Stroder planned the trip and secured permission to enter land overlooking the gap. A durable Dodge carryall was ideal for the ride over rough country, and the pleasurable company more than compensated for the vehicle's lack of springs.

At the renowned Chisholm Trail crossing of Red River Station, lawyer Glenn O. Wilson of Nocona, Texas, offered valuable assistance. Wilson is a native of the station and has made the study of its region a lifetime endeavor. On the other side of the river, Judge Otis James of Waurika, Oklahoma, guided me to several places on the trail in its first forty miles north of the Red.

Also in Oklahoma, at Geary, author-newsman Kent Ruth pointed me toward Jesse Chisholm's grave at the Left Hand Spring. Oklahoma City engineer James Cloud allowed me use of his Chisholm Trail survey—a new treatise that shows the progressive westward movement of the trail's main course.

In Kansas, Harvard Goodrich, manager of Abilene's cowtown attraction, introduced me to Glen French, who saw the light of day along the trail approaches to that settlement. He accompanied me some forty miles south of town and indicated still-visible Chisholm ruts and a sudden box canyon, where drovers always found water, and a supply of wood from sheltered timber on an otherwise treeless plain.

George Henrichs, curator of Dodge's City's Boot Hill and Front Street, also was a good historian. For photos he rounded up authentic appointments of the original Long Branch Saloon, and apprised me of remaining Dodge structures associated with the trail.

Mr. and Mrs. Will Spindler of Gordon, Nebraska, drove with me to Pine Ridge Reservation in South Dakota, where she was born and he taught for many years. Their acquaintance with Sioux history and with this area, which was a prime market for trail beef, was extremely helpful.

In locating material on John Wesley Iliff, Mrs. Katherine Halverson of the Wyoming State Archives and History Department at Cheyenne rendered yeoman service. Besides sharing manuscripts and documents, she put me in touch with Mrs. Dean Prosser, Jr., who with her husband owned the ranch south of town that once was an Iliff cow camp. After a tour of the ranch, Mrs. Prosser granted this Texas stranger a long loan of several rare books.

Snowbound at Torrington, Wyoming, in an early September storm, I was able the second day to make a short drive up the Platte River to Fort Laramie. Here Ranger-historian Robert A. Murray dug deep into his files for trail and beef bonanza material connected with this important supply post. He piloted me to points in the Rawhide Valley, along the Texas Trail, and for many months continued to forward additional information.

In Colorado I became greatly indebted to Dr. Harry Kelsey, then the state historian, for many contacts. Among them was Phil K. Hudspeth of

Pueblo, owner of the old Goodnight Ranch near that city. We spent a day going over this area, which Goodnight wisely had chosen as a swing station for his trail cattle.

Farther south, at Trinidad, two visits with the Baca House Museum director, Arthur R. Mitchell, were highly productive. On the second trip he was ready with maps and local cowmen to locate Charles Goodnight's homestead claim astride his trail on the Apishapa River. So nearly did we pinpoint this claim as described in Las Animas County records that Mitchell said he expected "Old Charlie to jump out from behind a cedar bush and tell us we were trespassing."

Artist Sidney Redfield of Roswell, New Mexico, who made frequent painting trips to the mountains, was indicated by his townsmen as the only man who could locate Bosque Grande, the first Goodnight and Loving headquarters. Redfield loaded me, the paints, and a lunch into his truck early one morning and headed for the Bosque. The thirty-five-mile trip over nearly impassable terrain required about three and one-half hours each way.

Back in Texas, Dallas attorney Joe McCracken, III, met me in Weatherford for a firsthand look at Oliver Loving's home country and his grave. McCracken, a Loving descendant, also arranged a difficult picture set-up of two rings Loving had made for his daughters from gold received for trail cattle. A relative of McCracken took one of the rings from Dallas to Abilene, Texas, where I photographed it beside its counterpart in the home of another Loving descendant.

On the Western Trail north of Vernon, Texas, ranchman Taylor Dabney, State Senator Jack Hightower, and then Vernon Chamber of Commerce Manager Joe Meador tramped the Red River Valley with me and bore the camera equipment. We concentrated on the area around Doan's Store and Crossing.

Another memorable trip to Doan's was made with the 1966 Longhorn Centennial Trail Drive on a horse named "Whiskey," borrowed from Charles Schreiner, III. Schreiner is the founder of the Texas Longhorn Breeders Association of America and, on several jaunts to his ranch near Kerrville, I have made pictures of his cattle.

Graves Peeler, another Longhorn breeder near Pleasanton, drove me over his brush-country ranch to snap antlered cattle in their legendary habitat. And Edwin Dow, who raises them near Fort Worth at his ranch located squarely on the old Chisholm Trail, extended me the same privilege.

Dr. R. D. Turk's contribution should be noted, too. This former head of Texas A & M University's Department of Veterinary Parasitology gave me a three-day cram course on the cattle tick—that mighty mite that dwelled on Longhorns, caused Texas fever, and cost billions of dollars to eradicate.

At my home town of San Angelo, Texas, Lloyd D. Witter made his splendid darkroom available to me for the processing of hundreds of photos taken in the course of this study. Lastly, and most importantly, the encouragement of my parents, Mr. and Mrs. J. T. Flanagan, and their understanding of my neglect of them during the preparation of these pages, have made this work possible.

Contents

Photographs

xviii

MAPS

Trailing the Longhorns

'THAT COW OUT THERE.' *A favorite of cowman tale-teller Shanghai Pierce, this phrase sums up the purpose of the cowboy and the ranch and bespeaks early methods of handling cattle. Wily Longhorns were wrested one by one out of the brush, and on the trail they moved as a long line of individuals, not as a herd. In range parlance all cattle were "cows." By 1865 they outnumbered Texans nine to one.*

'That Cow Out There'

No PERIOD IN AMERICAN HISTORY has maintained a stronger hold on world imagination than the brief twenty years following the Civil War, when national progress dammed up by the conflict burst suddenly upon the Plains. Pressures of the four-year delay in uniting East and West, compounded by the urgency to rebuild a workable North-South economy, forced immediate action over orderly development. The historical approach to this era, said a noted student of the times, "cannot be monographic; too much was happening at once."[1]

Also, the happenings were in the only area of the United States mainland that had escaped the shackles of civilization as the nation expanded westward. "The West," to the American people, lay beyond the settlement line more as a challenge than a direction. With the Pacific Coast fairly well populated after 1865, "the West" became the midcontinent that had resisted white men for three centuries. This region between the Missouri River and Rocky Mountains, the Canadian border and the Red River of Texas, was romanticized as the last frontier, where all American frontier experiences were rolled into one.

Extending the rails, subduing the Indians, and slaughtering the buffalo were but a few of the era's exciting and interdependent movements paving the way for settlement. Visiting eastern journalists gave flamboyant height to the actions which, indeed, had not occurred in earlier frontier processes. Eastern manufacturers, meanwhile, responded with new products designed specifically to subdue this obstinate and uncommon land.

Yet from the many-faceted, moving scene, only the cattle industry arose immortal, becoming the single American enterprise of any period to evoke a literature, a mythology, and a graphic symbolism.[2] For speed of expansion there is perhaps no American parallel to the raising of range cattle. The method, begun in pre-Civil War South Texas, spread in the decade after 1866 over western Texas and large parts of eleven other present states: Oklahoma, Kansas, Nebraska, North and South Dakota, Montana, Wyoming, Nevada, Utah, Colorado, and New Mexico.

The industry's dramatic climax came with the great Longhorn trails, which gave birth to the modern cowboy, and rise to the open range —the underpinnings of this whole cattle kingdom.

The trails, those long stretches of cowhide from Mexico to Canada, were the first vertical spans of the Plains. Their reign of less than a generation was long enough to create an unshakable image of freedom and individualism flourishing in a vastness where space still was an earth word. Both the image and the western landscape have grown more appealing as modern living has become more regulated and congested. Offspring of the trails today are giant examples. The cowboy has been canonized as the nation's number one folk hero, and more romance still centers around ranching than attends any other occupation.[3]

The factual evolution of range popularity is traceable only to about 1890, when a nation old enough to long for the days of its youth gave way to nostalgia and idealized the story. Census figures that year held the startling disclosure that the frontier was gone—vanished in a decade! All the continental United States reported population enough to be in a later stage of development. Frederick Jackson Turner frightened thinkers of the day with his theory that the American intellect owed its striking characteristics to a continuing frontier: "Dominant individualism, inventiveness of mind and the exuberance which comes from freedom" were

3

among the frontier traits and were called out elsewhere because the frontier existed. Would these, too, pass away?[4] Americans said "no."

The range and the cowboy—the last frontier and the last frontiersman—had reached their zenith at the proper time to receive the mantle of national affection, descending to keep their spirit alive.

Theodore Roosevelt was setting the stage in 1888, when he mourned that the open range could hardly outlast the century. "The great free ranches," he said, "with their barbarous, picturesque, and curiously fascinating surroundings . . . must pass away before the onward march of our people; and we who have felt the charm of the life, and have exulted in its abounding vigor and its bold restless freedom . . . must also feel real sorrow that those who come after us are not to see . . . what is perhaps the pleasantest, healthiest, and most exciting phase of American existence."[5]

The dime novel already had espoused the cowboy when a British traveler described him in 1887: "The cowboy has at the present time become a personage; nay, more, he is rapidly becoming a mythical one. Distance is doing for him what lapse of time did for the heroes of antiquity . . . his genuine qualities are lost in fantastic tales of impossible daring. . . . Every member of his class is pictured as a kind of Buffalo Bill . . . who makes the world to resound with bluster and braggadocio."[6]

The term "cowboy" had an almost traitorous American meaning at its Revolutionary War inception, applying to cowbell-tinkling tories who lured milch-cow-seeking patriots into New York bushes. Half a century later and two thousand miles away, "cowboys" after the Texas Revolution in 1836 were bands of border cattle thieves and raiders ruthlessly preying on ranchers of Mexican descent. Actions of these ruffians brought forty years of bandit revenge and reprisal to the Texas side of the Rio Grande. The remembered cowboy, however, is a product of the post-Civil War cattle trails, and he rode over the divide into legend even in his own day. On the trail he won his spurs for quick-thinking heroism, and at the trail's end his infamous reputation for cowtown carousing.[7]

Often forgotten or overshadowed by his glamor is the commodity that gave him prominence: Texas Longhorn cattle. Fierce, lean-flanked, slab-sided, and countless, the critters were inspiring examples of freedom fighters. Dislodging three a day from the bristling defense of their brush country home was a good day's work for any man. As one writer declared, "The cranky, armored Longhorn made heroes out of cowboys. . . . A tamer breed of cattle would never have given rise to the cowhand's glory."[8]

In fact, the cowboy story is Texas based because a system of raising already-storied cattle had evolved there more than because the cowboy was a native son.[9] In fiction, not so. Even after the trails spread both cattle and system through the High Plains, where both were altered and the lasting open range picture distilled, the belief persisted that any cowboy's first profession was being a native Texan.[10]

An 1880 *Scribner's* article on the abundance of cowboys in Dodge City reflected the early trend: "Everywhere stared and shown the Lone Star of Texas—for the cowboy, wherever he may wander, and however he may change, never forgets to be a Texan, and . . . in some way recognize the emblem of his native state."[11]

The first crop of enshrined cowboys, nonetheless, did not all wear the native label. They —the estimated 35,000 men who went up the trails during the Longhorn exodus—apparently were 40 and perhaps 50 percent Texans made, not born. About one-quarter hailed from other parts of the South, over 10 percent from the North, and more than 5 percent from Europe. Approximately one-third were Negroes and Mexicans.

About one hundred of the largest drovers, with their connections, are credited with moving seventy-five percent of all cattle driven to Northern markets. A surprising number of these leaders were of Northern origin. Charles Goodnight from Illinois and Oliver Loving from Kentucky were the duo who extended the first major trail for Texas cattle after the fraternal war. In Texas in 1853, New York-born Richard King began ranching as it is known today, soon taking as his partner Mifflin Kene-

HOME ON THE OPEN RANGE. *In 1883, a pale, weak-eyed Harvard graduate came to hunt buffalo in Dakota's Badlands. Captivated by the country and its cattle future, he quickly bought free-range improvements of the Maltese Cross Ranch south of Medora, North Dakota. His steep-roofed, story-and-a-half ranch house, built partly of railroad pilings, later was moved to town. He lost money here but found "abounding vigor and bold, restless freedom." His name was Theodore Roosevelt.*

dy, a Pennsylvanian. Other big operators included John T. Lytle, also a Pennsylvania native, and J. O. Dewees, an Indiana emigrant.[12]

The reason for the cowboy and his methods had been building since the second voyage of Columbus in 1493, when he brought a few Andalusian and Castillian cattle along with Arabian-barb horses to the West Indies. Horses in 1519 and calves in 1521 made their debut on the North American mainland, landing in New Spain at Veracruz. Hernando Cortés, conqueror of Mexico, reportedly used the first cattle brand on this continent, marking seven calves—tradition says—with three Christian crosses.[13]

In any event, the progeny seemed blessed to increase. In Mexico by 1537, Spain had established the *mesta*, a stockmen's association to deal with mounting numbers of livestock. The *mesta* was an integral part of colonial administration, and governed, among other things, cattle branding and brand registration. The system had worked well in Spain since the thirteenth century.[14]

Horses also had flourished in a climate and land similar to their native habitat. Conquistadores were raising fancy equestrian stock before the Indians of southern Mexico were subjugated. Greatly expanded activity on Mexico's open ranges required more manpower, and Indians were mounted as cow-workers. They were the vaqueros from whom the cowboy would learn his trade.

Coronado easily collected fifteen hundred horses and five hundred cattle for his journey into the Southwest in 1540. His cattle were the first to cross present Texas, but they were marked for conquistador steaks and few, if any, escaped. Initial planting of cattle seed stock in Texas came in 1690, when two hundred head were taken to a hastily constructed mission in eastern Texas. Within twenty-five years, thousands of cattle and horses were reported in the vicinity.[15]

In 1716, Spain began more permanent types of missions in eastern Texas. In the next forty years, some twenty formal compounds were built, including a number in South Texas. Settlements grew up around these installations, where friars taught stock raising, as well as Christianity, to Indian neophytes. The missions became the real foundation of the Texas cattle industry. Community-mission roundups were held twice a year, and by the 1770's, cattle were the principal source of wealth, not only to the church but to all of Spanish Texas. Mission Espíritu Santo, near present Goliad, claimed forty thousand branded and unbranded cattle, nearby Mission Rosario thirty thousand.[16]

Trail driving was pioneered at the missions with Louisiana, under Spain from 1763 to 1800, receiving herds as large as two thousand head from South Texas mission ranges.[17] The South Texas area also had developed into a reservoir for wild horses, whose ancestors had escaped from early Spanish expeditions. Spaniards settling along the Rio Grande in 1747 noted a few wild horses on the Texas side, but by 1777 the numbers astounded travelers. On early nineteenth century maps, land from the Nueces to the Rio Grande was marked "Wild Horse Desert," or simply "Vast Herds of Wild Horses."[18]

As Spanish power waned, mission activity contracted, roughly, to within a one-hundred-mile radius of San Antonio. Most of the missions were secularized in the 1790's and their cattle fell prey to Indian depredation or ran completely wild. The progeny of escaped mission stock were the feral cattle south of San Antonio that would be the major source of Texas beef for well over fifty years.[19]

When Anglo colonists came in 1821, they described "wild," "Spanish," or "mustang" cattle from Red River to the Rio Grande and from Louisiana to the Brazos headwaters. The animals seldom were seen in daylight and kept in small bunches, usually in thickets. Descendants of this kind eventually were called "Texas cattle" and, finally, "Longhorns."

Longhorns were primarily a mixture of two cattle types brought from Spain: black animals with small close-fitting horns set forward like the buffalo's, called Spanish or Moorish cattle; and an oxen type with broad, heavy horns, known as Mexican cattle. Milch cows and oxen coming in with American settlers had some effect on Longhorn bodies but failed to modify

MISSION RANCHING. *Mission Espíritu Santo, moved to present Goliad in 1749, had the largest ranch in Texas by the 1770's, ranging 40,000 cattle. Although conquistadores brought cattle seed stock to the present United States, the modern cattle industry owes its foundation to Spain's mission system.*

ON WILD HORSE DESERT. *Horses as a means of moving Longhorns were as vital as cows to cattle kingdom evolution. Escaped Spanish horses multiplied in such numbers that Texas below the Nueces River was labeled "Wild Horse Desert."* Mesteños *(wild ones) were "mustangs" to Texans who broke them as cow ponies. Some four hundred wild horses resembling the strong-legged, short-statured mustang yet range in the area, but are* galiceños, *brought from Yucatán several years ago.*

ARMED FOR FREEDOM. *Equipped with spirit and headgear to do battle for his liberty, the Longhorn made heroes out of cowboys successful in his capture. Frank Reaugh, who essayed the Longhorns in art and painted them from life, frequently saw men on foot treed by the ferocious beeves. "This would have happened more often," he said, "had there been more trees."*

FIRST ANGLO-TEXAN RANCH HOUSE. *Early travelers on the lower Texas-New Orleans road noted near Anahuac the home of J. T. White. Begun in 1827, "in advance of a tract of woodland," the cypress house has beaded siding, giant framing timbers, corner pilasters, and newel porchposts. A second story was added in 1852.*

their nature.[20] They remained extremely dangerous to a man unmounted.

Wild cattle had no yen for, and sometimes killed, domestic bovines that tried to join them. Longhorns native to southern Texas carried further insurance against new blood. Ticks, which immunized them at birth and resided on them thereafter, spelled death or devastation to pampered cattle crossing their path.

"The Longhorn became what he was with only a limited influence beyond Mexico," says his biographer, J. Frank Dobie. Cattle in Texas grew mightier and heavier-horned than their Mexican counterparts, largely because Americans began to select calves for breeding, as they had done with smaller farm herds. Spaniards and Mexicans castrated few animals, leaving for bulls any calves that would not make good steers.[21]

James Taylor White, though French, is credited with being the first American cattleman in Texas. He raised the black Spanish breed. Coming from Louisiana about 1819— before Texas was opened officially to settlement—White located near Galveston Bay. He was near the main route to New Orleans and trailed herds there in the 1830's. A visitor in 1831 wrote that White had about four thousand cattle, which three or four men drove "occasionally toward the house." The whole business of Texas cattle raising, he observed, was reduced as it was in the land of Canaan to letting them take care of themselves until the owner chose to claim tribute of their flesh, hide, and horns.[22]

Because many of the cattle had never felt a rope, and those claimed by large Mexican ranchos along the Rio Grande were not enclosed, accurate count was impossible. An 1830 estimate places the number in Texas at 100,000 —one-fifth American cattle and four-fifths Spanish-Mexican cattle.

Ranching was foreign to colonists arriving mainly from the agrarian South but, finding

9

that Spanish land grants for intent to ranch were ten times the acreage given for intent to farm, they all declared for ranching. Although cattle raising as a business received little attention until Texas won independence from Mexico, Texans depended on cattle almost as the Indians did on buffalo.

Besides supplying beef, tallow, rawhide, and leather, the bellowing natural resource was an accepted form of legal tender. As colonizer Stephen F. Austin pointed out, cows and calves could always be found, "but money was out of the question." By gentry understanding in the province of Texas, a cow and calf came to stand for ten dollars, and a settler's promise to deliver was scrawled on a piece of anything. The homemade currency, "cow paper," was circulated until someone decided to redeem the claim and collect the cattle.[23]

More cattle began to be harvested in the East Texas-Gulf Coast area in the late 1830's, the stock descended from that left by the Spaniards or from Louisiana herds of similar blood. Some raisers, like White, trailed overland to Louisiana markets, but rangy steers often were rounded up and sold for hide and tallow. Among the earliest businesses near today's Beaumont was a crude plant where cattle were slaughtered, tallow was rendered, hides were dried, and meat was dumped into the river. With no inhabitants along its banks to be offended by floating carcasses, the Neches River made "an admirable open sewer" where beef-fattened catfish were legion.[24]

Through the 1840's, several attempts were made to find markets and uses for the ever-increasing cattle. John Jay French, a Connecticut trader and manufacturer, came to the Neches in 1842. He saw shoe leather and jackets in the thriving herds and established himself where tanning oak was plentiful. With cowhides from nearby ranges and a fourteen-vat, one-horse-powered mill, French and his son turned out most of the shoes worn in eastern Texas for a time.

In the spring of 1843, Captain M. C. Houstoun brought from England an "extensive apparatus for packing beef according to a late invention." For the process in which saline solutions were injected into veins and arteries of slaughtered stock, the captain announced that he would erect a large beef export establishment at Houston. The newspaper *Morning Star* predicted an inexhaustible market for prairie cattle "which have hitherto been almost as useless for exportation as the wild buffalo."[25] During this time, another English beef-packing concern, Jones and Company at Liberty, Texas, was being supplied by James Taylor White.[26] These efforts were local and short-lived.

By far the most imaginative exploration into a general market for Texas cattle was the "Meat Biscuit," which Gail Borden, Jr., formu-

OFFICIAL 'COW PAPER.' *In money-scarce Mexican Texas a cow and a calf were accepted mediums of exchange and handwritten notes called "cow paper" substituted for currency. Small wonder that Texas as a republic carried on the cattle theme in her monetary system. This 1841 two-dollar bill—showing a rider racing after a horned steer—may be the first artist's conception of a cowboy.*

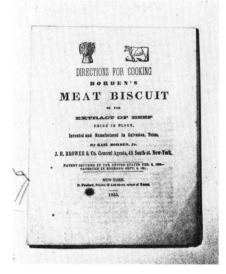

EARLY MARKETING ATTEMPT. *In 1855, Gail Borden, Jr., printed a combination prospectus and cookbook to push the sale of his Meat Biscuit. The hard, unsavory concentrate won international acclaim for nutrition, but no steady customers.*

lated in 1846. By boiling 120 pounds of beef down to 10, mixing flour with the extract and baking the substance, Borden arrived at a product that resembled a light-colored sugar cake. The inventors admitted that the item—made without salt or other condiment—was "insipid and without flavor"; but flavor could be added when the biscuit was pulverized, "diffused" in water, and boiled into soup. The nutritious stock also could be used for gravies and pies, and for making custard without milk.

A party of forty-niners tried Meat Biscuits on their desert trek to California, as did Dr. Elisha Kent Kane on his Arctic expedition. Many physicians and military officers recommended the biscuit highly. One captain bought fifteen hundred pounds for use on his steamer. Encouraged that large contracts were eminent, Borden built a plant at Galveston, "where prairies abounded in neat cattle at a price so low as to justify the manufacture of beef in concentrated form." When the Meat Biscuit won an award at London's 1851 International Exhibition, Borden secured agents there and in New York, New Bedford, Boston, and St. Louis. Cooking instructions were printed and widely circulated; yet the concentrate was not taken up by armies, navies, and hospitals.

After ten years of promoting and living-hand-to-mouth, Borden was forced to abandon the biscuit, but in the process he had discovered a way to condense milk in vacuum. With 1856 patents, he opened a Connecticut milk factory, which failed twice in two years. Finally, with

new backing and another plant, he gained wealth and fame when the Civil War brought great demand for his milk. Before his death in 1874, he authored his own epitaph: "I tried and failed, I tried again and again and succeeded."[27]

Borden's epitaph could summarize Texans' activity from statehood late in 1845 to the post-Civil War period as they sought again and again to link the growing cattle surplus to lucrative ends.

In 1846, Texas had almost 400,000 taxable cattle valued at less than $4 per head, and some 35,000 horses rendered at slightly more than $42 per head. By 1850, combined cattle and horse numbers on tax rolls were up 300,000, while the census estimate for the total was one million. The increase had taken place despite a number of spotty outlets.

The first northward cattle drive of record was made in 1846 by Edward Piper, who took 1,000 Longhorns to Ohio. Sporadically, other drovers followed. The New Orleans demand, while continuous, was not great, and swamp trailing was difficult. Heelflies bit the cattle until the enraged animals tore through the timber, often leaving their cocklebur-matted tails. By 1848, steamers could carry the beasts from Texas ports to New Orleans, but the volume was never large. A 900-pound steer would lose 100 to 125 pounds en route.[28] The Mexican War was a temporary boon, with American troops needing beef and horses. Texas mustangs by this time had reached their

11

numerical peak—about a million head, according to one source.[29]

In the decade following 1850, when prospectors flocked to California, probably 50,000 Texas cattle were driven to highly speculative markets on the Pacific Coast.[30] Beeves bringing $5 to $15 at home might net $25 to $150 in California to those who ran the risks and took the losses from desert and Apaches.[31]

By 1853, drives to Missouri and beyond no longer were novel, but two events of that year were destined to have vital effects on the nation's cattle future.

In June, three thousand Longhorns were turned back from western Missouri by hostile citizens who feared "Texas fever" would be communicated to their cattle. This was the first in a long series of protests against Texas cattle that would bring bloodshed, quarantines, and ultimately the most expensive and sustained eradication campaign ever made on a parasitic enemy of man.[32]

Texas fever—least romantic of the trail elements—was transmitted by a tick with which Longhorns were infested and to which they were largely immune. Thriving in other Southern States as well as in Texas, the tick was not known then to be the culprit; but the hideous malady he inflicted had appeared under various names for half a century. In 1796, a Pennsylvania outbreak was attributed to cattle driven in from South Carolina. Later, rare occurrences in the East of "dry murrain," "bloody murrain," "Spanish fever," or "splenetic fever" always were linked to apparently healthy cattle arriving from the south Atlantic or Gulf states.

Not until 1853 did similar accounts come from the Midwest, as more and more Texas cattle were driven toward Missouri. Examina-

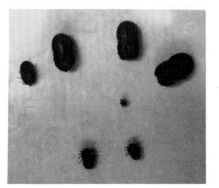

CATTLE TICKS. *Trails about to open were closed before* Boophilus annulatus, *the cattle tick infesting Longhorns, was known to cause "Texas fever." Quarantines against the disease diverted trails faster than fences or rails. Average tick life is three weeks. Females (top) attached to cattle, engorged, and dropped off to lay thousands of eggs and die. Minute larvae covered the next grazing cattle, molted to nymphs (center), then adults. Males (bottom) were small.*

SANTA GERTRUDIS CREEK. *Along this stream, only the second source of living water in more than a hundred miles north of the Rio Grande, ranching as a United States industry was born in 1853. Captain Richard King was the progenitor. The scene is directly behind the present ranch house, which is on the site of King's first large headquarters.*

tion of animals mortally stricken with the disease often revealed "not a single red blood disk."[33] In five to ten days all red corpuscles in a thousand-pound steer could be destroyed, the dead corpuscles enlarging the spleen, liver, and gall bladder and frequently blocking the kidneys.[34]

With fever sometimes 110 degrees, the cattle suffered frantic delirium, tossing their heads and cracking their horns. Others were too weak to do injury, or even to keep off flies. They pressed their heads against each other, neck muscles rigid on one side, relaxed on the other. They showed great debility and emaciation and would not feed, standing braced with spines arched on nearly paralyzed hind legs. Still others were unable to rise—heads drooping, eyes glassy, breathing rapid. Hot-based horns were cold. Death came to 90 percent of the acute and 10 percent of the chronic cases. With the great poverty of blood, survivors recovered slowly.

To Northern farmers who watched helplessly as their Durhams, Herefords, and Holsteins fell in the Longhorns' wake, the plague was "Texas fever." And Texas fever it historically remained, adding odium to the lanky bovines and to their drovers.[35]

Also in 1853, far-sighted Richard King turned his attention from steamboating on the Rio Grande to ranching on Wild Horse Desert. With his purchase of 15,000 acres on Santa Gertrudis Creek, he reached beyond the free, open ranges that were yet to bloom and set the more solid ownership pattern of present-day ranches. For the initial tract he paid $300, or less than two cents per acre. The next year, for $1,800, he added 53,000 acres. From the beginning, the King Ranch employed vaqueros and incorporated proven Mexican methods of handling large numbers of livestock. As the founder cut needless wastes from the system and steadily increased his holdings with clear-title land, ranching in the United States turned into an industry—there on the Santa Gertrudis.[36]

New York had a look at Longhorns in 1854, when Tom Candy Ponting unloaded 150 select head. The year before he had driven 700 Texas cattle to Illinois, wintered them, and trailed the best to Indiana, whence they were rail-shipped to the metropolis. While each animal brought about $80, trailing and shipping costs were $19 per head. New Yorkers across the board were unimpressed with the grass-fed horn-tanglers and by 1860 not more than 2,000 had made the distant journey.[37]

With mounting difficulties, trailing continued to Chicago and Missouri railheads at the rate of thirty thousand to sixty thousand head annually.[38] An 1855 outbreak of Texas fever had left scores of native cattle dead along the route. Enraged owners formed vigilance committees to stop upcoming herds. The Missouri legislature moved quickly to pass a quarantine law, but the anti-Texas fever measure, prohibiting "diseased" cattle from being driven into the state, unwittingly exempted the Texas breed. Longhorns, though tick-infested, were well cattle.

Little test was made of the quarantine in the next two years because the fever strangely subsided on its own. Then, in 1858, when an estimated 48,000 Longhorns were trudging through Missouri, the fever broke out in epidemic proportions—far worse than earlier onslaughts. Thousands of fine cattle perished in the shadow of Texas horns. Missouri farmers, strapped for finances, resorted to the more effective shotgun quarantine as legislation proved unenforceable.

To avoid open conflict, Texas drovers veered west of the Missouri line, only to find that eastern Kansas, also losing cattle to the plague, was up in arms. The Kansas territorial legislature in 1859 made Longhorn trailing illegal in four eastern counties from June to November—the only time of feasible weather to make the drives.[39]

The marketing outlook for Texas cattle thus was bleak in 1860 as a more stringent quarantine, the coming Civil War, ground North-South commerce to a halt. The various attempts to find a steady and profitable outlet had come to naught; the trailing experiment largely had failed.

Assessed cattle, which had jumped from 750,000 in 1855 to 3.5 million head, shortly were to be left untended while their keepers fought two foes.[40] By 1861, able-bodied Texans

SEA OF HORNS. *Untended during the Civil War, Texas cattle multiplied and developed their legendary characteristics. With no market at home, an estimated five million Longhorns overran the state by 1866. Then destitute Confederate veterans began gathering herds for northward drives. The movement was a gamble, but the only chance for financial rebirth.*

either marched with Southern armies or rode with the Frontier Regiment to protect the settlement line that was receding as Indian marauders took advantage of the national preoccupation. A few stockmen were exempted to supply beef to the Confederacy, but practically no cattle left the state after New Orleans fell to Union forces early in 1862.

It was in these turbulent years of 1861-1865 that Longhorns developed their legendary characteristics. Early chronicles referred generally to cattle in Texas as black, but as the nineteenth century wore on, less was said about all blacks and more about those with brown sides, or with yellow or white stripes down the back. Reds, browns, blues, and sometimes pintos appeared in the Mexican-type. Without roundups and branding during the war, they grew wilder and reinforced their ability to fend for themselves. Massive horns became longer and stronger with spans of three and a half to nine feet. They were tall and big boned; backs swaying from the length of their bodies. Yet they were built for speed: trim legs, stag muscles, and hard hooves.

Variegated coats, running the color spectrum except for green and purple, made the ultimate Longhorn-look unusual. There were brindles, whites, pale reds almost orange, and many kinds of paints. There were mulberries and ring-streaked and speckled blues. *Grullas*, a slate hue, were named for the color of sandhill cranes. Duns were dark, faded, or Jersey-like creams approaching yellow. Browns with bay points often appeared in reverse. Blacks came in solids or marked with white, brown, and red. Red-and-white peppered *sabinas* were common, as were all varieties of red. No two were alike.[41]

Like the men who would drive them, they were not a breed but a kind, growing rugged and self-reliant in their struggle with a challenging environment.

A Northern-born Texan, A. H. (Shanghai) Pierce was not typical of the drovers, but he somehow epitomized the expanding postwar spirit and the romance attached to it by early writers. His height was right for the concept— six feet four—and his gangling legs, like a Shanghai rooster's, earned him the cowboy moniker he kept.

Since stowing away on a Texas-bound boat in 1853, he had come to know cattle from horn tip to tail switch, and he was never molested by modesty. He shared his experiences with gusto—in time, from the Rio Grande to the British possessions. The volume of Shanghai's Rhode Island twang was the human sound easiest to recall, said the Old Trail Drivers of Texas when they set down their memoirs in the twentieth century.[42]

Pierce had a common bond with many of the men caught up in the swirl of trail dust: he had been attracted to Texas by the lure of free land and cattle; he had seen hard, even destitute, times. But unlike the majority, who never rose in status above the pommel of a saddle, he would become nationally known for his trail activities.

During the war he was "regimental butcher" for the First Texas Cavalry. Although Confederate annals list no such station or its equivalent, in that capacity he served, getting beef for soldiers by whatever means. After the war he was called "Colonel" because he looked the part and was a leader. Many prominent trail men carried legitimate or illegitimate military titles, not by choice, but by the respectful designation of their cowboys.

The ink at Appomattox was only four months dry when Shanghai shed the poverty of a Confederate veteran and graduated from the strictly cowboy class.[43] His dress was pseudo-Southern, a colonel in high-heeled boots, as he moved from range to range contracting South Texas herds for boat shipment to the meager markets in Cuba, New Orleans, and St. Louis. Cattle-poor owners, looking on him as a redeemer, were glad to sell their stock at any price. The means arrived in style with his Negro servant, Neptune, leading gold-laden burros.

Despite his showmanship and bluster, Abel Head Pierce was the only Texan—adopted or otherwise—in the immediate postwar years to wrangle unlimited credit in gold, and he managed it well. To insure delivery as contracted, he stayed several days at each camp. The sellers remembered these singular days of sale, but the cowboys remembered the nights. They retold and took to their graves tales that he related around the campfires.[44]

Shanghai could have boasted of *Mayflower* ancestry, or kinship with Henry Wadsworth Longfellow and former President Franklin Pierce.[46] He chose instead to expound on his self-made side: "I'm Webster on cattle by God, Sir." All cattle were "cows" in range parlance, and Pierce's long and lusty stories invariably concerned and could be reduced to one recurring phrase—"that cow out there." These four words summed up the reason for the cowboy, for the trails about to begin, and for much of America's economy during the next score of years. Certainly, in 1866, "that cow" and five million mangy others of her kind in Texas offered the only immediate hope of recovery anywhere in the South.

'THERE STANDS OLD PIERCE.' *Always looking toward the future, A. H. (Shanghai) Pierce made sure his image would survive along with the memory of his bugle voice. Five years before his death in 1900, he erected on his chosen grave site at Blessing, Texas, a statue larger than that of any Confederate general's. It is "an exact likeness of myself," he said. "You will recognize it when you see it and say: 'There stands Old Pierce.'"*

17

Goodnight-Loving Trail: 1866-1867

THE FIRST MAJOR OUTLET for Longhorn cattle after the Civil War led from Texas to New Mexico and Colorado. This long and tortuous route, called the Goodnight-Loving Trail, carried the names of two of its early travelers. Charles Goodnight and Oliver Loving indeed extended the route into Colorado, but sufficient evidence exists to show that the way between Fort Sumner, New Mexico, and North Central Texas was opened by an obscure pioneer, James Patterson.

Ohio-born and Illinois-reared, he migrated to New Mexico shortly before the Civil War. By 1864, he had joined Thomas Roberts in supplying meat to the military in New Mexico Territory. The same year Patterson formed a partnership with Texas ranchman William Franks to drive cattle to New Mexico. Thomas P. Murray, who in 1865 assisted Franks in driving a herd to Fort Sumner, remembered meeting Patterson on the Pecos with wagonloads of merchandise, headed for Stephenville to buy cattle. Robert K. Wylie also met Patterson in 1865—near the mouth of the Concho—and entered his service to trail beeves to Sumner.

That at least two Texas herds reached the territory safely is borne out by a September 2, 1865, letter from the commander of the Department of New Mexico. General James H. Carleton wrote the quartermaster at Fort Union that Patterson, a "contractor for furnishing fresh beef to the troops at Forts Sumner and Stanton . . . is about to return to Texas to procure another lot of beef cattle. He is obliged to cross the great prairies through the Indian country both going, and on returning." The party was not sufficiently armed, said Carleton, and he authorized a loan to its members of twelve to fifteen Sharps carbines. "You can let them have for *cash* a reasonable amount of ammunition for use with these guns," he added.

"It is desirable to encourage the introduction of cattle from Texas to New Mexico now partly reduced in stock from Indian depredations—and this enterprise of getting cattle across the plains from that state which has already been twice successfully accomplished by Mr. Patterson, is the beginning only, it is hoped, of a great and profitable trade."[1]

Goodnight, too, sensed the challenge of this new direction and, in 1866, chose it with its dangers over well-worn paths that earlier had carried the trade to Louisiana and Missouri. While he knew the Southern states were destitute of cattle, he knew also that they were bankrupt; and he believed "the whole of Texas would start north for market" over the troublesome trails beaten before the war. Within the year he was, unfortunately, something of a successful prophet. Some 260,000 cattle were turned back on the old Shawnee Trail from Texas to Missouri by farmers armed against the Texas fever threat.

When he and Loving pointed their herds toward the mining region—where there was money and likely cattle country—they gave substance to the strongest desire of their day and residence: to find a market for Texas cattle that outnumbered Texans nine to one.[2] The partners were singularly equipped for the task.

Goodnight had been a Texan twenty years when his trail activity began. As a nine-year-old, he moved with his family from Illinois to Texas in 1845. For the next ten years his interests centered a hundred miles west of the village of Dallas, in the Comanche-plagued Texas Cross Timbers, where he and a stepbrother ran cattle on shares.[3]

Indian raids on Texas increased, and by 1859 he was serving in frontier defense with a ranging regiment—seasoned outdoorsmen developing the plainscraft art of survival. Thorough Plains scouts could go as directly to

INVENTIVENESS. *Young Charles Goodnight brought plainscraft scouting and an inventive mind to the Goodnight-Loving team. For their initial drive in 1866, he built the first chuck box ever used on a cattle trail. The original box is believed to be the one in the Panhandle-Plains Museum at Canyon, Texas. Its hinged lid, resting on a folding leg, made a cook's table. Inside staple bins left room for a sour dough keg.*

a destination in darkness as in daylight and, as a master of the skill, Goodnight put it simply: "I never had a compass in my life. I was never lost." He also could judge accurately the distance and direction to water by watching animals, and their migrations told him much about the range beyond. By observing plant life he could estimate his elevation and approximate latitude and longitude.[4]

At the outbreak of the Civil War the Confederacy was too busy elsewhere to defend the Texas frontier, which was receding before the Indian onslaught. The state legislature took matters in its own hands in December, 1861, creating the famous Frontier Regiment of ten companies to protect the far-flung settlement line from Red River to the Rio Grande. In the fall of that year, Goodnight sustained a severe leg injury in an encounter with a wild hog, but as soon as he could ride, he joined this regiment.[5] If, in effect, he sat out the Civil War, he did so in the saddle.

His service expired in 1864, and he returned to his cattle, which now should have numbered five thousand. But his borderland range in Young County had become a fertile field for deserters and cow thieves who had reduced his herd to a thousand head.[6]

All Texans were disfranchised after the war. They champed at the bit of carpetbagger courts that took possession of their affairs, none harder than Charlie Goodnight. He was ready to leave the country with two thousand big steers by late summer, 1865, but Indians again swooped down, driving off the cattle and destroying his trail plans for the year.[7]

Although he never had been to the Rocky Mountain West, Goodnight had sufficient experience from his days in frontier defense to blaze a direct trail northwest to Colorado. Because Comanches and Kiowas commanded that route, he took instead a course almost twice as long: swinging south to avoid certain Indian encounter, moving down the abandoned Butterfield stage road to Horsehead Crossing on the Pecos, then turning up the Pecos to the Rockies and paralleling the mountains north.[8] Outfitting for the drive, the thirty-year-old bachelor built a chuck box, his own innovation that within five years would become standard equipment on all cattle trails.[9]

Oliver Loving, also gathering a herd, asked Goodnight if he could join him. Loving, then fifty-four and the most experienced cowman in the area, was welcomed by the younger man.

Born in Kentucky and married to a Kentucky girl, Loving had visited Texas in 1844 and moved his household there in 1845. He raised cattle, farmed, and bought and sold cattle and horses. As a freighter for the United States government, he hauled supplies to frontier military posts. In 1850 he went with the soldiers who established Fort Belknap on the Brazos. On this and subsequent trips he became familiar with the rugged, wild, and ample lands west of Fort Worth. Loving was the father of nine children in 1855, when he relocated in a valley near Palo Pinto, Texas. Bordered on the east by heavy timber and on the west by a row of naked hills, the spot later was named Loving's Valley.

LOVING'S VALLEY. *The eastern reaches of the Goodnight-Loving Trail began near the home ranges of the men whose name it bore. Bordered on the east by heavy timber and on the west by a row of naked hills, Loving's Valley, near Mineral Wells, Texas, was some thirty miles from the Goodnight range. Goodnight and Loving merged trail herds about twenty-five miles southwest of Fort Belknap.*

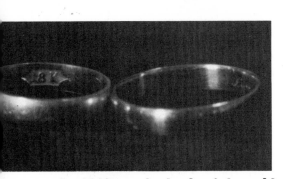

GOLD FROM CATTLE. *Loving had driven Longhorns to New Orleans and, in 1860, to Denver. With gold dust from the latter sale he had five rings made, one for each of his daughters. These two rings remain. They belong to Loving descendants Mrs. Betty Bergquist of Abilene, Texas, and Miss Mariana Roach of Dallas.*

In 1860, on the heels of the gold rush, Loving and John Dawson drove cattle to Denver over a direct route. This was the first Texas herd to enter the Colorado Territory. The Civil War began before Loving could start home and, as a resident of a secessionist state, he was granted permission to return to Texas only through the intervention of such friends as Kit Carson. Traveling alone with a small trunk of gold dust under his wagon seat, he reached Texas safely and celebrated his first venture into the West by having five rings made from the gold, one for each of his daughters.

The Confederacy dissolved in 1865 owing Loving more than $100,000 for beef supplied to Southern armies. His affairs complicated by this debt, he was as anxious as Goodnight to find a road to lucrative cattle markets.[10]

With ranges less than thirty miles apart, the two men were a balanced but unusual team. Loving was mild-mannered and gravely religious, Goodnight restless and profane. Loving probably never would have become a cattleman in the strictest sense, for his interest lay more in the marketing than in the raising of cattle.[11] Not so with Goodnight. From the outset he studied every element of cow nature with the goal of producing a better product.

On June 6, 1866, with two thousand cattle and eighteen men, they left the Texas frontier on the new trail for Longhorns. The first three hundred miles to the Pecos were costly indeed.

Joining their herds in Young County, the partners trailed easily past the abandoned posts of Camp Cooper and Fort Phantom Hill, through Buffalo Gap, and by old Fort Chadbourne. Crossing the North Concho River twenty miles above present San Angelo, the herd rested at the Middle Concho headwaters. Ahead lay a waterless stretch of ninety-six miles that came to be known as the worst part of any trail driven by Texas cowmen. Three days and nights of ceaseless movement by both cattle and men were required to cross the blistering waste. Three hundred Longhorns died of thirst en route.[12]

Toward the end of this greasewood plain were the flat-topped Castle Mountains. A large natural nick in the line of that higher plateau is called Castle Gap — a mile-long canyon visible for many miles. Twelve miles be-

EXPERIENCE. *Oliver Loving, a thoroughly experienced cowman, joined Goodnight in 1866 on the first post-Civil War cattle trail. Loving had made improvements, including this well, on his Palo Pinto range in 1855. The Loving home place is nine miles north of Mineral Wells in Loving's Valley. A West Texas county also is named for him.*

NINETY-SIX MILES TO WATER. *Of the two thousand Longhorns in the first Goodnight-Loving drive, three hundred died of thirst between the Middle Concho headwaters and the Pecos River. Three days and nights of constant trailing were required to cover the waterless stretch.*

CASTLE CANYON. *The mile-long canyon of Castle Gap is aimed directly at Horsehead Crossing on the Pecos, twelve miles away. Thirsting trail cattle often smelled a damp breeze in the canyon and stampeded toward the river. One owner lost an entire herd of one thousand here in 1872 when a light shower crazed the animals and caused them to refuse to water. Their bones marked the canyon for many years.*

ORT PHANTOM HILL. *Fifty miles down the trail the ghostly himneys of Fort Phantom Hill stood in 1866 as gaunt reminders of the ower of drouth. Water shortage had caused the post's abandonment in 854. The fort was burned, but the site was used later as a Butterfield age station and as an outpost of Fort Griffin. Frontiersmen called the lace "Phantom Hill" long before the military arrived.*

23

HORSEHEAD CROSSING ON THE PECOS. *A universal picture of bleakness, desolation and sinister dread is painted of this West Texas ford by the chronicles of several centuries. Goodnight called the salty river "the graveyard of the cowman's hopes." In 1850, Captain John R. Bartlett noted horse and mule skulls at the crossing, and as early as 1853 it appeared on maps as "Horsehead."*

yond the gap lies Horsehead Crossing, once the most noted and most feared landmark in western Texas. Unmerciful to all men alike, the Pecos here had taken its toll of Indian warriors, Spanish explorers, Mexican salt haulers, and Anglo sojourners of all types.[13] Goodnight and Loving were no exceptions.

Their thirst-crazed cattle smelled water at Castle Gap and stampeded toward the river, tumbling over six-to-nine-foot bluffs into the turgid flow. Many drowned. A veritable dam of horns and flesh writhed in the river's quicksands for two days while owners and cowboys fought desperately to pull them out. Cattle successful in the crossing, meanwhile, were finding the isolated and highly alkaline ponds for

which the valley is notorious. Cows dropped dead in their tracks minutes after drinking the poisonous water. Deciding they must move on if any cattle were to be saved, the drovers left a hundred head mired in the jaws of the Pecos, the skulls soon to join others bleaching along the briny banks.

The herd moved slowly up the east side of the river to the Texas-New Mexico line and Pope's Crossing, one of the few Pecos fords in several hundred miles. On the opposite bank, they trailed north across the Delaware and Black Rivers and near the site of modern Carlsbad. By switching back to the east bank of the Pecos, they put the river between them and the Mescalero Apaches, who ranged in the Guada-

24

JUAN CORDONA SALT LAKE. *A fifty-acre salt lake, several miles above Horsehead Crossing, was a trail hazard, though not on the trail. Plains Indians who camped here for long periods curing their buffalo meat soon discovered the new trail and its traffic. Salt deposits in the lake bed are four-inches thick. About 1848, Anglo freighters began hauling the commodity to other Texas points.*

lupe Mountains to the west. Without further trouble they passed the great cottonwoods of Bosque Grande and entered Fort Sumner.

At the fort they found a ready steer market contracting to Thomas Roberts and subcontractors James and Tom Patterson at eight cents a pound on foot. They netted a sizable profit despite trail losses of nearly twenty percent of the herd.

Fort Sumner, established three years earlier as a Navajo and Mescalero reservation, had 8,500 half-starved Indians. The government contractors, however, would not take the remaining 700 or 800 stock cattle, and the Texans proceeded with their original plan. Goodnight would make the 600-mile saddle trip back to

Texas for another herd before winter, while Loving moved the stocker cattle on to Colorado.[14]

Loving drove to Las Vegas, following the Santa Fe Trail north over Raton Range and skirting the base of the Rockies to Denver, where he sold to Colorado's most prominent ranchman, John Wesley Iliff. Goodnight took the twelve-thousand dollars in gold from the steer sale and, two weeks after reaching Texas, had put together another herd of twelve hundred steers. Within forty days he had them at Bosque Grande, forty miles below Fort Sumner, where Loving joined him. As they went into winter camp, they became the first Texans to locate a southern New Mexico ranch.[15]

25

BOSQUE GRANDE. *Mexicans living in the area gave the name "Bo[s]que Grande," Big Forest, to a concentration of large cottonwoods in the Pecos Valley, thirty-five miles northeast of present Roswell, New Mexico. Several trees—one with a circumference of twenty-seven fe[et]—remain today. Goodnight and Loving chose this spot for winter quarters in 1866, and John Chisum located here after Goodnight mo[ved] to Colorado.*

NEW MEXICO'S PECOS VALLEY. *Trailmen found the Pecos Valley in New Mexico wider than its Texas course and kinder to their cattle. Haystack Mountain, visible twenty miles in the distance, is opposite Bosque Grande, where Goodnight and Loving located for a season.*

FORT UNION. *Loving's trail north of Las Vegas, New Mexico, was by Fort Union. The weathered adobe remains now stand like an American Stonehenge, reflecting forty years of frontier drama, 1851-1891. At the Santa Fe Trail's fork, the post guarded prairie commerce and became the Southwest's largest supply depot. At Union, Goodnight met Colorado cattleman J. W. Iliff, who had fort beef contracts. Snyder Brothers of Texas also sold beeves there.*

28

'THE ONLY BANK.' *Built in 1865, the First National Bank of Denver was flourishing the next year when Loving arrived. Goodnight, in southern Colorado by 1867, noted that it was still the territory's "nearest and only bank." At Fifteenth and Blake streets, the building now is Denver's oldest and Colorado's "Constitution Hall." State principles were drawn up on the second floor in 1876. The mansard roof was added later.*

The 1866 drives had been extremely profitable. The partners sold some cattle during the winter on government contracts and the next spring sent five hundred head to graze the broad Capulin *vega*, in northeastern New Mexico, while the owners returned to Texas with plans for bigger drives.

But in 1867, Goodnight recalled, "the sign just wasn't right." News of their success encouraged others to follow their route. Indians discovered the trail, attacking the partners on the trek back to Texas. Their next herd was reduced by three stampedes—one caused by redmen, two by fierce lightning and rain.[16]

It was the end of July when they reached Horsehead, and cattle contracts were to be let at Santa Fe in August. Loving went ahead to be present for the bidding but was mortally wounded in an Indian ambush. After three days on the desert—bleeding, hiding, fighting, starving—he was discovered by Mexicans who took him 150 miles by ox wagon to Fort Sumner. Goodnight, arriving there before Loving died on September 25, promised to continue the partnership for at least two years so Loving's remaining debts might be paid.[17]

Their cattle were still far south of Sumner, and Goodnight had missed the contract-letting.

CAPULIN CRATER. *From 1866 drives to Bosque Grande, Goodnight and Loving sent cattle the next spring to graze on the broad* vega *west of New Mexico's Capulin Mountain. After Loving's death, Goodnight joined the previous herd at Capulin with more steers and moved over Raton Pass to begin ranching in Colorado. He soon found a shorter, easier pass over the range by trailing almost due north of the extinct volcano's cone.*

RATON RANGE. *Loving descended into southeastern Colorado over Raton Pass, the only established route through the high mesa country dividing New Mexico and Colorado. Wagons on the Santa Fe Trail's northern branch had inched across the mountains here for decades. In the summer of 1866, Loving was among the early customers of Dick Wootton's toll road over the pass.*

30

WOOTTON'S ROADHOUSE. *In 1866 Uncle Dick Wootton built a twenty-seven-mile toll road over Raton Pass, and a roadhouse on the Colorado side. The Wootton house burned about 1880, but soon was restored on the original adobe walls.*

Hurrying the steers northward, he joined remnants of the previous herd held by his men at Capulin *vega*. Then, as they moved thirty miles northwest, Charles Goodnight had his first glimpse of Colorado.[18]

It was late fall, 1867. He gazed down from Raton Pass on a great infinity of grass stretching northward to the Arkansas River valley. The west was rimmed by the rugged profile of Spanish Peaks, the Greenhorns, and Pike's Peak. In this cow-promising plateau he would have "the world to himself," but not before he grappled verbally with Uncle Dick Wootton. Wootton, a giant mountain man (6 feet, 4 inches, 260 pounds) with the grim visage of Daniel Webster, had set up a toll station on the Colorado side of the pass. The charge was 10 cents per animal. Goodnight, tall but weighing only 200 pounds, muttered that he would find another pass. Wootton laughed; there was no other.

North of the pass the country was broken only by arroyo-like streams, aimed north and northeast at the Arkansas. With this choice of water Goodnight singled out the Apishapa and, at the head of its canyon forty miles northeast of Trinidad, began the first extensive cattle ranch in southern Colorado.[19]

Apishapa Canyon, though not extremely deep, was almost inaccessible except at the ends of its twenty-mile length. Here also Goodnight established a pattern of ranch location he would follow many times. He always searched out a place that nature had fenced, sheltered and watered, allowing him to dominate a large range area beyond. This ranch would be his swing station on the trail for wintering horses, gathering cattle, and holding his steady men. He set cowboys to work at once locating the herd and building a cabin, while he turned back five hundred miles to Bosque Grande for more cattle. By Christmas Eve he was back

31

APISHAPA RANGE. *In 1867, Goodnight located at Apishapa Canyon and began the first extensive cattle ranch in southern Colorado.*

with a thousand head to release on the Apishapa, but this time the snow on Raton Pass had exacted a greater toll than Wootton.[20]

Losses of the 1867 drives had been heavy for the firm, and the promise to clear Loving's debts weighed heavily on Goodnight. Although Loving's son, Joe, had charge of their cattle at the *bosque*, grave problems arose from holding cattle in two widely separated points in a wild country. Imminent military abandonment of Fort Sumner would mean loss of a market, as well as protection. Only John Chisum and one other ranchman had moved into the area. Goodnight decided to shorten his line of operation by contracting to receive, at Bosque Grande, Chisum's drives from Texas. The arrangement was on a fifty-fifty basis, allowing Chisum a dollar a head extra for his trail risks. With a cattle supply assured, Goodnight turned his attention to the range and the speculative end of the business, delivering to ranchmen and other contractors throughout the Western Plains.[21]

But first he carried out Loving's last wish: that he not be buried on foreign soil. Returning to Fort Sumner, Goodnight and other trailmen carried Loving's body back to Texas to its final resting place.[22]

Together, Goodnight and Loving had insured a course that became a prominent trail almost in a season, and within six years 300,000 cattle had passed that way.[23] Drovers from various parts of Texas moved to intersect the route and travel its length, or go beyond to Arizona Indian reservations and the Pacific Coast or ranges opening up in Wyoming, Utah, and Nevada. Still the new trace had not escaped the scourge of Texas fever. As some measure of protection for its native herds, Colorado invoked a limited quarantine against Texas cattle in 1867. The restriction was not strong enough to slow the increasing flow of Longhorns into Colorado Territory.[24]

Goodnight, with his ability to grasp quickly every significant factor in climate, topography, and animal nature, would continue to make the route more practicable, constantly reinvesting his knowledge and inexhaustible energy wherever grass lay unbroken.

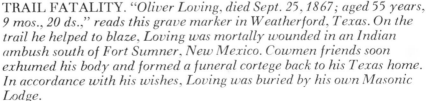

TRAIL FATALITY. *"Oliver Loving, died Sept. 25, 1867; aged 55 years, 9 mos., 20 ds.," reads this grave marker in Weatherford, Texas. On the trail he helped to blaze, Loving was mortally wounded in an Indian ambush south of Fort Sumner, New Mexico. Cowmen friends soon exhumed his body and formed a funeral cortege back to his Texas home. In accordance with his wishes, Loving was buried by his own Masonic Lodge.*

Chisholm Trail: 1867

ALTHOUGH the Goodnight-Loving drives of 1866 were successful, no truly dependable cattle market had been developed by early 1867. Yet more and more Texans looked to the glut of Longhorns as the only means of bolstering their sagging economy.

To recover or build herds, the cow hunts of prewar years were resumed. The hunts were long and hard, lasting two weeks to three months, while cowmen captured wild cattle that still roamed free of domestic herds and castrated the males. From these roundups on a fenceless range, established men in the business also cut out animals wearing their own brand and marked the calves while they were still identifiable with their mothers. The calf crop always was prolific because many Longhorn heifers calved as early as fourteen months of age. In summer these armored cattle were forced to the prairie's edge by mosquitos, but they hid in the brush during the spring, when trail herds had to be gathered if they were to reach some northerly destination before winter.[1]

The aura of freedom associated with range work vied with economics as the major factor in luring men to the life in the open. They liked drifting from range to range or with a herd of Longhorns, the silent spaces free from the social restraints of cities, and the challenge of pitting themselves against nature's unbridled forces. Whether they were simply reckless and bold or possessed an understanding of the odds against them, all sensed the lack of restraint possible on the ranching frontier.[2]

The cow hunt and the trail required young men, and the pursuits captured the imagination of the very young. "There is not a boy of American parentage learning a trade or reading for a profession west of the Colorado," grieved a South Texas correspondent. "The little children, as early as they can walk, pilfer their mother's tape and make lassos to rope the kittens and the ducks. The boys, as soon as they can climb on a pony, are off to the prairie to drive stock. As they advance toward manhood, their highest ambition is to conquer a pitching mustang or throw a wild beef by the tail."[3]

This contagious desire to conquer and drive the cow found its fulfillment in the Chisholm Trail, which opened in mid-1867 and which lives on in motion pictures, television, and millions of printed words. The annual take of such media exceeds the 200-million-dollar total from all Longhorn drives of the period.

The trail carries the name of an honorable man, but one, ironically, who had no connection with the cattle business. Jesse Chisholm was a seasoned guide and interpreter in 1865, when he joined his trading posts with a 220-mile wagon road from the North Canadian River in Indian Territory to the present site of Wichita, Kansas. His path followed generally that of Black Beaver, the Delaware scout who in 1861 led Union troops away from Confederates advancing on Forts Cobb, Washita, and Arbuckle.

Of Scottish and Cherokee parentage, Chisholm spoke twelve Indian dialects and was a wise and generous counsel to the tribes. Known

JESSE CHISHOLM, 'GOOD SAMARITAN.' *On a bleak March day in 1868, trader Jesse Chisholm was buried on a knoll overlooking Johnny Left Hand Spring, six miles northeast of present Geary, Oklahoma, having succumbed to ptomaine poisoning from eating brass-kettle-cooked bear meat at his camp here. He died without knowing his 220-mile wagon road would be part of a great cowpath, immortalized as "the Chisholm Trail." In 1939, his grave was marked with Texas granite, Oklahoma cement, and water from the Left Hand Spring. The inscription: "No one left his home cold or hungry."*

for his straight tongue among all races, he had assisted in many treaties between white and redmen, and was a pilot for American army engineers laying out supply routes and division lines for the rapidly changing territorial structure.[4]

The ruts of Chisholm's wagon road were only three years deep at his death in March, 1868, and very few cattle had passed that way. While his road was included in the new trail to Abilene, Kansas, the opening in August, 1867, was too late in the season for herds to start from Texas. The first herd to use the new route had moved earlier in the year from San Antonio, where Colonel O. W. Wheeler had purchased 2,400 Longhorns and 100 horses. Two associates, 54 trail hands, and the California colonel pushed safely up Chisholm's wagon road and on to Abilene. With the Chisholm name firmly attached to part of the trail, its extended application to the whole route was a matter of evolution.

The trail was known vicariously by many names in the early days. To some Texans it was McCoy's Trail, for Joseph G. McCoy, who developed the Abilene market. To others it was the Kansas Trail, the Abilene Trail, or simply the Cattle Trail or The Trail. Kansans referred to it as the Great Cattle Trail, the Texas Cattle Trail, the Great Texas Cattle Trail, and, later, as the Wichita Trail.

The name Chisholm Trail, probably in oral use long before it appeared in print, began to crop up in Kansas papers in the spring of 1870 and in Texas news four years later.[5] The trail title was subject to further conjugation by the name similarity of John Chisum, a Texas rancher who supplied cattle to trail herds. Thus, the Chisum Trail was added erroneously to the list of labels for America's most renowned cow road.

The Chisholm Trail resulted from the efforts and nimble leg work of Joseph McCoy, an Illinois cattle dealer and promoter. Still in his twenties, McCoy recognized the ripe potential awaiting someone who could link the bawling Texas herds to a steady market. Trailing cattle to a railhead was the quickest way to meet the great Eastern demand for beef, but McCoy was aware of the Texas fever problems caused by the Longhorns' earlier route through settled

areas to Missouri railheads. He looked beyond Missouri at the broad Kansas prairies to the west, where Union Pacific tracks were extending faster than the settlement line.

In the 1867 spring, the vigorous McCoy visited all stops along the new rails. He secured the railroad's promise to install a switch at a location of his choice and negotiated with a connecting line for cheaper shipping rates to the East. Settling in mid-June on Abilene as the site for his Texas cattle market, McCoy imported lumber to the treeless village of thirteen businesses and a few huts. By September 1, a barn, an office, and shipping yards for a thousand cattle were complete. A stable, hotel, and bank were under construction.

While the building was underway, he called on the Kansas governor and outlined his plan. McCoy explained that the country around and below Abilene was thinly settled, even though the town itself lay sixty miles east of the line established that year by a new Kansas quarantine against Texas cattle. He was smoothly persuasive and came away with the governor's hearty personal approval and semiofficial endorsement, which avoided legal hassles for a time.

To acquaint Texans with the new trail and market, McCoy circulated handbills to many Southwestern towns. He sent a stockman riding south to spread the word and intersect upcoming herds.[6]

Great controversies arising since the close of the Chisholm Trail still rage over the trail's Texas route, which varied considerably more than its name. The trail did not follow a narrow line, year after year, from a single starting point to a single destination. A veteran trail driver recalled that "at times so many herds would be on the trail they would spread out on either side and some herds went all the way to Abilene without being on the trail except occasionally." His "occasionally" referred to fords on major rivers that were the only feasible crossings for cattle, to trail towns necessary for supplies, and to landmarks, visible from long distances, that pointed the way.[7]

The trailing movement touched every frontier process on the Plains, finding markets at the Indian agencies, the forts, the gold rushes, and the railroad camps. These outlets were in

SOUTH TEXAS PRAIRIES. *Many sources cite Chisholm Trail beginnings as springtime on the prairies near Lockhart or Cuero, Texas. A veteran student of the trailing movement wisely added that this trail or any other "originated wherever a herd shaped up and ended wherever a market was found."*

CATTLE BUYER'S HOME. *Colonel Dillard R. Fant went into the cattle business in 1866 near Goliad, where Texas mission herds once ranged and trail herds were gathering. He soon bought Lloyd Vivian's house, slave-built about 1840. Commission buyer Fant took 200,000 cattle up the trail in fifteen years and reportedly was the second man to wire-fence a Texas pasture. He enclosed his range in 1874.*

37

BRUSHY CREEK ON A RISE. *Twenty-eight miles north of Austin, Texas trail cattle crossed Brushy Creek at Round Rock, where a solid stone bottom continues to the west about half a mile. Still-visible ruts were cut in the stone by drover and freight wagons; also by stage travel. High bluffs and boggy land narrowed the cattle crossing to this section, drovers often camping on the south side while the creek ran down.*

'CHISHOLM'S POOL.' *Near the trail east of Georgetown, Texas, Snyder cowboys had a favorite swimming hole, "Chisholm's Pool," on the San Gabriel River. The devout Snyder Brothers allowed no work on Sunday and held regular church services for their men, but the waddies later slipped off for a dip.*

'MUTTERING THUNDER.' *In 1876, the greatest recorded loss of trail cattle was credited to a black cloud showing above the foothills on an intermittent creek southwest of Waco, Texas. A thunderstorm at four o'clock in the afternoon unnerved the cattle, which "showed their fear by those low bellowings, ominous to the experienced cattle man as the muttering thunder." At ten o'clock that night the bedded herd rose with a single purpose and a simultaneous roar. Next morning 2,700 were dead in a ravine still called Stampede Gully.*

PERPETUATED HISTORY. *Almost within sound of the city, five miles northwest of Fort Worth's limits, Longhorns continue to graze along the Chisholm Trail. Limestone hills and rich creek bottoms still sustain without extra feeding a descendant herd of the history-making cattle. In 1966, Edwin B. Dow ran Tarrant County's first registered Longhorns here, although the late Amon Carter had fine steers of the kind before registration began in 1964.*

addition to the millions upon millions of Long-horns that went up the trail as stocker cattle for the Western and Northwestern ranges, and as beef to the railheads for the tables of Eastern consumers. As the late trail student T. C. Richardson pointed out, "We shall get rid of a good deal of geographical difficulty at once by recalling that the trails originated wherever a herd was shaped up and ended wherever a market was found. A thousand minor trails fed the main routes, and many an old-timer who as a boy saw a herd of stately Longhorns, piloted by bandanaed, booted, and spurred men, lived with the firm conviction that the Dodge or Chisholm Trail passed right over yonder."[8]

Drouth, intense rain, or heavy trail traffic determined the main route in any given year. On the theory that cattle would gain weight along the way, they were moved at a grazing speed of five to fifteen miles per day, depending upon conditions and terrain.

The course of the Chisholm Trail in Texas was new only above the Brazos River at Waco. To the south the trail was identical with the prewar Shawnee Trail to Missouri, used both by drovers and traders since the 1840's. Some herds came from ranges along or beyond the Rio Grande and were trailed north through the brush country, either on the old Beef Trail past Beeville, Gonzales, and Lockhart to Austin or westward to San Antonio.

Feeder lines from either side joined the trail above San Antonio, and at Austin, where more feeders intersected. The herds usually crossed the Colorado at Montopolis ford and moved on toward Brushy Creek and the San Gabriel and Lampasas rivers. The mighty Brazos, longest of the rivers rising in Texas, was encountered in the vicinity of Waco. It delayed many a herd with the drainage from its fingering head-waters. Smaller routes from the east and west swelled the northbound stream of cattle at Waco, where many swam the Brazos; others were trailed on to Fort Graham or Kimball before crossing the river.

Fort Worth, to the northwest, grew quickly as an outfitting point for drovers and a place of cattle exchange. The main trail, veering northwest again, crossed the West Fork of the Trinity River, then followed the borders of Wise and Denton counties east of Decatur. Beyond Denton and Clear Creek lay the brakes of Red River.[9]

A trickling of cattle crossed the Red into Indian Territory at Sivell's Bend, in Cooke County, or farther west at old Spanish Fort, in Montague County. But the vast milling majority came into Red River Station, also in Montague County, with feasible approaches from the southeast and southwest.

As trail herds increased, Red River Station became the end of a giant funnel fanning southeast to Houston and southwest to Uvalde through which Texas cattle poured out en route to Kansas. Herds did not follow directly one behind the other and, as the funnel filled almost to overflowing, the trail at this point was virtually as wide as the county. Red River Station, a Civil War outpost for the Frontier Regiment, had attracted three hundred persons to settlement on the crest of the trail. Even they, however, had not planned for so great a flood of cattle: The school house had to be moved because constantly passing herds prevented the children from reaching its doors.

Waiting to cross the river, cattle bedded down on rightly named Panther Creek, five miles away. At least one stampede was caused there by trail hands shooting to silence the big screaming cats.

Inexperienced trailmen in the first years of the drives drew many lessons from the ruthless "Big Red." Heavy cattle losses and several cowboy drownings cooled the impatience of others. Fewer and fewer tried to cross the river at flood stage, frequent in the spring trailing season. At best, the current was swift, the quicksands deep. Longhorns refused to cross any river unless they could see the other side, but they milled uncommonly in this wide stream's middle. When drovers learned that cattle at Red River Station were blinded by the morning sun during certain times of the year, they waited until afternoon to attempt a crossing.[10]

Into Indian Territory, the Chisholm Trail crawled across rolling country with plenty of grass and water. Timbered streams, except in the northern part, relieved the camp cook of carrying firewood or relying on cow chips. The

PANTHER CREEK. *When Red River was up, herds waiting to cross often bedded down on nearby Panther Creek, which cowboys said was rightly named. "I heard the most horrifying yell that I had ever heard in all my life," remembered a night guard. "It came from a bending tree about sixty yards from the herd and was the scream of a panther. Next morning we told the boss we would rather swim Red River than to stand guard assisted by panthers."*

43

CROSSING AT RED RIVER STATION. *The Chisholm Trail's focal point for herds leaving Texas was Red River Station. At the old Indian crossing where a Confederate outpost had been located, cattle were put into the river bend with the current to help move them across. The deep channel was next to the Texas side, steep-sloped in most places. With several smaller channels separated by sand bars, the crossing from bank to bank was a mile wide.*

44

MONUMENT ROCKS. *Some twenty-seven miles north of Red River,*
early drovers marked the trail in Indian Territory by stacking sandstone
slabs which nature had strewn about an almost flat mesa. Visible for
miles, the stacks became known as Monument Rocks. A storm caused
one stampede at the site, cowboy fun another. Trail hands pitched their
boss's tent over a polecat bed, tying the tent front when he retired.
His quick demolition of the shelter is trail legend.

RUTS OF THE TRAIL. *The course that Longhorns carved through Indian Territory remains at several points. Treeless, rolling prairie is yet unplowed north of Monument Rocks and four miles east of Addington, Oklahoma, and here the earth still swags from trail traffic of a century ago. The grass-grown ruts are more than a hundred yards wide.*

THE ICY WASHITA. *Some eighty miles north of Red River cowboys encountered the Washita, the first major river in Indian Territory. Tu drovers reported all streams in the vicinity frozen hard in an early April blizzard. At Hell Roaring Creek, to the south, a remuda of sixty-five horses froze "in a space no larger than an ordinary dwelling house." On a sunnier day at the Washita, trail men met forty Comanches, each with a parasol, returning from a treaty-making.*

THE CIMARRON. *South of today's Dover, Oklahoma, the trail crossed the Cimarron, or Red Fork of the Arkansas. Banks were accessible but quicksand danger was great, and drovers often found the river wide and getting wider from spring rains. The trail, which had forked at the South Canadian River, became as one again on the north bank of the Cimarron.*

SALT FORK OF THE ARKANSAS. *Placid at normal stage, the Salt Fork on a rampage vied for first place among the meanest rivers on the trail. Cowboy-author Charles Siringo told of a time when driftwood almost mauled the cattle at the Oklahoma crossing near Pond Creek. A horse went under, scaring the lead steers and "causing the whole herd to turn back amidst terrible confusion." The cattle would not take water again that day.*

BUFFALO RANGE. *During the 1870 and 1871 trailing seasons, Long-horns encountered vast numbers of buffalo between the Cimarron River and the Salt Fork of the Arkansas. One trailman recalled buffalo passing for two hours just ahead of his herd: "Sometimes they would be one behind the other, and then they would come in bunches of 300 or 400."*

TOWARD ABILENE. *During peak seasons, herds stacked up on the Kansas prairies waiting their turn to get into Abilene. Though they grazed the whole area for miles around, the main trail still dimly shows some thirty miles south of town.*

second night's camp north of Red River was Monument Hill, or Rocks, from whose summit cowboys could spot trail herds strung out ten to fifteen miles in either direction.

Beginning with the Washita, trail outfits had five sizable rivers to cross in Indian country, where often the Kiowas and Comanches demanded payment for passage over their land. A wise trail boss paid the fee by cutting out a few steers, which he sometimes saw butchered and devoured on the spot. This compliance with the redman's wishes eased the threat that he might return to stampede the cattle and drive off the horses. Even so, trail night guards heeded every sound.[11]

In the early 1870's the trail split at the South Canadian River because, as one drover wrote, "grass and water were hard to find for so many herds and herds were getting mixed up."[12] The west fork, which was part of Jesse Chisholm's wagon road, also was used by stagecoaches. It passed Fort Reno near the North Canadian. The east branch went by present Yukon, Oklahoma, and a recent study of 1871-1875 geological survey maps shows that the path at some time went as far east as modern Oklahoma City.[13] The forks came together again at the Cimarron River, and lead steers stepped out on a single trail to the Salt Fork of the Arkansas.

Trail hands said this northern part of the

ROLLING COUNTRY. *Twenty-seven miles south of Abilene, the central route led to a surprise fault, dropping seventy-five feet below the gently rolling plains.*

territory and southern Kansas were "literally covered" with buffalo in the early 1870's. Several herds lost heavily from cattle and horses getting into buffalo drifts which, like the cattle, were moving northward in the springtime.[14]

The trail entered Kansas near present Caldwell, and herds had little trouble with streams north to Abilene: the Chikaskia River, Slate Creek, Ninnescah River, Cow Skin Creek, and the Arkansas. The box canyon of Elm Springs, twenty-seven miles south of Abilene, was a fine campground and shelter with ample wood and water. Herds at times were stacked up from Elm Springs into town, waiting for shipping accommodations in the young village that

would be the trail's end from 1867 to 1871.[15]

With some combination of lightning, stampedes, cloudbursts, blizzards, Indian raiders, cholera, prairie fires, and hail, the Longhorns were brought into Abilene ninety days after leaving San Antonio. And the cowboy who had been "up the trail" could be pardoned for the slight swagger in his walk.

The Chisholm Trail [says the Longhorn's biographer, J. Frank Dobie] was a canal out of the mighty dammed-up reservoir of Texas beef to meat-lacking consumers with money to buy. That Trail became a fact when in 1867 Abilene, Kansas, with a railroad carrying stockcars eastward—and with construction pushing rails on towards the

51

BOX CANYON AND ELM SPRINGS. *The sudden box canyon that broke from the prairie was an ideal holding place for cattle, and the only place nearby with wood and water always in abundance. Deeper inside the canyon was a splendid camp site, where the constant drip of cool springs forms a stream of living water that ultimately joins the Smoky Hill River and flows past Abilene.*

52

TRAIL'S END—ABILENE! *The Chisholm Trail's first Kansas terminus reigned supreme as the queen of cowtowns from 1867 to 1871. By 1870, rowdy Abilene boasted ten saloons, ten boarding houses, five general stores, and four hotels. A double row of false-front buildings lined Texas Street, paralleling the railroad. Merchant's Hotel, a "goodly sized frame building," opened that year, and a marshal was hired to deal with the increasing quarrels caused by whiskey and six-guns.*

Pacific—established a definite, dependable market for Texas cattle. The Chisholm Trail . . . initiated the greatest, the most extraordinary, the most stupendous, the most fantastic and fabulous migration of animals controlled by man that the world has ever known or ever can know.[16]

A move was on to mark this storied route in 1931, when the Old Trail Drivers of Texas went on record as saying that the proper designation was the "Eastern Texas-Kansas Trail." Their formal resolution stated that the Chisholm Trail did not begin until after cattle were crossed into Indian Territory. Drover President

George W. Saunders was more emphatic. "The famed Chisholm cattle trail," he declared, "about which more has been written than any other southwestern trail cannot be traced in Texas for the reason that it never existed in this state."[17]

The "eastern" trail advocates made a case for geographical purists, since a western trail had been blazed in 1876. But like many dictionary definitions trampled under by popular usage, neither resolution nor declaration could shorten the Chisholm Trail's line of lore extending from the Rio Grande to the Kansas prairies.

53

MOVING TO MARKET. *In the exciting eight years from 1868 to 1875,
trail driving became a profession and almost a science. Improved
methods greatly reduced the cost of trailing northward and new
markets increased the demand. New ranges, rail construction crews,
reservation Indians, and, in the West, soldiers and miners were added
to the beef call from Eastern tables. Answering Longhorns totaled 2.3
million on the Chisholm, 600,000 on the Goodnight Trail.*

54

Changing Times and Trails: 1868-1875

As the Goodnight and Chisholm Trails heralded the northward advance of cattle, the Plains west of the frontier line fairly seethed with other movements that were somewhat interdependent. Under the 1867 Treaty of Medicine Lodge, certain wild tribes were moved from the region between the Platte and Arkansas rivers to reservations in Indian Territory and elsewhere. Forts established before the Civil War to protect immigrant and trade routes were strengthened to help watch over the Indians and keep down hostilities; the buffalo slaughter and the westward march of rails were beginning. Agrarian settlement followed in the wake. All combined in a many-faceted pincer attack on the Plains.

The Indians' removal from parts of Colorado, Kansas, and Nebraska cleared the way for rail development and opened the area for stock raising. The forts, Indian agencies, and railroad crews became prime markets for cattle. While the army was not powerful enough to keep the Indians on reservations as long as the buffalo—their customary food, clothing, and shelter—roamed, points along the new rails gave immediate outlets for buffalo hides and sped destruction of the great herds. Meanwhile, the Longhorn stood ready as heir-apparent to bison grazing grounds.[1]

Diverse individualism, riding the crest of these activities, had but a few years to flourish before being caught in the inevitable trend toward economic centralization and specialization. Opening of the Chicago Union Stock Yards late in 1865, replacing several smaller yards, was but one step in that gigantic movement. As early as 1867 cattlemen themselves began organizing to deal with mutual problems such as rustling and, ultimately, to speak politically as one unified, powerful voice.[2]

Neither the trails nor the range cattle industry they helped develop had time to standardize—so swift was their rise, so enormous their proportions, and so rapid their decline.[3] While trail ends changed as railheads were extended south and west and as more northwest territory opened to ranching, the fear of Texas fever moved faster than other elements in relocation. Early in 1867, six states and territories raised additional quarantines against the trailing of Texas cattle. Fortunately for drovers on the new trails, restrictions in Kansas and Colorado were less severe than in Nebraska, Missouri, Illinois, and Kentucky.

The southwestern quarter of Kansas was left open to Longhorns. With a $10,000 bond posted against damage to local stock, and the drovers' promise to keep five miles away from any settler, the cattle could be driven on north to Union Pacific shipping pens. Abilene's market was threatened, nonetheless, by an 1868 fever outbreak in Illinois, attributed to Texas cattle. The ingenious Joseph McCoy averted collapse with a rail-traveling Wild West show, playing in St. Louis and Chicago, which stirred feeders to more interest in than fear of his Kansas market. For five years Abilene was the Chisholm Trail's main terminus, with the Texas drives doubling each year, from 35,000 head in 1867 to 600,000 in 1871. Many cattle were shipped to Kansas City, which had opened its first packing plant in 1868, but more went to stock new ranges, where the demand for cheap cattle was described as "so hungry it was grasping at almost anything that looked like a cow."[4]

Since the trade was contributing heavily to territorial coffers, Colorado compromised in 1867 with a limited quarantine admitting only "wintered" cattle. Though the tick remained anonymous as the fever culprit, it was common knowledge that wintering cattle away from Texas removed the danger. Many herds did

BEGINNING AT THE APISHAPA. *John Wesley Iliff's, $40,000 cattle purchase from Charles Goodnight on the Apishapa in 1868 marked the beginning of large-scale ranching on the Plains. Iliff had army, railroad, and Indian beef contracts to fill. Goodnight could assure a constant cattle supply. As he made the first delivery, he stretched and straightened the Goodnight Trail to the full length of Colorado.*

THE PLATTE AND THE CROW. *Trailing to Cheyenne, Goodnight swam his herd across the Platte at the mouth of Crow Creek. He was to recall that those old Texas steers with only part of their heads and horns above water "looked like a million floating rocking chairs."*

winter on the Pecos in New Mexico, but it was impossible to prove that others did not. The ineffective law spurred Boulder, Arapahoe, El Paso, and Fremont County stockmen to form the Colorado Cattle Association and, in April, 1869, to warn: "fifteen hundred men . . . have pledged themselves that no herds of Texas cattle shall pass over the main thoroughfare between the Arkansas and Platte Rivers." Goodnight already had shifted his trail east of the association. He was able to drive without serious trouble, although settlers east of Denver once shot into his herd at night, stampeding and killing a number of cattle.[5]

In the spring of 1868, John Wesley Iliff offered forty thousand dollars for the cattle held on Goodnight's Apishapa Ranch delivered to Cheyenne, Wyoming. It was the largest cattle transaction for either man to that time. Loving had trailed from Pueblo to intersect the Platte at Denver; Goodnight now drove almost due north over the divide from Pueblo, leaving Denver to the west. Near present Greeley he struck the Platte at the mouth of Crow Creek and moved up the Crow to Cheyenne, a bustling railroad town born the year before, when the Union Pacific arrived.

These Goodnight cattle going in February to Iliff were the second Texas trail herd to come up through Colorado into Wyoming. In 1866 Nelson Story had trailed across Wyoming en route to Montana, but Indian troubles prevented further travel in that direction for some time.[6] Although Goodnight personally moved only one more herd to Wyoming—at Chugwater—he continued to supply beef for Iliff's railroad and Indian contracts, delivering twenty-five to thirty thousand Longhorns in the next three years. His practical route came into general use.[7]

There were striking similarities between these young and thorough cattlemen. In 1868, Iliff was thirty-seven—five years Goodnight's senior. Both bore a remarkable resemblance to Ulysses Grant, who that year would be elected President of the United States.[8]

They exemplified the rugged individualism of American business leaders; a case in point was their use of public lands for grazing. While both men shared grass with other ranchmen, the land they actually owned was small compared with that which they controlled. The secret was selective purchase of water sites, exempting them from the ranks of "range pirates" who turned cattle loose without title to water and hence to proscriptive range possession.

At Iliff's death in 1878, he dominated a triangular-shaped range of 150 miles from Julesburg to Greeley, yet he had purchased only 15,558 acres. In this total were 103 land parcels in 54 locations, monopolizing water along the South Platte and its tributary lakes and streams.[9] Goodnight ultimately bought considerable land as the free range passed, but his initial water acquisitions made easier the purchase of surrounding country, as it would have for Iliff, had he lived.

Although they developed many other economic interests, neither left cattle management to their cowboys. Like Goodnight, Iliff "rode the range and followed the roundup."[10] At the same time, they pioneered in cattle breeding, using Herefords and Durhams to upgrade the crusty Longhorns on which their empires were built.[11] Although both had reverential faith and were generous in Christian philanthropies, neither was a church member. Iliff had "no tolerance for *pretended* Christians," and Goodnight was impatient with "institutionalized religion."[12]

The skill with which men like Goodnight and Iliff assumed the risks of land and capital in a rapidly changing time allowed them to move successfully with its opportunities. They were symbols of expansion in an industry which remade the map of the West and rewrote its history. Without their kind there would have been no cowboys.[13]

After his initial trade with Iliff, Goodnight rushed up another herd on an altered route from the south. He trailed fifty miles east of his old path in New Mexico, making a shorter distance with better grass and water from Bosque Grande to Capulin crater. The old volcano cone lay almost due north. Turning up the South Trinchera, he found a passage across Raton Range, a full two days' drive shorter than by Wootton's toll road. Once out of the mountains, Goodnight pointed northwest to his Apishapa range, some fifty miles away.[14]

Trinchera Pass proved to be the outlet he

CHALK BLUFFS. *Half a mile south of the Colorado-Wyoming line, about twelve miles south of Cheyenne, lay Iliff's Chalk Bluffs cow camp. The camp, one of several scattered over his vast domain, was ideally located for receiving and working cattle. Still contained and protected by the sudden canyon walls is a spring with the only living water for many miles.*

'HOODOO ON THE HORIZON.' *In 1868 Goodnight extended the trail north of Cheyenne to the Chugwater Valley, where shortly the open-range bubble would rise and burst. By 1883 this bold rimrock guarded Swan Land and Cattle Company headquarters. The huge Scottish company, called by former manager John Clay a "hoodoo on the horizon," failed in 1887, shaking the whole industry. Indian legend says bison, driven over the bluffs to avenge a chief's death, made a "chug" sound as they tumbled into the creek.*

59

GOODNIGHT HILL. *The trail blazer also altered his route in New Mexico, driving about fifty miles farther east. With better grass and water, this way was shorter from John Chisum's cattle supply at Bosque Grande to Capulin crater, but past the Canadian River an abrupt mesa rose seven hundred feet in a quarter mile. Goodnight pointed his herd directly up the incline. He passed on his experience to others, who named the hill for him. Cattle would balk unless the climb was made in the morning, when they were rested.*

60

CIMARRON SECO. *Ten miles north of Capulin Mountain, Goodnight's new trail in 1868 intersected and followed the Dry Cimarron westward several miles. The twisting course of the small stream bed gave ample opportunity to view the back side of Capulin, now labeled America's most perfect volcanic cone.*

HISTORIC VALLEY. *Turning north up the deep valley of the South Trinchera, Goodnight noted a long, rock wall formation, unlike anything he had ever seen, that "looked like it had been laid up by human hands." Trinchera, Spanish for "trench," was named by conquistadores who dug trenches there for protection against Ute Indians. In 1843, dried steer hides were used as units of land measurement for the Sangre de Cristo grant, of which the valley was a part.*

TRINCHERA PASS. *Welcome spring broke from the very crest of Trinchera, Goodnight said, as he topped the pass into Colorado in 1868. With easier grades this toll-free mountain outlet—thirty miles east of Raton, visible in the distance—saved two full days of needless driving.*

61

was seeking. The grades were easier, the trail was shorter, and the tolls were absent. The cattle trade from Texas and New Mexico began to pour through the new cut to such a degree that Wootton offered to let Goodnight pass his cattle free if he would return to the old route. It was Goodnight's turn to laugh.[15]

He continued to drive by this route until 1875, when he found it advantageous to blaze a course to the railroad at Granada, Colorado.[16]

In December, 1868, Goodnight headed for Texas to discharge the final trust to his late partner, paying Loving's family half of the $72,000 profit he had made since Loving died.[17]

Thirty thousand dollars was in his saddlebags the next spring when he continued his quest for cattle. He bought two thousand head on the Canadian in New Mexico and hired three of the herd's men to help trail them to Colorado. But they gambled all night—a pastime Goodnight never allowed—and at dawn he paid them off. The veteran trail blazer was among the most ardent extollers of the feeling of freedom that surrounded the trails, yet he kept a tight rein on his men. "I had a system on my drives," he said many times; "the most successful drives were always systematically ordered." Goodnight drilled his cowboys before starting up the trail, outlining in minute detail the duty of each hand at every hour of the trail day. "The men ate in squads," he noted, "as a certain number of them were constantly on guard. Every movement was almost military precision."[18]

Longhorns were bringing $27.50 a head in the territory when Goodnight abandoned his Apishapa claim in 1869 and bought from Charles Peck another strategic location for the trail swing station, five miles west of Pueblo.[19] While a broad virgin range lay on both sides of the Arkansas River, to the north it was unprotected, and Goodnight's seasoned eye looked south. There the line of the Rockies jogged east with wooded foothills—fine cover for cattle.[20] Calling the new place Rock Cañon Ranch, he began immediate improvements. He built a residence in early 1870 but for several years kept ranch headquarters west of the house at the canyon.

After entering his PAT brand on Pueblo County records and setting more herds on the trail, he married Mary Ann Dyer in July, 1870. Molly, as she was called, was one of a large family her lawyer father had moved from Tennessee to Texas, where she met Goodnight. This slight little woman one day would be the first of her race and sex to live in the Texas Panhandle.[21]

The entry of Iliff into Wyoming's South Pass gold rush had not lessened his demand for beef, and Goodnight's trail work continued. He shared the Pueblo range with H. W. Cresswell and the Thatcher Brothers and joined with these neighbors in buying out squatters.[22] In 1871, he ditched the valley for irrigation, imported apple trees by stage from Missouri, and set out the first orchard in southern Colorado.[23] He built a stone barn and stone corral that were monuments to permanency.[24] When the Denver and Rio Grande Western's three-foot narrow gauge came through his ranch,[25] Goodnight shipped in a few Durham bulls and purebred cows, branding them P A T M for Molly.[26] In July, 1872—when he registered their brands as far south as Las Animas County[27]—life was good on the Goodnight Trail.

While the Chisholm route remained unaltered until the 1872 trailing season, nearly 1.5 million cattle had deepened its ruts since 1867, and signs of progressive change appeared along the trail.

Down in Texas, the Snyder Brothers had a trail office in Georgetown to feed their cattle-contract operation which, since 1871, had been headquartered in Wyoming. Waco's new suspension bridge across the Brazos was the talk of the country, and by 1872 cowpokes could get mail on the trail at Tannahill Stage Station near Fort Worth.

The Waco span, begun a year before New York's Brooklyn Bridge, was completed in 1870. Optimistic owners erected holding pens so the great trail herds could be released on the cabled superstructure in orderly procession. But, except during high water, the five-cent-a-head cattle toll caused most Longhorns to go under instead of over the bridge. Herds headed in at Goode Ford on the west side could, with

ROCK CAÑON RANCH. *Where the Arkansas cuts through a narrow rock canyon, five miles west of Pueblo, Colorado, Goodnight bought a ranch in 1869 and made it his new swing station on the trail. The horseshoe of high bluffs receding from the river made a sheltered valley below the level of surrounding plains—ideal for holding cattle. He ran about three thousand head, besides, and owned a bridge here where "many thousand" crossed.*

63

the normal drift, emerge downstream at Norris Ford, passing directly under the bridge during the half-mile swim.[28]

In 1870, the Cheyenne-Arapaho Agency had been located astride the trail in Indian Territory, near present El Reno, and already had become an important market for drovers. Others turned off farther south on the government road to Fort Sill, established in 1869 to protect the nearby Comanche, Kiowa, and Kiowa-Apache Agency.[29]

When the Plains reservations were established, the government began issuing beef as a major item of annuity goods, hoping that this buffalo substitute would keep the Indians content with their new home. The "pinto buffalo,"

as redmen called the Longhorns, did their share in this respect with beef rations totaling more than 12.5 million pounds in 1870. During the next year, when 266,000 Indians were on reservations and all but a fraction were west of the Mississippi, nearly 27.5 million pounds of beef were contracted for them. Competition was keen among cowmen, especially for the big Sioux contracts, which alone amounted to almost that figure by 1880.[30]

Trail hands were astonished at the speed with which Indians could slaughter, skin, and pack off a steer; ten minutes was average time. For biweekly issues at the Wichita Agency—south of the Cheyenne-Arapaho and about thirty miles west of the trail—the agent divided

SNYDERS' TRAIL OFFICE. *From Georgetown, Texas, where they built a trail office, J. W. and D. H. Snyder ranged a wide area of the Western States. They drove the Goodnight Trail in 1868 and the Chisholm in 1869 and were the first to go to Nebraska's Union Pacific pens in 1870. After the next year's drive to Cheyenne, they made it headquarters for their upcoming Texas herds, bound for Wyoming, Idaho, and Utah. They also supplied cattle to Iliff and, after his death in 1878, managed his cattle interests for Mrs. Iliff.*

TRAIL ENDOWMENTS. *Though not a church member himself, Iliff
became interested in religious education through trail dealings with the
Snyder Brothers. Their generosity had enabled the Methodist Church
to acquire Southwestern University (above) at Georgetown, Texas.
When Iliff died, his widow carried out his request to establish a
ministerial school that young men of the West could attend at low cost.
Iliff School of Theology (left) at the University of Denver resulted.*

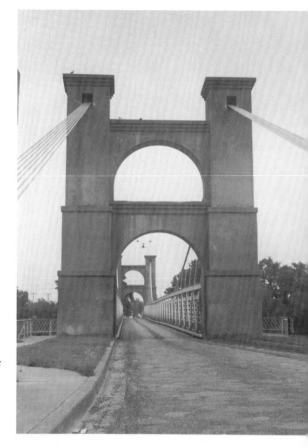

WACO SUSPENSION BRIDGE. *Built privately and opened in 1870, this still-standing span was the first across the Brazos River. The $144,000 cost included holding pens so trail herds would not be put across the bridge at a run. "Riding across faster than a flat-footed walk" was forbidden. The per-head cattle toll kept most herds swimming the river, except during high water, but the half-dollar fee for chuck wagons was preferred to wet grub.*

MAIL ON THE TRAIL. *Men who followed cattle resented most encroachment of civilization on the trail and range, but postal service was an exception. By 1872 trail drivers could get mail at a stage stop-post office called Tannahill Station, newly-built on the Chisholm Trail a few miles west of Fort Worth. The two-story stone structure also was an inn.*

68

CHEYENNE-ARAPAHO AGENCY. *Established in 1870 by Brinton Darlington, a Quaker appointee of President Grant, this important stop on the Chisholm Trail sometimes was called the Darlington Agency. The frame house, once used as agency headquarters, and several barns remain of the original structures about five miles northwest of today's El Reno, Oklahoma. An Arapaho school also was located here.*

his charges into "beef bands" of twenty-five to fifty Indians, and appointed a "beef chief" for each band. The chiefs helped with distribution, allotting one animal for division among twenty-five persons.[31]

The Indians were not confined, however, without much difficulty and bloodshed. An 1868 raid in western Kansas, attributed to the Cheyennes, gave George A. Custer the opportunity he was seeking to regain his brevet rank of major general, withdrawn at the Civil War's close. He attacked the sleeping village of Black Kettle's peaceful Cheyennes on the Washita River in Indian Territory, killing most of the braves and many of the women and children. Neighboring Kiowas, Comanches, and other tribes retaliated upon the white man at every opportunity during the next seven years.[32]

In the early 1870's, Forts Richardson, Griffin, and Concho in Texas frequently deployed troops as protective escorts for trail herds. Several trail men felt the Indian's stern reprisals, and at least 2 cowboys lost their lives.[33] Indians came upon the Snyders on their first trip up the Chisholm Trail in 1869 and drove off 140 cattle. The Osage Indians in 1872 "gave us an exhibition of what they could do to a Texas herd," said drover George Hindes. "They

69

killed about 100 beeves right there on the prairie, and scattered the others to the four winds."[34]

Again, the chief factor in placing the Indian upon a reservation and keeping him there was the buffalo slaughter—a factor ultimately assured at 2:47 p.m., May 10, 1869. At that moment the continent was spanned as the Central Pacific and Union Pacific rails joined at Promontory Point, Utah, and opened at once to traffic.[35] Plains buffalo that for eons had ranged the midcontinent, north to south with the seasons, now were divided into two great herds. Furthermore, the Union Pacific's southern division, the westward-moving Kansas Pacific, was almost across Kansas. With extension of the Atchison, Topeka, and Santa Fe south to Wichita and Dodge City in 1872, the southern buffalo range was sliced to bits. These lines brought in hordes of hunters and shipped out hundreds of thousands of buffalo hides until, by 1875, the southern herd of about four million was almost gone. Construction of the Northern Pacific in the early 1880's repeated the story for the smaller northern herd, which virtually was extinct by 1884.[36]

The railroads also went after the cattle trade. Snyder herds in 1870 were the first to cross the Kansas Pacific and go on to Schuyler, Nebraska, located on the Platte River and the Union Pacific. By the year's end U.P. promotion of Schuyler as a shipping point for Texas cattle was aimed at offsetting the Abilene trade.[37]

The Leavenworth, Lawrence, and Galveston, pointing south through Kansas, had reached the northern border of Indian Territory by June, 1871, and advertised its route in Texas papers. With good water and grass and no settlements, it was 125 miles nearer than Abilene and 80 miles nearer than Newton. Shipping rates were the same as from other points. "Don't be misled by Agents of Rival Lines," cautioned the advertisement.[38]

For a year the Missouri River, Fort Scott, and Gulf road had been shipping to Kansas City some cattle that had come up the old Shawnee Trail into Indian Territory. The fledgling Missouri–Kansas–Texas Railway— The KATY—also was in the race. By October this line had pushed from Sedalia, Missouri, and Junction City, Kansas, to Fort Gibson, in east central Indian Territory, and was carrying twenty to fifty carloads of cattle daily.[39]

In 1870, the year Texas was readmitted to the Union, the secretary of agriculture's report reflected some alarm over the Texas cattle trade, which he said had disturbed and deranged the general market. If the condition continued, states east of the Mississippi would be compelled to yield entirely the production of lower beef grades.[40] The condition was due in part to the railroad rate war of that year, when 300,000 Longhorns were trudging up the Chisholm Trail. Reduced freight costs allowed cowmen to make between $15 and $25 a head. The profits far outweighed the discomfort caused by body lice, which infested many drovers during the 1870 season.[41]

Flushed with the previous gain, drovers rounded up 600,000 to 700,000 cattle for the 1871 drives. More than 300 herds averaging 1,000 head had passed Red River Station by June 19. Cowboys reported that every available stream crossing was crowded between there and San Antonio, with each herd striving to be first, and that "grass along the principal trail has been closely eaten off and new trails are being made."[42] South central Kansas was inundated and running over with the bovine flood, and still it rose. "The line is now continuous from the Rio Grande," wrote one observer, and "fully half of the beeves passing here are ready for the butcher."[43] The fact that some of the cattle were sixteen years old, however, indicated that the reservoir of wild cattle was not depleted entirely, and that Texans were bent on selling anything they could rope.[44]

Yet trail driving was a dangerous pursuit fraught with tension, uncertainty, and unending weariness, causing many Texans to try again for home cattle markets. The resulting hide-and-tallow factories, which sprang up on the Texas coast immediately after the war and flourished for a decade, were the first of the larger ventures in processing the state's raw materials.[45] Unique in North America was this bizarre and voluminous business that slaughtered thousands upon thousands of cattle, largely for their hide and tallow.

70

MARGIN OF THE BAYS. *For over a decade after 1865, boat shipment of Texas cattle and cattle by-products centered around inlets on the Lone Star coast from Corpus Christi north to Houston. Live animals went by sea from Rockport to New Orleans and, in 1869, the first successful shipment of beef by refrigerated boat left Indianola for the Crescent City. In 1871 the nation's first mechanically refrigerated abattoir at Fulton launched American meat packers on a new road.*

In the better establishments animals were killed as the market demanded. Meat was salted, pickled, dried, or preserved as "mess beef" for the army; tallow was sold to eastern soap and candle makers; hides and horns were marketable for shoes, buttons, and combs. But at other factories countless cattle were killed for their hides alone. At that time, when Texas teemed with Longhorns in numbers beyond belief, a cowhide was worth more than a live cow.

Many "packeries," exporting through Rockport—the center of this activity—rendered the tallow and dumped the cooked meat into the bay or fed it to the hogs. Raw lean cuts, too, were available for hogs, or to anyone who cared to haul them away. A five-acre hill of discarded carcasses, covered with blue bottle flies and reeking of rotted meat, finally was sold to Yankees and shipped north as fertilizer.[46]

At these plants daily sales of 400 cattle were frequent, the owner receiving an occasional $8 a head, but usually $4.50. Buyers would take any animal that would pass the brand inspector, and his cut of 25 cents a head often amounted to $100 a day. This office was begun in 1868, when the military government in Texas took note of the new industry.[47]

Rockport hide-and-tallow factories were constructed hastily of rough pine shipped from New Orleans. The main building housed steam tanks, platforms, hoists, and tallow vats. Boiler rooms normally were enclosed. The structures were flanked on the landward side by a network of pens and chutes and on the bayside by loading docks and long wharves.

"Packery" operation also was simple. Forty men could handle about 250 cattle a day with a minimum of machinery. As the animals passed through chutes, the spearman from a platform above struck downward and, if skillful, severed the spinal cord, killing the beef instantly. On skinning platforms the horns and hooves were cut off and the hide ripped from the legs and neck. A horse or mule with block and tackle did the rest. Butchers, markers, and axmen sliced the carcass into pieces that were

hoisted into big iron steam tanks holding about 25 beeves. Tallow drained into vats below the tanks and was stored in hogsheads to await shipment.[48]

Less elaborate hide-and-tallow factories were on the big ranches of Texas, which at that time were all on the coast. Captains King and Kenedy, then operating separate ranches, were in the group, as was Shanghai Pierce. Allen and Poole, on Galveston Island, had the largest known factory, killing 20,000 cattle in 1870 and 1871, and discarding everything but the hides and tallow. The exact number of these plants was never tabulated, but they reached from Houston and other East Texas points to Corpus Christi Bay.

During the early 1870's, the waste of Longhorns for hides in South Texas was equaled only by the buffalo slaughter then in progress on the Plains. Excluding all other Texas ports, Corpus Christi and Rockport shipped out almost 300,000 hides in 1872, a figure equivalent to the combined number of cattle driven north in 1874 and 1875.[49]

There were other experiments in the beef-use field, but none of the hide-and-tallow magnitude. In 1868, Frances Stabler's Beef Packery at Indianola had a process of canning meat while it was still warm with animal heat. With six hours between slaughter and soldered can, Stabler was independent of outside temperatures and thus could work through the summer without meat spoilage. Demand apparently was not sufficient to require many summers of labor, although he did obtain a U.S. Navy contract.[50]

The San Antonio Meat Extract Company, also formed in 1868, had a New York depot and was paying shareholder dividends when it was incorporated in 1870. Company advertisements for "Extract of Meat of Texas" ran a month in local papers before the product sank into oblivion.[51] Another attempt, the Liebig Meat Extract Company, received passing mention in an 1871 list of home manufacturers.[52]

Far-reaching developments in the field of refrigeration had begun in 1867, when the first

COASTAL SHOWPLACE. *During 1872-1876 the $100,000 mansion of cattleman and refrigeration pioneer George W. Fulton went up at Fulton, Texas. A civil engineer and cousin of the steamboat inventor, Fulton designed his copper-roofed home with central heating, lighting, and air conditioning; hot and cold water; and a sewer system. On concrete and steel foundation, exterior walls resembling stone actually are cypress—vertical boards with thick corner blocks. Black walnut, marble, jade, and ebony accented the interior.*

BIG BUSINESS. *John Grant Tobias's 1875 painting of Marion Packing Company at Fulton shows penned cattle, cylindrical rendering vats and wooden buildings of a large hide and tallow operation. Tallow was packed in 1,000-pound barrels. Typical schooners carried about 2,000 hides, 20 tons of bones, 4,000 horns, tallow, and some mess beef. More than 100 million pounds of tallow and 2.5 million dollars' worth of hides left the Texas coast in 1874, and the 1875 value of exported hides rose to $34,730,000.*

74

FOR HIDE AND TALLOW. *A crumbling cistern at Fulton is all that remains of hide and tallow factories that mushroomed along the Gulf Coast in post-Civil War Texas. The elements have destroyed hastily constructed buildings and rusted away the iron vats where hundreds of thousands of cattle were slaughtered for hide and tallow alone. Much beef was discarded in the bay in the wasteful operation that was the first large venture in processing Texas raw materials.*

refrigerated rail car appeared. There was a lesson in the simple rolling icebox, in which meat discolored from ice contact and soon spoiled. In improved cars with separate ice and meat compartments, George H. Hammond was shipping refrigerated beef from Chicago to Boston by 1869. In four more years the nation's initial effort at long distance rail shipments of refrigerated beef would leave Denison, Texas, and arrive fresh in New York City.[53]

The Morgan steamship *Agnes* was fitted out with a cold storage room in 1869 by Dr. H. P. Howard of San Antonio, and thirty dressed beeves were shipped from Indianola to New Orleans in July. This was the first export cargo of refrigerated meat. Howard and investors from Texas and Pennsylvania had utilized a process patented by Wilson Brady of New York. Although their firm, the United States and West Indies Fresh Meat and Fruit Company, failed financially within two years, they had pioneered a field that shortly would revolutionize the American and British meat industries.[54]

Verbose General D. A. Maury, who pronounced the beef sweet on arrival in New Orleans, wrote this prediction back to Texas:

Henceforth. instead of driving your emaciated, footsore, and perhaps diseased cattle to an unfavorable or uncertain market. thousands of miles away. you may establish your slaughter houses . . . kill and dress your beeves with all their juices and freshness in them, hang them in your great refrigerative ships and send them in perfect preservation to New Orleans. Liverpool. the coast of Guinea. or Ceylon . . . and with due energy and judgment. you gentlemen of Texas may find your cattle independent of the malign legislation of the northern States. and once more a great staple production used by civilized men all over the world.[55]

The Texas livestock buying and shipping firm of Coleman, Mathis, and Fulton believed that cattle demand would increase with the use of refrigerated boats, and looked upon that means of marketing as more desirable than the long trails to Kansas. In 1869, George Ware Fulton of that firm had patented a plan that would allow meat to be ready when the ships came in. His "Improvement in Apparatus for Slaughtering and Curing Meat" called for a double-walled abattoir with nonheat-conduct-

ing material between the walls. An "apparatus" to discharge cool air into the slaughterhouse would enable carcasses to be moved from room to room without temperature increase.

Practical application of Fulton's plan was made in 1871, when the Holden brothers—D. L., E. G., and C. M.—opened the first artificially cooled abattoir in the United States at Fulton, Texas.[56]

In Kansas, meanwhile, many changes were in the offing for the Chisholm Trail. Abilene tired of the boisterous trade that had made it and formally asked the drovers to take their cattle, cowboys, and entertainment elsewhere. Nesters, coming in during the cowtown's five-year supremacy, joined with townsmen in the February, 1872, resolution:

We, the undersigned members of the Farmer's Protective Association, and officers and citizens of Dickinson County, Kansas, most respectfully request all who have contemplated driving Texas cattle to Abilene the coming season to seek some other point for shipment, as the inhabitants of Dickinson will no longer submit to the evils of the trade.

The action opened Kansas in the next three years to a ping-pong game of cattle markets played by railroads and rival towns. Like the proverbial ball, the trade bounced between Newton on the southward-going Santa Fe to Ellsworth on the westward-sweeping Kansas Pacific, back to the Santa Fe farther south at Wichita, and returned briefly to the K.P. more westwardly, at Hays City. Solomon, Salina, and Brookville also had a share in Longhorn shipping. Of the cattle-center towns, Wichita was the longest lived and most important, but bore more than a mite of color. "The end of the trail" now was a phrase fanning out over the western two-thirds of Kansas like the frayed tip of a mammoth rope.

Newton's glory was limited to less than a year by the pressing timetable of expansion. The Santa Fe reached there in 1871 in time to tap some of the Abilene traffic, but by May, 1872, the same line had facilities at Wichita—twenty-six miles closer to Texas. Twenty buildings went up in the first month, and Joe McCoy came down to supervise construction of stockyards large enough to hold four thousand cattle. So Texas cowboys would feel at home,

ELLSWORTH JAIL. *Completed in July, 1873, the calaboose in
Ellsworth, Kansas, was the finest in the West. The local paper exclaimed
that it was the most comfortable place in town but warned readers that
not too many should crowd into the building at one time. Remembering
Abilene, where cowboys had torn down walls of a jail under construction, Ellsworth's was two-story stone and solid.*

saloons and gambling places took names of their Abilene predecessors, with "The Alamo" leading the line. Paid partly from a fund raised by gamblers, two justices of the peace, a couple of constables, and a deputy sheriff did little to retard the wild night life. There were few fatal shootings, though, until that August night in Perry Tuttle's dance hall, when in a matter of moments eight men littered the floor, dead or dying, in a tragedy always referred to as the "General Massacre."[57] Two thousand drovers and buyers were reported in and around Newton at the time, and cattle shipments were predicted to reach forty thousand head.

During the 1871 season, the older town of Ellsworth, which had straddled the Kansas Pacific since 1867, shipped 35,000 Longhorns, and took over much of Abilene's trade and some of its buildings when that market closed. The Drover's Cottage, a 3-story frame hotel at Abilene, was dismantled, loaded on flat cars and set up for business in the town farther west. And the business came: 100,000 cattle in 1872.[58] "Here you see in the streets," gushed the *Ellsworth Reporter*, "the tall, long haired Texas herder . . . the dirty, greasy Mexicans . . . the gambler from all parts of the country . . . the honest immigrant . . . the keen stock buyers; the wealthy Texas drovers; dead beats; cappers; pick-pockets; horse thieves; a cavalry of Texas ponies and scores of demimonde."[59] Ellsworth obviously needed a commodious jail, and one was begun.

Eyeing the Santa Fe's advance, the Kansas Pacific pitched in to promote Ellsworth. The railroad surveyed a cutoff trail to Ellsworth, leaving the Chisholm between the Salt Fork of the Arkansas and Pond Creek, in Indian Territory. Labeled the Ellsworth Trail, the new route saved twenty miles. It was advertised by the K.P.-published *Guide Map of the Great Texas Cattle Trail from Red River Crossing to the Old Reliable Kansas Pacific Railway*, copies of which were circulated throughout the Texas ranching country.[60]

Ellsworth's major rival was Wichita, the booming settlement on the banks of the Arkansas, where Jesse Chisholm had set up his first trading post. An outsized, coffeepot smokestack and heavy cowcatcher dwarfed the first little locomotive that pulled in on May 11, 1872, but Wichita citizens were overjoyed. Regular service began two days later, and herds were on the way from Texas. To spread the word, the city council hired a cowman to ride south for drovers, and Joe McCoy to go north and east for buyers. Bugle-voiced Shanghai Pierce and two others were engaged by the Santa Fe to look after its cattle interests.

Boasting nearly two thousand inhabitants, Wichita was more solid than earlier cowtowns. Presbyterians had completed a church in 1870. Congregations of Methodists, Episcopalians, and Catholics were preparing to build. Despite the ecclesiastical influence, bankers assured all comers that the new shipping center would not emulate Abilene in driving the cattle trade away. Signs were posted on the trail south of town: "EVERYTHING GOES IN WICHITA." In anticipation of the rowdy element, a jail was ready when the first cowboys came in.[61]

The *Wichita City Eagle* was sure in July that, "notwithstanding all the blow and fuss and feathers made by new and ambitious points to gain the Texas cattle trade, Wichita practically controls the whole thing." Ready for a grand opening was the two-story hotel erected by prominent Texas cowmen to accommodate themselves and buyers and called, of course, the Texas House. Chutes and gates were going up at the Arkansas River bridge to "provide against such a rush of Longhorns as might breakdown or damage the structure."[62]

More than 350,000 Longhorns were moved north in 1872 and, for the majority of Texas drovers, it was a profitable trail year. Wichita did lead the field as a shipping center, sending off 70,600 head, compared to Ellsworth's 40,161, but at least 100,000 cattle bound for Nebraska, Wyoming, Utah, and even California, changed hands in Ellsworth. Sixty to 70 percent of the total drives were mixed herds rather than beeves, indicating that most of them were to stock new ranges instead of being shipped east.[63]

A number of cattle also were sent that year by rail from Hays City, on the Kansas Pacific. The town was dominated by nearby Fort Hays, which had helped to guard Santa Fe Trail commerce before the cattle period.[64]

WELCOMED COWCATCHER. *Town folk of Wichita, Kansas, proudly watched the first train—Santa Fe's small, brass-trimmed, diamond stack—puff in on May 11, 1872. Drovers banned by Abilene in February flocked to the new end of the Chisholm Trail. Locomotive No. 1, an 1880 replica of coal-burning power that launched the Santa Fe in 1868, weighs 108,500 pounds. Note running lamps and oil headlights.*

NEW END OF THE LINE. *Wichita's original railroad station was ready in 1872, when the first locomotive arrived. The 2,000 aggressive citizens, led by Jesse Chisholm's associate, J. R. Mead, were unwilling to watch steady streams of Longhorns pass them by. They floated bonds to build from Newton 26 miles of track, which the Santa Fe preleased. Overnight, Wichita became a major shipping point, sending 70,600 cattle east in 1872.*

FOR WICHITA WORSHIP. *Appropriately, a church was among the earliest structures in the Kansas town founded by the Southwest's good Samaritan, Jesse Chisholm. This Presbyterian house of worship, built in 1870, was sold to a Catholic congregation in 1873 and made into a rooming house before being saved for posterity in the 1940's.*

FOR LAW AND ORDER. *Anticipating the 1872 cattle trade, Wichita's first jail went up in 1871 at a cost of eight hundred dollars. The six-cell affair of strong, stacked-plank construction was far from escape-proof; the outline of exit holes cut by early inmates shows today. The Munger House, at right, was the city's first dwelling, and boarders were accepted with the cattle boom. The log house is chinked with Arkansas River sand, lime burned from mussel shells, and buffalo hair.*

Cattle moved in 1872 trail drives were down from the disastrous peak of 600,000 the previous year, when Texans, encouraged by 1870's good prices and lower freight rates, had flooded the market with rough cattle. By 1871, the railroad rate war was over. Since feeders already were stocked up from the year before, buyers were scarce and choosy. Drovers unwilling to sacrifice their stock waited in Kansas for a market rise that failed to come. Instead, a concentrated blizzard sweeping down the Plains froze everything in its tracks—jackrabbits, wolves, ponies by the hundreds, and Longhorns estimated at between 100,000 and 250,000[65]

The 1871-1872 winter was severe and dry in the south. Texans came to speak of the 1872 spring as "the die up." By early April the word had spread and Denver's *Rocky Mountain News* quoted the *New Orleans Picayune* report that "late cold weather and drought has occasioned immense cattle losses in Texas. Texas papers estimate 200,000 head died in the last few weeks . . . [and] the loss is fearful between the Guadalupe and Nueces Rivers. In Goliad alone 25,000 animals have been skinned."[66] One outfit skinned four thousand dead cattle, and nearer the coast, a cowboy commented that he had seen as many as a thousand carcasses in one day's ride.[67]

Although the Texas loss of Longhorns was unprecedented, cattle skinning was not. "Consideration of it belongs in any account of what was doing along the range at the southern end of the trails—and of what many trail drivers did with their time during the winters of the 70's," says J. Frank Dobie. Several factors caused South Texans to know "skinning wars" and the "skinning season" as naturally as they knew the branding season. Accepted range practice allowed "fallen hides" to be taken from dead animals regardless of brand or where they were found. With all the country open and unfenced, many cattle drifted toward the coast each winter, banked up along creeks and bayous, where they grazed off the grass, bogged down, and died.[68]

Cattle-wise Joe McCoy observed that some Longhorns arriving at Wichita in 1872 from northern Texas had blockier bodies and shorter horns and were more civilized in general. He believed they were graded up with Durham

bulls on the home range.[69] Bovine imports could have survived then in North Texas, where winters were cold enough to kill the cattle tick, but more probably Texans' efforts at selective Longhorn breeding, and the winter's heavy culling hand of 1871-1872, were paying off.[70]

Trail driving had become a more regulated business since 1870, when state officials established a Texas office of hide and cattle inspection. The governor was authorized to appoint inspectors in counties that needed them. To facilitate inspection, drovers were required to mark their cattle with a lighter "road brand," and to have a "bill of sale" describing each animal. This closer check was necessary with so many cattle on the trails. Herds were getting mixed and, deliberately or not, were being swelled in number by animals from ranges along the trail. One rancher lost three hundred cattle to passing trail herds in 1869, and a lady near Red River Station typified the many who were irate because "the pesky drovers" had driven off her milk cows.[71]

Another item was added to trail staples when Bull Durham was introduced in 1871. Before the advent of this tobacco, complete with rolling papers, trail hands sometimes skinned prickly pears to get wrappings for their cigarettes. Aside from the smoking pleasure "Bull" brought to the trail, it was useful, too, when rubbed in the eyes of tired waddies to keep them awake. Their regular work was nearly eighteen hours a day, or twenty-four if the night was bad.[72]

About this time, trail driving ceased to be an exclusively male endeavor, and a few hardy women also accompanied the cows.

Among the drovers to Wichita in 1873 was Mrs. Margaret Heffernan Borland of Victoria, Texas, the only woman actually known to have commanded a cattle herd on any trail. Though frail, she was a lady of resolute will and self-reliance long before 1867, when she assumed management of the A. Borland ranch on the death of her last husband. Fortune finally had smiled upon her in a pecuniary sense, but exceptional trials and adversity followed her all her forty-nine years.

As an infant she had come to Texas with her father, who steered his own ship from New

FORT HAYS. *The stone blockhouse at Fort Hays, Kansas, dates from 1867, when the Kansas Pacific came in. The town of Hays grew up around the post and became a minor market for Texas cattle. It was here, too, that William F. Cody earned his legendary moniker. The railroad hired him at $500 a month to furnish buffalo meat for its laborers. Cody killed 4,280 of the shaggies in 17 months and rail crews dubbed him "Buffalo Bill."*

York harbor to Matagorda Bay about 1825. He was slain in the 1836 Texas Revolution by General José Urrea's advancing forces, but his children, who spoke Spanish fluently, passed for Mexicans and thus escaped the Goliad massacre. Thrice widowed, Mrs. Borland lost several children in infancy. Then the 1867 yellow fever epidemic claimed a son, two daughters, and two grandchildren.

She owned upwards of 10,000 cattle in 1873, when she readied a trail herd of about 2,500 and gathered up the remnants of her family to make the drive. With her went two sons, Alex and Jesse, both under 15; a daughter, Nellie, about 7; and a 5-year-old granddaughter, Julia Rosa Rose. Employing a Negro camp cook and a group of trail hands, Mrs. Borland climbed into a buckboard and headed north.

"It is believed," wrote her son-in-law Victor Rose, "that this journey and the attendant responsibilities proved too severe for her mental and physical resources, as she died soon after reaching the long looked for goal; and before she had sold her cattle." Another family member called her malady "trail driving fever," while the *Wichita City Eagle* of Thursday, July 10, said simply:

Mrs. Boling [Borland], the lady who brought a drove of cattle to this point from Texas a few weeks since, died in this city on last Saturday of congestion of the brain. Her body was taken to Texas for interment.

The cowboys accompanying her cared tenderly for the two little girls, dressing them as best they could in ladies clothes — the only ready-made garments they could find. Fashionable long drawers were tied around the children's necks.[73] The Borland boys, who later became livestock dealers, erected in the Victoria cemetery a handsome marker inscribed

Our Mama
Margaret Heffernan Borland
Born Apr. 3, 1824
Died July 5, 1873

Gone, but not forgotten.

The trails dealt harshly with all women, whether left on lonely ranches to worry about their husbands' safety or accompanying them, as a few did, on the long, rough drives.

In conventional cases, women on the trail were wives of the bosses or herd owners. A small tent was set up for the lady at night; she rode in a buggy or buckboard during the day. The female presence was loooked upon as a bad omen by most trail hands, perhaps because cowboys in the main were over-protective of their womenfolk. Also, when the herd was ready to move on, having to extricate a lady from her newly-found patch of wild flowers or plums was as hard as punching cattle. Mrs. W. F. (Amanda) Burks, Mrs. James M. Holmsley, and Mrs. Mary Taylor Bunton were among trail wives of this sort.[74]

Mrs. D. M. Barton, who persuaded Mr. Barton to take her and their young child up the trail in 1874, was a slight deviation from the norm. With the cook as baby sitter, the infant cooed happily in the chuck wagon while Mrs. Barton rode as a trail hand.[75] Mrs. Charles Goodnight twice rode the trail to Dodge City in the two-horned side saddle that Goodnight designed for her.

The stork hovered over the Chisholm Trail in 1871, when Mrs. George Cluck, great with child, prevailed upon George to take her and their several children on the drive. Cow waddies rode double with the youngsters while she mounted a pony and swam Red River, then rising and nine hundred yards wide. Her son, Ewell, was born at Abilene in October, none the worse for his prenatal trailing.[76]

Another headstrong but extremely feminine example of womanhood on the trail was Mrs. Lizzie Johnson Williams, known for her love of frilly silks and satins. Better at business than Hezekiah, her handsome spouse, she kept her property and brand separate from his. Three times they drove the Chisholm Trail together as man and wife, and as two independent cattle owners.[77]

In the trails' latter days a girl disguised as a boy joined a herd at Clayton, New Mexico, and made a top hand until homesickness overtook her. Revealing her secret to the astonished trail

MORE CIVILIZED. *Longhorns arriving at Wichita, Kansas, in 1872, had shorter horns and squarer bodies, said trail promoter Joseph McCoy. He attributed the improvement to Durham bulls on home ranges; yet if the few Durhams brought into Texas by that time survived Texas fever, they lacked the time to effect upgrading. Spanish practices allowing all animals to breed had been discarded by King, Pierce, and many others. Using the best cattle at hand, they were producing Longhorns with better meat qualities.*

WOMAN'S MARKER ON THE TRAILS. *Mrs. Margaret Heffernan Borland's determination to drive her own cattle to Wichita in 1873 earned her the distinction of being the only lady trail boss, but it also caused her death. Cowboys returned her body, her small daughter, and her granddaughter to their home in Victoria, Texas. Mrs. Borland is buried in the city's oldest cemetery beneath an imposing marble and granite shaft.*

GOODNIGHTS' GEAR. *In the 1870 summer Goodnight designed for his bride the second-horn side saddle, which she twice rode up the trail. The saddle, made by C. Gallup of Pueblo, Colorado, was safer than the old type and less severe on horse and rider. A regular man's saddle tree was used, the horn replaced, and an adjustable side horn added for the left knee. The design became universal and won a London prize. Goodnight's saddle, at left, was a gift from Mexico.*

84

boss, she explained that tales of her father who had been up the trail caused her craving for the same adventure.[78]

In the wet year of 1873, every river on the trail was up, but the contrast of prices—$8 a head in San Antonio against $23.80 in Kansas—drew 405,000 Longhorns to the trail.[79] This was the big year for Ellsworth, where some 150,000 cattle were moved, although the loadings were less than half of Wichita's 66,000. Great Bend and Hutchison, in Kansas, also had a taste of cattle shipping, along with Granada, across the line in Colorado.

More herds probably would have gone by rail from Kansas, but the Panic of 1873 fell with all its fury in September, paralyzing the cattle market and leaving thousands of Longhorns unsold. The economic plunge was set off in the East by the failure of Jay Cooke and Company, a securities and banking firm that had floated big government loans during the Civil War and now had over advanced for railroad construction. Like falling dominoes, the New York Stock Exchange closed, banks were broken, and many individuals were out of work or bankrupt.[80]

Writing in 1874, McCoy estimated that Texas drovers lost 2 million dollars in the panic and that nearly every man who drove cattle in 1873 shared in this loss. Cows and thin, rough steers sold in some instances from $1 to $1.25 per hundred weight.[81] As a result, the hide-and-tallow industry reached its peak; the drives to Kansas dropped to 166,000 head in 1874, and to 151,000 in 1875. While the cattle market slumbered these 2 years, significant events on the Plains and in the nation bore heavily on the future of the trails.

Many historians peg November 24, 1874, as the most important date in the development of the West, for on that day, a patent was granted for the first practical form of barbed wire. Innovator Joseph F. Glidden, a tight-lipped Illinois farmer, called his simple wire barb twisted onto double-strand wire, "The Winner," and so it was. After nearly a century, Glidden barbed wire has proved to be the most popular of some four hundred varieties made in the United States since the first in 1867. Modern domestic styles differ little from his original design.

There was nothing new about fencing in America. Over 1,200 patents for farm and field fences had been issued in the first seventy-five years of the nineteenth century, and more than two-thirds of that number after 1865. As farmers crowded in on the eastern edge of the Plains' new cattle ranges, the need for cheap fencing grew more urgent. The process was expensive at best. Fence material on the Plains in some cases was three hundred percent higher than in other regions.

Cowmen believed that farmers should fence their crops against cattle, and farmers argued conversely that cattlemen should fence and let the fields lie open. Depending upon material available locally, there were worm fences, rock fences, mud fences, rail fences, plank fences, and fence hedges of bois d'arc and Cherokee roses. There also was a great deal of unsatisfactory smooth wire fencing, which expanded and sagged with the heat and was no match for a Longhorn. None of it lasted more than ten years except the slow-growing hedges that took more space than other types of barriers and depleted the soil.

It was the thorny hedge, however, that inspired barbed wire and thus the fencing controversy, which from 1874 through the 1880's occupied more newspaper space in the Plains and prairie states than any other issue.

Retaining royalties, Glidden sold his interests to Washburn and Moen, a Connecticut company that quickly perfected production machinery and monopolized barbed wire patents. In the same year, 1876, the Bessemer-steel process was developed for a cheaper and more durable material that revolutionized the wire business. The cost dropped from 18 to 8 cents a pound, putting "the devil's rope" within reach of the poorest sodbuster. Wire manufacture climbed from 10,000 pounds in 1874, to 2.8 million pounds in 1876, to a staggering 80 million pounds in 1880, as the bloody encirclement of the range went on.

Cattlemen from the beginning labeled as "vicious" this farmer contrivance that cut up their stock, but soon they were forced to fence. Free access to grass and water was part of the unwritten law of the open range, and when water holes were walled off from general use, fence-cutting wars raged the length of the

'THE WINNER.' *Visitors to the Texas Panhandle still may see, near Amarillo, stretches of the first practical barbed wire, patented in 1874, and the first erected in that region. With Glidden as a silent partner in 1881, H. B. Sanborn surrounded 250,000 acres with 150 miles of "The Winner," extra-heavy Glidden wire. Their Frying Pan Ranch, developed as a demonstration by, for, and with barbed wire, then was an unprecedented enclosure. Its success affected all of the Plains at the opportune moment in range expansion.*

86

A VANISHING AMERICAN. *The last all-wooden windmill in the Texas Panhandle was moved a few miles in 1966 from the Harrell Ranch to Potter County Historical Park, northeast of Amarillo. The "vertical aspect of an otherwise horizontal landscape," as one author describes the windmill, is fast disappearing even in its all-steel form. Its role in western economic development, as dominant as its silhouette, is being passed on to products of rural electrification, and in some cases to gasoline pumps.*

87

Plains. The death toll was high in Wyoming's "Johnson County War." Out of New Mexico's "Lincoln County War" grew the legend of Billy the Kid. The conflict came to a head in the Lone Star State in 1883, when headlines in far-away Chicago summed up the reason Rangers were called out and the legislature assembled in special session: "HELL BROKE LOOSE IN TEXAS—Wire-Cutters Cut 500 Miles in Coleman County."

The cowboy's hate of wire was as fierce as the barbs, and he gained stature as a freedom-loving man who wouldn't be fenced in. But the days of the trail, the open range, and the Longhorn were numbered by the speed of fencing.[82]

Harnessing the wind to draw water to the otherwise arid face of the Plains became a broad practice about the time of Glidden's 1874 barbed wire patent. An American adaptation of the windmill had been made in 1854 and used in construction of the Pacific railroads, but demand did not require large-scale production until the mid-1870's. The mill that young Daniel Halladay, a Connecticut mechanic, designed was intended only as a water pump and was much smaller than its European counterparts, known since 1185. The invention of well-drilling equipment in the 1870's allowed tapping of the water table, which in many places lay too far beneath the surface for dug wells. It set the stage for widespread western use of windmills. Agents for all-wooden windmills followed closely behind barbed wire salesmen, and drilling crews came after fencing crews.

Steel blades that could be curved to capture more wind force, developed in 1883, rapidly replaced the wooden-bladed wheel. In company with barbed wire, the windmill opened up prime agricultural land to the homesteader. As the *1870 Texas Almanac* had predicted, before many years irrigation by wind power enhanced prairie land values hundreds of millions of dollars.

Windmills also allowed expansion of the cattle industry into areas where the shortage of surface water had rendered ranching almost impossible. No longer dependent upon a central water hole, pasture subdivisions made for more even grazing and for livestock improvement through selective breeding.

Easily the most romantic of man-made installations on the range, the gothic thrust of an isolated windmill dwarfed against the sky accents the charm of the lonely vastness. Moreover, to those who know personally the meaning of drouth, a windmill presiding over life-giving water is a comfortable sight; its singular creaking, especially at night, is reassuring music to sleep by.[83]

In Kansas, the 1874 arrival of Russian Mennonites, and with them the hard Red Turkey wheat and the tools to cultivate it, signaled the agricultural trend that ultimately would overgrow the trails and make Kansas the "wheat state." The Mennonites came at the fervent insistence of the Santa Fe Railroad, which sent crews of land agents east and a representative to Europe. The Santa Fe, like other Western lines and unlike Eastern roads, had extended much faster than the settlement line. The lack of settlers to create business along the rights-of-way largely precipitated the Panic of 1873.

WHEAT THRASHING STONE. *This innovation of the Russian Mennonites, who came to central Kansas in 1874, was used to harvest the Red Turkey winter wheat which they had brought to the Plains. The saw-tooth stone wheel is about eighteen inches in diameter and three feet long, with side pieces arranged to hook up to a horse or mule. Only burr mills incapable of grinding such hard wheat were in Kansas then, but a roller mill—the first of many—soon was set up near Abilene.*

88

'SO LARGE A RANCHO.' *Early in 1874, a Corpus Christi paper diagnosed King's 78,225-acre Santa Gertrudis as "so large a rancho." The stable, said the article, is "capable of accommodating . . . sixty head of animals," and land around the "large and commodious dwelling . . . resembles a well cultivated park." Equipped for work "from the forging of a horseshoe nail to the erection of a first class house," the rancho was independent of cities. Nearby, King had bought 196,775 more acres.*

The Santa Fe's sale of sixty thousand of its three million acres to the Mennonites was but the beginning of a flood of immigration to the Plains encouraged by railroads and by government land offers.[84]

By 1874, connecting rail lines provided through passenger service from St. Louis to Dallas and Houston, while Captain Richard King was completing major ranch improvements that are enviable even in the present day. King cattle had not moved up the trails until 1870 because the ranch owner, like many others, had hoped for markets nearer home. Shortly after the 1871 trailing season he had invested in the International Railroad Company that later became the Missouri Pacific, risking his cattle profits to get rail connections to South Texas.[85]

Selling his trail herds before the 1873 crash, King gave his attention to other elements of his diversified ranch while the cattle market recovered. In the hard year of 1874, he marketed hide and tallow, horses and mules, and wool from his sheep.[86] "The Captain has endeavored to arrange his matters as to render himself entirely independent of all the annoyances connected with the successful operation of so large a rancho at so great a distance from a City," observed the *Corpus Christi Gazette*. According to the report, King then owned about 50,000 cattle, 6,000 mules and jacks, 30,000 sheep, and probably 7,000 hogs. These were sustained on 275,000 clear-title acres where smooth wire fencing was complete on 65,000.[87]

Young braves of the southern Plains tribes, becoming restive in 1874, staged a general uprising that struck fear particularly into personnel of the Cheyenne-Arapaho (Darlington) Agency. Army troopers camped nearby and in 1875 located Fort Reno southwest of the agency as a permanent guard against the Cheyennes. In June, 1874, about seven hundred Cheyennes, Kiowas, and Comanches, having attacked a hunters' camp in the Texas Panhandle, were repelled in a five-day fight known as the Second Battle of Adobe Walls. The attack spurred the military into a major campaign to confine or kill all Indians. In April, 1875, the last remnants of the Comanches came into Fort Sill. The Texas Panhandle and Indian Territory now were safe from savage marauding, while the lordly and roving Comanche—whose name from the Ute meant "anyone who wants to fight me all the time"—was reduced to a new and sedentary role.[88]

Maneuvers on the northern Plains likewise indicated a showdown with the Sioux and, if the whites were successful, more room for the roping man on horseback and the one who carried a pick and placer pan. Indian attacks on surveyors of the Northern Pacific Railroad gave the army an excuse to order reconnaissance of the Sioux's Black Hills and, incidentally, to investigate persisting rumors of gold. Lieutenant Colonel George A. Custer led the military foray with a contingent of scientists, newspapermen, photographers, and some miners.

They found gold deposits on French Creek in Dakota Territory, and Custer proudly reported in August, 1874, that anyone could duplicate the feat. In accordance with the 1868 treaty at Fort Laramie, soldiers attempted to keep prospectors out of the Sioux lands until September, 1875, when the Indians refused the government's six-million-dollar offer to buy the Black Hills.[89] Then gold seekers, pouring in despite military warnings, created a great demand for meat and poultry products.[90]

The cattle market was looking up in 1875 when the first shipment of American dressed beef reached England in good condition.[91] Men who trailed to Kansas that year received about $22 a head for their cattle. Their trailing costs were 2 to 3 times less than the earliest drives, so efficient had trail driving methods become. A herd of about 2,500 cattle would make 300 to 500 miles a month and, if properly handled, would gain weight on the way. Most estimates figured that cattle could be driven 1,200 to 1,500 miles for 60 cents per head or $1 to $1.25 for each mile traveled by the whole herd.[92]

Trail driving had developed into almost a science. No longer did a lone rancher shape up his own herd, get a crew together, and start up the trail. Some stalwarts like Captain King entrusted their herds to competent drovers, then went ahead to the place of market, negotiating a sale well in advance of the herd's arrival. But the trend was for professional trail drivers who served as brokers to contract with various ranchmen for their cattle and road-brand and drive them in a combined herd. And

90

FORT RENO. *During the 1874 Indian uprising, cavalry troopers en-camped at the Cheyenne-Arapaho Agency in Indian Territory and located Fort Reno nearby in 1875. The log headquarters used by General Philip H. Sheridan was built the next year. At times soldiers were dispatched from the fort as far as South Texas to escort beef herds for the Indians. Cowboys unseated by their mounts or otherwise ailing made use of the post's medical facilities.*

gone were the days when the transactions took place in gold, or in mule-packed silver, making it necessary to know that 1,000 silver dollars weighed 62½ pounds. More often the drover took possession of the cattle on credit and in 5 to 7 months settled up with the ranchmen at prices agreed to earlier.[93]

There were few instances now of small northern buyers or stock raisers coming to Texas and themselves trailing cattle back as Tom Ponting did in 1853, Nelson Story in 1866, and—that most unusual of all cases—the Mason Brothers in 1870. The Masons, from Missouri, came to Texas with six wagon loads of Seth Thomas clocks and did business with

every family that had a cow to spare for many miles around Waco. For a small, spring-run clock they asked a cow and a calf; for a larger clock run by weights, two cows and calves; and for a still larger one with weights, three cows and calves. These were the first timepieces brought into the state since the Civil War's start. Many children never had seen one; many adults had forgotten how it was to hear one strike. The brothers readily disposed of their ticking cargo. After that, so the story goes, you could get the time of day at any Texas cabin in their wake.[94]

To strengthen marketing positions, more and more partnerships of the big trail operators

91

FRENCH CREEK. *Along this short, glistening stream near today's Custer, South Dakota, an 1874 military expedition found gold in the creek bed and in deposits no deeper than the roots of grass. Army attempts to hold prospectors back were futile after September, 1875, when negotiations broke down to buy the Black Hills from the Sioux. The miners' stampede to the region was followed closely by another by cattlemen.*

RED CLOUD BUTTES. *Red Cloud Agency, adjacent to Camp Robinson, Nebraska, from 1873 to 1877, was silhouetted by buttes also named for the controversial Sioux chief. Near here in September, 1875, he helped thwart the U.S. attempt to buy cheaply the gold-rich Black Hills, but Red Cloud could not stem the tide of meat-hungry miners already flowing into that region.*

were being formed: Millett and Mabry, Ellison and Dewees, Schreiner and Lytle, and many others.[95]

Chief Red Cloud, as he helped scuttle September negotiations to buy the Black Hills, indicated that some Longhorns were reaching the Sioux agency, and that he had savored their steaks. Besides many more millions than the government could pay, the symbolic Sioux asked the Great White Father "for seven gen-

erations . . . to give us Texan steers for our meat."[96]

Wichita again was the leading shipping center for Longhorns, but this was its last season. The Kansas legislature once more advanced the quarantine line against Texas cattle, leaving Wichita well behind the barrier. By 1876 southeastern border towns of that state were closed completely to the Texas trade.

A new trail was needed.

The Western Trail: 1876-1897

MANY EVENTS IN HISTORY seem timed to meet man's needs. Such was the advent of the Western Trail, opening—like the Red Sea—at a crucial moment in Plains development.

Unless a new route with new outlets developed quickly, the 1876 Kansas quarantine that placed Wichita beyond the pale of Texas cattle threatened to flatten again an industry barely risen to its knees from the Panic of 1873. Also facing economic reverse was Dodge City, 120 miles west of Wichita, but overlooked earlier as a cattle market. Reached by the Santa Fe in 1872, Dodge had grown from a pile of buffalo hides into the major shipping center for that commodity. But it now was declining with the southern bison herd. With rail expansion halted by the panic, the raucous settlement in 1876 remained the end of the line.

Far north of Dodge, happenings in that year of the nation's centennial added incentive to the quest for another trail. The June massacre in Montana of Custer's Seventh U.S. Cavalry brought a clamor for change in Indian policy on the northern Plains. The army in the West was increased to enforce an ultimatum handed to the Sioux: no appropriation for their subsistence unless all lands were ceded outside their reservations, and cession made of the Black Hills reservation land. Thus meat-hungry miners—thick in the hills since the 1875 Deadwood gold strike—and the once-forbidden grasslands of Montana, Dakota, and Wyoming beyond the Platte now beckoned to drovers and cattlemen.

The Western Trail became the solution to Longhorn marketing problems, the remedy for dwindling Dodge, and the means for range expansion. Miraculously, it was ready for general use in the 1876 trailing season.

The last of the great cattle thoroughfares, the Western Trail was the longest, and longest lived, its farthest extremes reaching from Mexico to Canada. This new route, roughly a hundred miles west of the Chisholm Trail, was the easiest course the cowboys pursued, for rivers requiring "time, patience, and profanity" to cross were narrower nearer their source.[1] Furthermore, the drive from San Antonio direct to Dodge was twenty to thirty days shorter than the time needed to reach markets on the old Chisholm Trail.[2]

Unlike the other two post-Civil War cattle trails, the Western had no proven progenitors. Among the pathfinding claimants were Hige Nail in the early 1870's, Maxwell and Morris in 1871 (or 1874) Frank Collinson with John Lytle Longhorns in 1874, James H. Cook trailing in 1876, and D. S. Combs driving Ellison and Dewees cattle the same year.[3]

That the army knew much of this route was apparent in 1874 when the Lytle herds advanced to Fort Griffin, Texas, and were furnished a military guide to Dodge City.[4] Trail drivers met in San Antonio two years later and sent a scout to perfect the way to Dodge but, unable to make improvements, he followed the same course.[5]

The real engineers of the Western Trail were the buffalo. Their centuries of migration from north to south with the seasons had determined the most practical, primitive highway up the Plains—between the ninety-eighth and one hundredth meridians and from the Missouri River to the Rio Grande south of Uvalde, Texas. Drovers previously demurred to follow so far from the settlement line, but in the decade after 1876 they extended the trail to Indian

UP FROM THE RIO GRANDE. *The Western Trail, like its Shawnee and Chisholm Trail predecessors, had its southern extremity in the far tip of Texas along the Rio Grande. Many herds on this route were "wet cattle" swimming across from Mexico at this and other points near Brownsville. The coming together of Mexican cattle and mounted, six-shooter-armed Texans formed the elements of an industry carried by the Western Trail even to the "British Possessions," as the cowboys referred to Canada.*

95

ARROYO COLORADO. *A deceptive-looking stream, over fifty feet deep for much of its thirty-seven mile length, dictated cattle routes above Brownsville, Texas. Herds veered west past the brackish arroyo's head or followed the coast to cross at the river's shallow mouth. Wagons often ferried here at Paso Real on the main road of northern travel. American troops had established the ferry to move men and supplies south for the Mexican War.*

THE COAST ROUTE. *Herds choosing to parallel the gulf shoreline up from Arroyo Colorado had about a week of easy trailing on the sand-packed beaches before being forced west by the arms of Laguna Madre. Ideal campgrounds with good grazing were found each night at small, fresh water lakes a few miles inland.*

THE NUECES. *Longhorns moving north on either route from the Rio Grande struck and followed the Nueces River to its southeast divergence near Oakville. The 30,000 King Ranch cattle trailed to market in 1876 used this crossing near San Patricio.*

agencies, forts, railheads, and remote new ranges on the northern Plains, wherever the call for cattle led.[6]

The Western Trail began, as did the Chisholm, on the Rio Grande in far South Texas, near Brownsville. It ambled north to the Nueces by one of two courses: inland past present Alice, or up the level gulf beaches past the King Ranch. Gathering cattle from adjoining ranges, the trail aimed for San Antonio, then bore northwest to Bandera and Kerrville, where it was met by a more westerly branch from Uvalde. Beyond Pegleg Station, a San Saba River stage stop, the path straight-lined north to Red River.

In this stretch to the Red were the budding towns of Coleman, Albany, Fort Griffin, and Seymour. At Fort Griffin the trail was joined by a strong feeder cutoff from the old Chisholm Trail at Belton.[7] When the cutoff diverted Longhorn traffic from Fort Worth, that cowtown began the "most extensive cattle yards in the state" in an effort to keep the trade. The Fort Griffin-Fort Worth rivalry, meanwhile, produced some of the most rambunctious editorials in Texas newspaper history.[8]

Doan's Store opened in April, 1878, on the Texas side of Red River, becoming, with the exception of Dodge, the most storied stop on the trail. The Doans, Jonathan and his nephew,

BANDERA'S JAIL. *Burly Bandera was a growing hamlet of strident force on the trail, thirty-eight miles northwest of San Antonio. A place of incarceration for rowdies opened in 1881, following the design of architect Alfred Giles whose plan snugly fitted the tastes of the citizen majority. Bandera was settled largely by Polish and German immigrants.*

ROVED ON THE PLAZA. *The Governor's Palace in San Antonio— e only remaining example of an aristocratic Spanish home in Texas —witnessed a peculiar sight in 1877. While trail herds were passing, arbed wire salesman J. W. "Bet-a-Million" Gates called a wager that is product could not hold Longhorns on the prod. He fenced the plaza onting the palace and goaded some wild cows into a charge. It was the ost colorful moment in barbed wire history when they fell back ewildered, and Texas wire sales started to soar.*

LONG-TIME LONGHORN RANGE. *As the trail pushed northwest to Kerrville, it passed several ranches of Captain Charles Schreiner, an 1852 immigrant from Alsace-Lorraine, France. He established a famous Kerrville mercantile store and was prominent in trail activities, sending more than 150,000 cattle north with John Lytle. Charles Schreiner, III, maintained in 1974 one of the nation's largest privately owned Longhorn herds on his YO Ranch north of Kerrville.*

COLEMAN'S OLDEST HOUSE. *Coleman, Texas, was located on the Western Trail in 1876, its first year of discernible cattle traffic. Townspeople sent riders south during the trailing season, inviting drovers to linger in the town where the main street had been laid out wide enough to accommodate a herd of Longhorns. This stone house, built by M. B. Polk, was new in the 1876-1880 period, when Coleman County's population increase of a thousand percent was due mainly to trail activity.*

ALBANY'S COURTHOUSE. *The first business in Albany, Texas, opened in 1876, when the first northbound herds arrived. One outfit loaded up with dried fruit—a new item to the cook—and he filled a kettle with shriveled apples that swelled until all camp vessels, including the wash basin, were full. Orienting its economy to the trail, the town drew about half the county population, which rose from 2,000 in 1880 to 5,000 in 1881. Taxable real estate doubled also. A majestic courthouse was built in 1883.*

FORT GRIFFIN BAKERY. *Huge baking ovens were part of Fort Griffin's original installations made for six cavalry companies in 1867. Perched on a hill overlooking the Clear Fork of the Brazos, Griffin was a center of General Ranald S. Mackenzie's Indian campaigns and furnished many troop escorts and guides to surveying parties and cattle drives. So important was the post to the Western Trail that it sometimes was called the Fort Griffin-Dodge City Trail.*

'THE FLAT.' *Below the hill where Fort Griffin stood was the town of Fort Griffin, a cluster of adobe and frame shacks usually called "the Flat." A remaining wooden structure was one of several general stores that at times averaged daily sales of $2,500 to buffalo hunters. Early trail outfits took on enough supplies here to get them to Dodge City. As Frank Collinson wrote, "Fort Griffin was the last town with any semblance of civilization on the western frontier of Texas, and that semblance was very thin."*

CLEAR FORK OF THE BRAZOS. *Fort Griffin lay in Shackelford County, the last organized Texas county on the trail, and all herds had to be inspected at the nearby river crossing. This crossing of the Brazos, one drover recalled, was "high up where there was not much water in it, and . . . it was so salty our cattle would not drink it." As the buffalo disappeared, some hunters turned to horse thieving, and Fort Griffin vigilantes hanged as many as possible from trees along the Clear Fork.*

102

SEYMOUR CENTER. *Born on the trail in 1878 and catering to its trade, Seymour, Texas, had a thousand percent population growth in ten years. Stone blocks were added later to this 1879 structure, which served as the first schoolhouse, cafe, and justice-of-the-peace office. Here also, the Methodist Church organized and court was held. The town was named for Seymour Munday, a cowboy whose line camp was nearby.*

EDITH'S POINT. *Highest of the graduated tablelands that frame Red River Valley's most celebrated cattle cut is at left on the Texas side. At Doan's Crossing fully three million Longhorns chugged the murky waters from 1876 to 1885 en route to Kansas shipping centers or to Nebraska, Colorado, Wyoming, Montana, and Dakota ranges. The lookout-landmark is about eighteen miles north of present Vernon.*

DOAN'S. *Beside their famous trail store near Red River, C. F. and J. J. Doan added this adobe house in 1881. "These walls could speak many a tale of border warfare," said the builders, who lived here half a century, giving sanctuary to governors, English lords, and tramps, but mostly to cowboys. The walls were pockmarked by insects in the 1960's. Doan's Store—last chance south of the Kansas line for drover mail, Winchesters by the case, sow bosom, and flour—burned years ago.*

104

'OH, BURY ME NOT ON THE LONE PRAIRIE.' *A yet unplowed bit of prairie in a cotton field near Doan's Crossing inspired this lasting ballad. Here in 1879 a mortally wounded trail hand begged not to be buried on Red River's solitary range, but his friends had no recourse. Two of them, however—Pink Burdette and Jesse James Benton— immortalized him in the mournful song that became an instant success. "Even the horses nickered it and the coyotes howled it," recalled a cowboy of the 1880's.*

SUNDOWN AT DOAN'S CROSSING. *On a tranquil evening, the quiet, majestic grandeur of Red River was deceptive of her merciless nature. Several channels—not more than one swimming—exposed shallow, intervening sand bars, and only the size of driftwood lodged high on the banks hinted at her force when angry. At this and lower trail crossings on Red River, the lives of more cowboys were lost by drowning than on all other rivers combined.*

105

INTO RED RIVER. *Cattle always were pointed into a river with the sun to their backs and enough daylight to see the opposite bank. Drovers learned the hard way that Longhorns would balk and mill in a crossing if blinded by the sun, or if unable to see land.*

TRAIL BREAK. *Because the Longhorns' trail day began early, they were allowed to rest during the noon heat. Making five to nine miles in the morning, trail bosses tried to arrange a lunch stop near a watering place, where cattle could drink and lie down or be at ease. The temperature along the trail often exceeded one hundred, shadeless degrees, and the animals would lose weight if trailed at midday.*

MOVING 'EM OUT. *As shadows lengthened, the herd got up slowly and moved on to graze. Shortly they were turned back into the trail for a steady drive of another seven miles or so before nightfall.*

107

WICHITA MOUNTAINS. *Past Doan's on the South Fork of Red River, the trail continued up the Red's smaller North Fork about four days' drive before crossing that stream and passing through a gap in the Wichita Mountains. This stretch was well-watered country where drovers often encountered Comanche Chief Quanah Parker, demanding a yearling for passage over his land.*

THE GRASSY WAY. *West of present Vicki, Oklahoma, the cattle-carved route of the Western Trail still marks the earth, which grows the same forage that Longhorns relished. The grasses changed along the trail in Indian Territory from the buffalo varieties to the more nutritious bluestem and gramma types.*

108

INDIAN TERRITORY. *Toward Camp Supply, the grazing looked good to drovers—particularly in 1877—when a dry, cold winter in Texas made the skinning season so heavy that one cowboy remarked, "it looked like our herd would all be hanging on the fence." In Indian Territory, said another, our cattle began to fatten and "you could see their hides moving away from the bones, but . . . it thundered and lightned to a chilly finish and these storms had a tendency to make a fellow feel homesick."*

Corwin, provided branding pens and corrals, secured a post office, and set up a wagon ferry at the crossing that soon bore their name. Weather frequently aided business at the store. The cardinal example came in 1882, when a violent night storm raised and mixed eleven bedded herds—33,000 cattle and 120 cowboys. Ten days at Doan's were required before the Longhorns could be shaped up and ready to move on. Cattle coming all the way from the southern tip of Texas had, at this point, trav-eled more than 600 miles and been on the trail 6 weeks to 2 months.[9]

It was a good month's trek from Doan's to Dodge, with only one sign of white habitation along the way—Camp Supply in northern Indian Territory. During this time drovers usually were met by tribal members asking tobacco, beef, or both. Other callers could be expected, too, when cattle owners traveled directly to Dodge, arranged a sale, then went back to meet their advancing herds. A mem-

CAMP SUPPLY. *Over 150 miles north of Doan's, the next white habitation on the Western Trail was Camp Supply, Indian Territory. Established in 1868 as an outpost from Fort Dodge, Kansas, the camp buildings were all-wooden for nearly 3 decades. The tiny, log fire house that accommodated a fire-fighting hand cart was not enough in 1876, when seven officers' quarters burned. The trail from Supply to Fort Dodge was a well-marked military and teamster road.*

110

THE CIMARRON. *Snaking out from its New Mexico source, the Cimarron River makes a small loop north into Kansas before diving southeast into Oklahoma. The Western Trail crossed the stream in Kansas near Dull Knife's old campground, where another cutoff from the Chisholm Trail intersected. A whiskey-selling roadhouse called Longhorn Roundup grew up on the site, causing some cowboys to qualify for the literal application of* cimarrón—*"wild and unruly."*

111

orable visit of this kind from Jim Ellison was set down by the boss of his herd: "As we proceeded on our journey Mr. Ellison came to meet us in a buggy. He remained all night with us, and we slept on a pallet together. Mr. Ellison undressed, but I did not, as I always slept with my entire outfit on, pants, boots and spurs, so as to be ready for any emergency. During the night the cattle made a run, and when I started to get up one of my spurs caught in Mr. Ellison's drawers and he was rather painfully spurred."[10]

Along the whole of any cattle trail were dirt, dust and dull routine, a few exciting moments, and much hard work.[11] Yet few trail drivers complained; in their later years the great majority longed to make the drives again, following perpetual spring through ever-changing country from the rise of grass in Texas to the first rich sprigs of grazing in the meadows of Montana.

Springtime on the trail, however, was not without its difficulties; it also was calving season. Tottering little calves could not keep up with the herd. Some were given to settlers, if any lived near, but most calves were killed on the bedground. To a man, trail-hardened cowhands winced at the gruesome task, and at least one drover changed his habits as a result of this practice. "I had a pistol and it was my duty to murder the calves each morning while their pitiful mothers were ruthlessly driven on," he said. "Being the executioner so disgusted me with six-shooters that I have never owned—much less used one from that time to this." And steering clear of cowtown shoot-outs, he added, "unpreparedness has kept me peacefully inclined."[12]

Calves found a soft spot also in flinty Charles Goodnight, who took great pains as soon as practicable to insure not only their lives, but to keep them from being orphaned or "dogied." "I hated to kill the innocent things," the colonel declared after his early drives, "but there was no loss financially, as the calf was not counted in the sale of a cow." When cattle became more valuable, he had calf wagons built to pick up the newborns as they were dropped; at night they were turned out with the cows, to be roped in the morning and put back in the wagon.[13] If truly successful, this operation required another, for a cow would not accept her calf after its scent had been mixed by jostling with others. Goodnight's remedy was to place over each calf a loose sack, marked for use day after day on the same animal. Calves thus retained their proper scent and were recognized by their mothers when the covering was removed in the evening.[14]

A similar wagon was used for Longhorn offspring by Colonel William Day's outfit in 1878. Although the herd reached Dodge City in good shape, the cowboys called it "a wretched trip as the calves gave us a lot of trouble."[15]

Dodge, the geriatric of cowtowns, has maintained a greater afterglow than all the others combined. Rehashes of its early chronicles run to millions of words and as many feet of celluloid. In its ten years as the cowboy capital, 1876-1885, Dodge was a magnet drawing zealous reporters from around the globe to investigate the incredulous movement of cattle that was affecting world markets.

Few accounts rival the *Scribner's Magazine* description of Dodge in its 1880 heyday. Most of the irregular buildings lacked foundations, and many "sat visibly perched upon awkward corner props, as if fearing a flood." Bounded by the railroad, the town proper spread with "a succession of yellow pine board pens, filled with cattle—antlered, uneasy, alien looking cattle—out over the level bottom land, pen after pen, until the boards became shadows, the beasts lost their identity, and all that was left was a queer, sinister, perplexity of uplifted and tossing horns." For Dodge was "a cattle town, that novel frontier village which belongs to a branch of commerce and an aspect of life unknown elsewhere under the sun."

The town was dominated by the arriving cowboy, "no longer the easy-going, mild-demeanored type of native Texan languor, and the anomalous self-repression of the trail. He 'turns loose,' as he calls it, and appears to change his disposition in the act of shifting his garments, so rapidly does he challenge every restraint of society and sound every depth of vice and shame. Perhaps the sight of civilization, after so much of the desert and its high, haunting sky, stuns and dazes his moral nature."[16]

Tumbling out of Dodge into the American

THE TROUBLE WITH CALVES. *"If you have never driven a herd of two thousand cows in the spring you just can't imagine the time we had,"* moaned a cowboy en route to Dodge. *"We would leave from five to ten calves on the bedground every morning and the cows would have to be roped and hobbled to keep them from going back the next night to their calves, and this thing lasted until we reached Indian Territory."*

UNSTEADY STEPS. *Calves on the trail were a gnawing problem of delay, whether in a herd of stocker cows or in mixed herds with steers. A cow did not keep pace with a steer, and a wobbly, newborn calf hardly kept step at all. Drovers killed thousands of baby bovines until cattle prices justified wagons to pick up calves as they were dropped.*

113

BEDGROUNDS. *Thirty miles north of the Cimarron, trail country changed in color and character. Red-clay outcroppings gave way to unbroken plains of grass extending to the Arkansas. On the south bank opposite Dodge, cattle were bedded down while drovers arranged sales. One waddie left here with a herd told of a July Fourth hailstorm that killed yearlings and "knocked over jackrabbits like taking them with a rifle. We nearly froze to death," he said, and "had knots and scars all over."*

114

FORT DODGE. *Some trail cattle were sold to the fort established by General Grenville M. Dodge in 1864, five miles east of the town that bears his name. During heavy seasons, herds waiting to get into Dodge City backed up for miles, and drovers often camped ten days opposite the fort. Post-Civil War skirmishes were usual wherever hot-blooded, ex-Rebel cowboys came in contact with "Blue Bellies." As fort commander, General George Custer lived in this stuccoed stone house built in 1867.*

THE ARKANSAS AT DODGE CITY. *For several years of Dodge's cowtown supremacy, 300,000 to 350,000 Longhorns annually plunged into the Arkansas at fords in this vicinity. The view looks south from town. Upstream dams now reduce the river's flow, but it never was a difficult water course on the trail. Except for spectacular canyons near its Colorado head, banks generally were gentle and ideal for crossing cattle. The Goodnight, Chisholm, and Western trails all encountered the Arkansas at some point.*

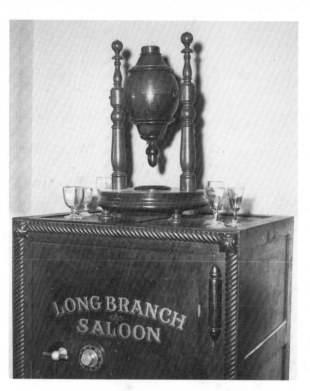

WINE, WINNINGS, AND CHANCE. *Dodge City's original Long Branch Saloon is gone, but much of its equipment remains. Many a hard-earned cow dollar went into the Long Branch safe, and the glasses are those that washed down trail dust. The wooden hi-ball gambling device, used to determine who would buy the drinks, could be played among individuals or against the house. As the suspended holder swung over, flat numbered discs inside shuffled and spilled out to tell the tale.*

OVER THE BAR. *Whether paintings in the Long Branch contributed to the number of cattle deals made there is not recorded, but two works by an unknown artist were alternated above the bar. One portrayed a nude woman in a Roman carriage driving a black horse and a white one. Animate subjects in the other appeared to be identical: the nude on a cart drawn by the horses. The Long Branch was grandly appointed and strict as saloons go—no dancing.*

'A CREDIT TO THE TOWN.' *Dodge City's business district was largely frame and later burned, but John Mueller's gray stone house stood. Mueller, a bootmaker who followed the trail trade from Ellsworth to Dodge, was carried away by tales of profit in the beef bonanza. He went broke in the cattle business and was forced to sell his handsome home, which the local press dubbed "a credit to the town."*

language were the words, *stinker, stiff,* and *joint.* The rancid odor of rotting buffalo hides was transferred to their hunters, the "stinkers" who headquartered there. "Stiff" was coined for the litter of dead men so often in the streets, and the *Dodge City Times* conjured up "joint" to describe the many saloons. The Long Branch, owned by Chalk Beeson and Bill Harris, was the finest saloon in town, but there were other spots famous for gambling, entertainment, food and drink: Delmonico's Restaurant, The Alamo, and The Lady Gay, to name a few.

More "ladies gay" were south of the tracks at the Red Light House, where gawdy crimson glass adorned the entrance and commanded wide attention. From this distinguishing feature the bland surroundings took their name, and Dodge City had the first of many areas to be called the "red light district."[17]

Not all the girls of easy virtue stayed in town; a number went out to meet the herds and camped several days with drovers holding cattle outside of Dodge. Into Tobe Odem's camp in 1877 rode a big coach with six finely dressed women from the East, while an excited cowboy made note that Odem "knew one of the ladies pretty well. . . . 'We want to see all the sights,' she told Odem. 'We are all good sports, have plenty to drink with us, and have some good singers and dancers.' "

That night, "two or three big dry steer hides were spread on the ground, out come the fiddle and two banjos, all hands joined in singing of the old-time songs, eating broiled ribs and drinking good whiskey. Believe me, them gals could sing and dance. . . . What was left of the night, they slept on the steer hides and seemed to enjoy it."

The narrating trail hand observed that "other camps weren't so lucky as us. As we neared Dodge City we seen another stage load of women going to another herd. We heard about it afterward, in Dodge City. These women were from England and talked funny and dressed peculiar. . . . They called them boys *hirelings* and acted mighty high-hat." The retaliating boys gave the visitors buffalo robes to sleep on, and the damsels cut short their stay, departing the next morning thoroughly infested with lice, and scratching.[18]

These and other exploits on the trail were adding fodder to the grist of fiction, which produced its first strictly cowboy novel in 1879. Written by Arthur Morecamp, *The Live Boys; or Charley and Nasho in Texas* tells of adventure on the cattle drives to Kansas.[19]

Dodge City's cowtown longevity was aided by Texas Panhandle development, which also began in 1876 with the sudden vacating of Indians and buffalo. Into this coveted grazing area, less than two hundred miles south of Dodge, Charles Goodnight led the vanguard of cattlemen. A victim of the 1873 panic, Goodnight had sold his Colorado ranch, returned to the trail in earnest, and watched for his chance to begin again. Securing the backing of John Adair—a wealthy Irish nobleman who had moved to Denver and wanted to invest in land and cattle—Goodnight located their JA Ranch in Palo Duro Canyon. Other ranches soon polka dotted the Panhandle, and trailed their products to the growing market in Dodge.[20]

Beyond that "Bibulous Babylon of the Plains," the Western Trail stretched another thousand miles. A fourth of the distance was consumed in reaching Ogallala—Nebraska's version of Dodge.[21] While Ogallala was born a railroad town in 1868, its name from the Ogallala Sioux, meaning "to scatter" or "to scatter one's own," was descriptive of its place on the trail as a cattle distribution point. Strategically located on the Union Pacific for cattle shipments to the East, the village was the hub of radiating branch trails. Valleys of the South and North Platte rivers, which sandwiched Ogallala on a narrow throat of land, made excellent trailing routes.

The extent of cattle business transacted at Ogallala belied its size. The permanent population never exceeded 100 persons during its decade as a trail town.[22] In 1876 the record number of cattle driven in a single year by one firm was made when Ellison, Dewees, Millett, and Mabry moved 100,000 Longhorns to Ogallala for distribution. Many of the 30,000 King Ranch cattle on the trail that year were sold there also.[23]

Ogallala's living tempo was geared entirely to the cattle trade. The town began to stir in June as the first Texas herds arrived. Facilities were taxed, however, when as many as ten

118

CANYON TRAILS. *Returning to Texas permanently in 1876, Charles Goodnight descended Palo Duro Canyon's 700-foot walls to establish the first ranch in the Panhandle. Cowboys and 1,600 cattle—including fine Durham bulls—carefully picked their way down the path of the old Comanche War Trail, still visible at left center. Wagons were dismantled and lowered piece by piece. Many ranchmen followed Goodnight's lead to the area, increasing the cattle supply to Dodge and other markets on the Western Trail.*

EARLY DEVELOPMENT. *As new Panhandle ranches were located, Goodnight got on with practical improvements, such as dugouts for his men. With cedar posts from Palo Duro Canyon, Leigh Dyer built the region's first house in 1877. He settled where Tierra Blanca and Palo Duro Creeks converge, and his home place later became headquarters for the vast T-Anchor spread.*

119

LIMESTONE FENCEPOSTS. *Faced with the problem of protecting crops from Longhorns advancing on a treeless plain, German and Russian immigrants north of Dodge created unique objects of the American prairie. Limestone was uncovered from outcroppings, sledged out by hand, notched and shaped while soft, and erected as fenceposts when hardened by the air. Corner posts often weighed more than a ton. In 1966, some forty thousand miles of barbed-wired stone posts could be traced through Central Kansas, where the shallow limestone stratum is found.*

SODBUSTERS. *Trail cattle above Dodge sometimes made their last charge at a landscape rise that turned out to be a sod house or sod annex to a dugout. Where the Plains were devoid of wood and stone, homesteaders built such shelters of prairie sod as it was turned by a plow or sod cutter (above). Sliced about four inches thick, and keeping the grass on top, the earth sections were laid in strips like brick. Grass continued to grow, the roots serving as cement.*

WILD HORSE SPRING. *In the forty Nebraska miles between the head of Stinking Water Creek and Ogallala, the only living water was a spring, "which curiously enough," a trail hand mused, "opens up right in the bald prairie." One lone tree guards the spot. The area around the spring is subject to severe storms that frightened one puncher into making premature notes for his obituary: "George Knight, struck and killed by lightning 20 miles south of Ogallala on July 20, 1879."*

121

BOOT HILL. *While every cowtown had its boot hill, progress often required cemetery relocation. Only in Ogallala, Nebraska, do "leathery knights of the dim old trail" have their original resting place as immortalized by cowboy poet Badger Clark in "On Boot Hill": "Up from the prairie and through the pines,/ Over your straggling headboard lines/ Winds of the West go by./ You must love them, you booted dead,/ More than the dreamers who died in bed—/You old-timers who took your lead/ Under the open sky!"*

herds bedded nearby, releasing about one hundred cowboys to roam the streets. Activities in Tuck's Saloon, The Cowboy's Rest, and The Crystal Palace contributed to the hamlet's reputation as the churchless "Gomorrah of the West." As the season reached its peak, Ogallala's activity rose to a fever that continued until the end of August, when the Texans headed home, and the floaters, gamblers, trades-people, and dancehall girls drifted on to Omaha or Cheyenne. One hotel, one supply store, and a single saloon remained open for the winter, while the community sank into slumber until the next spring.[24]

Fingers of the Western Trail extending out of Ogallala were called the Texas Trail in the territory through which they passed and are so marked in Wyoming today. Reaching generally for the big Dakota and Montana Indian agencies, the Black Hills gold region, and the millions of virgin range acres in Wyoming, Montana, and Dakota, these were the most scenic parts of the trail. The possible paths were many, with each herd determining its course in light of destination, need for supplies, current quarantine lines, and range conditions. Available army protection also was a consideration until the early 1880's, when the last of

122

NORTH OF OGALLALA. *Into and over the sand-hills region north of Ogallala trailed thousands of cattle bound for Indian agencies on the Missouri River. Soapweed bloomed in the sand hills and an abundance of antelope, elk, and deer offered trail drivers the most varied diet they had enjoyed since leaving home. Grazing ever northward, the herds continued over land drained by the headwaters of the Dismal and Loup rivers.*

HAZARDOUS HOLES. *A horse's hoof in a prairie dog hole often meant death as Teddy Blue described it after an 1876 stampede. "There was one man missing . . . we found him among the prairie dog holes, beside his horse. . . . horse and man was mashed into the ground as flat as a pancake. . . . We tried to think lightning hit him . . . that was what we wrote his folks. . . . But we couldn't really believe it . . . his horse stepped into one of them holes and they both went down before the stampede."*

123

APPROACH TO PINE RIDGE. *Red Cloud Agency in southwestern South Dakota was renamed "Pine Ridge" in 1878, more for political than geographic reasons. Approaching from the south as trail herds did, a sprinkling of pines does appear suddenly on hills below the Nebraska line. But the reservation is situated in a wide valley with no ridge, and trees only in ravines. The new name was to lessen identification with the Sioux chief who had troubled government officials over the agency location.*

the Sioux came into the reservations. It is interesting to note that almost sixty percent of the Sioux had some kind of firearms.[25]

In 1876 the first Texas herds reached the Missouri River agencies in Dakota Territory by trailing north of Ogallala past the Dismal and Loup River headwaters.[26] The more prominent traces were described succinctly by J. B. Kendrick, who was said to be the only man to ride the Texas Trail to the U.S. Senate, and who was taught to read and write by Jesse Borland, son of the unlucky lady drover.[27]

Emanating from Ogallala:

—one branch went down the South Platte to points in Colorado, with some herds leaving the Platte below Julesburg to follow Lodgepole Creek westward in Wyoming to Pine Bluffs, Cheyenne and the Laramie Plains;
—another branch continued up the North Platte to the vicinity of Fort Laramie, Wyoming, before crossing the river and heading north; many drovers turned north, however, near the Nebraska-Wyoming line at the Platte's intersection with the Sidney-Black Hills Road.[28]

FORT ROBINSON. *Original structures at Fort Robinson, Nebraska, are adobe officers' quarters built in 1874. Wooden siding was added later. Red Cloud Agency, located here in 1873, had immediate troubles, despite trimonthly issues of hardware, cloth, and Texas beef on the hoof. The agent's request for military protection resulted in the post establishment and the army's Sioux expedition. In 1947 the installation became Fort Robinson Beef Cattle Research Center.*

This road had been pioneered by trail drivers delivering beef to the Red Cloud and Spotted Tail Agencies. It came into wide use by prospectors and freighters during the gold rush. The course divided near Fort Robinson and the Nebraska-Dakota line, the eastern branch going to the agencies, the northern to Deadwood.[29]

In Wyoming, the Texas Trail, from its Pine Bluffs entry in the far southeastern corner, stretched the full length of the territory. Longhorns followed Horse Creek up from Pine Bluffs and swam the North Platte at the mouth of Rawhide Creek, or sixteen miles west, where chuck wagons could cross the bridge at Fort Laramie and be replenished. On up the Rawhide Valley, east of Rawhide Buttes, past Hat Creek Station, and down Old Woman and Lance creeks to the Cheyenne River and the crossing of the Belle Fourche, ran the well-worn path.

From this point the trail spread fan-like to the Dakotas; the Indian agencies; northern Wyoming; eastern, central, and western Montana; and the Canadian border—1,700 miles from the Texas ranges.[30]

The most heavily traveled route from the Belle Fourche crossing—at present Moorcroft, Wyoming—struck the headwaters of the Little Powder River and continued fifty miles along its valley to a Montana union with the Powder. At least twenty miles of this stretch was through the Powder River badlands—hills of red scoria outcrop and gray clay, greasewood-clad and eroded.

The Texas Trail in Montana did not vary as did the southern portion. Once across the Powder, it pointed northwest over Mizpah Creek to Pumpkin Creek. Herds grazing up this stream to the Tongue River followed its course past Fort Keogh and into Miles City, where the Tongue joins the Yellowstone on its way to the mother Missouri. Cattle bound for points farther north crossed the Yellowstone above the fort and traveled up Sunday Creek before spreading out to various ranges east and west. Miles City became the northern center for drovers and many famous ranches were developed in the area with Texas trail stock.[31]

Meanwhile, a rail extension breathed new life into a portion of the Chisholm Trail. In 1880, the Santa Fe completed tracks south from Wichita to Caldwell, Kansas. Caldwell was perched so neatly on the Kansas-Indian Territory border that the Texas fever quarantine, which had closed the trail to Wichita, had no effect. Thus, in the early 1880's, three streams of Longhorns were flowing northward, on the Goodnight, Chisholm, and Western Trails.

Well before 1880, however, the burgeoning cattle industry on the Plains of the United States had captured international attention, concern, and imagination. The rapid growth of ranching and the resultant increase in the beef supply encouraged refrigeration improvements. In the fall of 1875, New Yorker Timothy Eastman had sent the first successful quantity shipment of dressed beef to Europe. By 1877, the volume of this business had risen to 49 million pounds, while live-cattle shipments to Europe also were increasing. English and Scottish stock growers were alarmed. The price of meat in their countries had fallen 25 percent —from 8d. a pound in 1875 to 6d. in 1877.[32]

That spring the *Scotsman* of Edinburgh sped its animal husbandry expert to America to report on the true extent of this new trade with Britain. His stories had wide circulation in the British press and excited reader interest in the possibilities of Great Plains ranching.

The British government was so exercised that a Royal Commission on Agriculture was formed in 1879. Two members of parliament were instructed to continue the ranching investigation. Their official reports, telling of the Texas breeding grounds for cattle and the picturesque drives, glowed like the western sunset. "It is generally acknowledged," they concluded, "that the average profit of the stock-owner has been for years fully 33 percent," and that "for the present the American stockman in the West is possessed of singular advantages; land for nothing, and an abundance of it."

As a result of these missions, the craze in Great Britain to enter American ranching approached an epidemic. With the formation of the first two British cattle companies in 1879, the foreign stampede to the Plains was on.[33]

126

CRAZY HORSE

SCALP SHIRT OF CRAZY HORSE. *Crazy Horse was one of four tribal chiefs designated to wear a scalp shirt; decorations, however, are hair locks—not scalps. Conqueror of General Crook on the Rosebud and a leader in the Custer fight, Crazy Horse symbolized the fighting Sioux. His surrender and death at Fort Robinson in 1877 made the passage of trail cattle safer. Many believed this noted chieftain was white; his handsome physique, fair hair, and gray eyes never were photographed.*

BEEF FLATS. *At Red Cloud (Pine Ridge) Agency, Dakota, as at others, Indians looked upon beef-issue days as splendid sport. Trail herds moved slowly into pens, where weighing took all day. "The agent would call the Indians by name and each family would fall in behind his beef and off to the flats they would go," said an eye-witness cowboy. Steers sometimes were shot in the pens, for the Indian art of beef-skinning was fast. The big Sioux beef contracts exceeded 39 million pounds in 1880.*

127

THE BROAD NORTH PLATTE. *Quicksands with no bottom, treacherous with few crossings, the North Platte westward from Ogallala commanded drover respect. The river is more than a mile wide in places, and a cautious cowhand remarked that it seemed two miles wide "when we reached the place we were to cross. The range cattle on the other side looked like little calves standing along the bank."*

PINE RIDGE CHURCH. *At one time, Indian agents were selected by church groups. Episcopalians made the choice at Pine Ridge Agency and, in 1879, built this Church of the Holy Cross. A Texas cowboy arriving at the agency with a herd that year registered amazement at the number of redmen: "There I saw more Indians than I ever expected to see. The agent said there were about 10,000." Trail hands consistently called the large Sioux reservation "Red Cloud Agency," though the name was changed in 1878.*

129

COURT HOUSE AND JAIL ROCKS. *Some drovers followed the North Platte from Ogallala to Fort Laramie before crossing the river. Seventy-five miles from Ogallala stark bluffs of Wild Cat Ridge rise suddenly on Nebraska's high plains—rougher country that made the cattle skittish and the trail seem longer. Four thousand King Ranch cattle, used to Mexicans, jumped off the bedground near Court House Rock one night when "they got wind of the old negro cook."*

130

CHIMNEY ROCK. *Rising 475 feet above the Platte, a natural needle became a beacon for trail drivers as it had for earlier travelers. Chimney Rock, just northwest of Court House Rock in Nebraska, was a guiding landmark visible three or four days, or 40 miles in pioneer travel on the Oregon and Mormon trails. Few diaries of sojourners along this way to the West omit reference to the symmetrical tower, which gave incentive to reach a fine camp site located directly north, on the river.*

PINE BLUFFS. *In Wyoming's southeast corner a descriptive geographical name was given to a settlement that developed on the Union Pacific. Pine Bluffs, as a point where the Texas Trail entered Wyoming, became the largest livestock shipping center on the railroad. Mesa land to the south is broken abruptly by low, pine-covered cliffs, which descend as quickly to easy trailing country. Northward, the land is level to gently rolling and watered by several creeks.*

SEPTEMBER SNOW. *Late August and early September snows, not uncommon from the North Platte in Wyoming to Montana and beyond, were revelations to sun-baked Texans arriving with cattle: "Indeed something different . . . [that] I could not enjoy at all," admitted one. From this point at present Torrington, Wyoming, Longhorns crossed to the far bank up the river some five miles at the mouth of Rawhide, or at Fort Laramie, sixteen miles farther upstream.*

131

FORT LARAMIE. *The most important fort in the conquest and settlement of the West was forty-two years old and at its peak in 1876. Intense Indian campaigns that year had paved the way for Texas cattle to stock northern ranges. The garrison helped protect, and was a large market for, beef coming up the trail. In the 1850's some fifty thousand settlers annually had passed this way on the Oregon Trail. Laramie was abandoned in 1890; eleven of its sixty-five buildings are restored.*

132

'SQUAW WINTER.' *This log bunkhouse, built in 1885, still nestles in Wyoming's Rawhide Valley beside the Texas Trail. Dark, heavy foliage remaining on the trees indicates that the snow is an early one—the "squaw winter" that sometimes precedes Indian summer above the North Platte. While drovers hurried to reach their northern destinations at least by early September, they frequently were caught at that time in quick-melting snows.*

CHEYENNE-DEADWOOD STAGE STOP. *Stage passengers were not the only beneficiaries of this Wyoming relay station constructed in Rawhide Valley, southwest of today's Lusk, during 1876. The Texas Trail paralleled the stage route for many miles, and stage stops were welcome sights when cow ponies needed shoeing or chuck wagon axles broke. Like the forts, some stations had telegraph facilities, which drovers used more and more to contact their markets and home ranches.*

133

RAWHIDE BUTTES. *Red granite uplifts southwest of present Lusk, Wyoming, are legendary landmarks near the Rawhide River's source. Trail cattle pouring up the valley and past the buttes after 1876 gave a new dimension to the old "Rawhide" name. Early fur traders had prepared rawhides here for eastern shipment. Later, during the California gold rush, Indians are said to have skinned a white man alive among these crags, for the wanton killing of an Indian maiden.*

HAT CREEK STATION. *An 1875 army error became a drover blessing when the Texas Trail opened in 1876. Soldiers sent to establish an outpost on Hat Creek, in Nebraska, mislocated and built Fort Hat Creek on Wyoming's Sage Creek, north of present Lusk. With cattle and gold rushes to the former Sioux country, the fort became a stage and trail stop. The two-story log building—used as a blacksmith shop, hotel, store, telegraph, and post office—now is a ranch house.*

THE BIG POWDER. *Near its Montana junction with the Little Powder, the main Powder River is a majestic stream. Cowboys loved the Powder, for at its broadest point the river was shallow and benign. "Powder River, let 'er buck," they said, "she's a mile wide—an inch deep—swimmin' holes for grasshoppers—cross 'er anywhere—yeouuhh —yippee—she rolls up hill from Texas."*

135

FORT KEOGH. *Facing the parade grounds of old Fort Keogh, the Montana home of Colonel Nelson Miles stands as it did when the Texas herds arrived in 1880. The post was established in 1877, and Miles City, named for the fort's first commandant, grew nearby. S a roaring trail town, Miles City gained and yet retains national fa as a cattle market.*

POWDER RIVER VALLEY. *Headwaters of the Little Powder are framed by a series of long, low hills. As the Sioux retreated to reservations in 1877-1878, trail herds streamed into this valley stretching from Wyoming to Montana. The coveted grasslands were reached by a drive of three months and twenty days up from the Red River boundary of Texas. Many Texas cowboys stayed on this northern range to work as hands or to establish ranches.*

136   **PUMPKIN CREEK.** *Past the Powder River badlands in Montana, the reaches of Pumpkin Creek composed about thirty miles of the Texas Trail. Lands softened toward the creek's junction with the Tongue River, where the trail to Fort Keogh in the Yellowstone Valley became a ribbon of green.*

THE MIGHTY YELLOWSTONE. *The Texas Trail crossed this formidable river but once, a mile or so inside the foreground shown here, near Miles City, Montana. Yet the economy of ranges that developed in the region depended upon the resources generated by this great, contributing arm of the Missouri River.*

SUNDAY CREEK. *Herds bound for Canada or Montana points north of Miles City crossed the Yellowstone above Fort Keogh and trailed some forty miles up Sunday Creek before fanning out to various destinations. The creek and its country maintain the pristine grandeur that inspired an 1880 Montana newcomer to write: "No king of the old times could have claimed a more beautiful and bountiful domain." He, Charles Russell, stayed in Montana to record the West immortally in line and paint and plaster.*

138

HOTEL IN CALDWELL. *The Santa Fe's 1880 extension to Caldwell, Kansas, reopened the Chisholm Trail through Indian Territory. For the trade Caldwell soon opened the thirty-eight room Southwestern Hotel, with a "ladies parlor" on the second floor. Cowboy author Andy Adams, who spent some time in Caldwell, records this ditty: "Sure it's one cent for coffee and two cents for bread, three for a steak and five for a bed, Sea breeze from the gutter wafts a salt water smell, To the festive cowboy in the Southwestern Hotel."*

BOUND FOR NEW MARKETS. *Dodging Texas fever quarantines, Longhorns hurried northward in 1880 over all three cattle trails opened after the Civil War. "It was sure a pretty sight to see them strung out for about a mile, the sun flashing on their horns," said one of the working cowboys. Expanding foreign markets for refrigerated beef called attention to apparent range profits and caused a rush to the Plains of the rich and the titled. The day of the dude was at hand.*

139

Bonanza to Blizzard: 1880-1887

THE BLOOM OF EASY PROFITS was on the sage in 1880 over nearly a million square miles of Western and Midwestern Plains opened to ranching since the massive trail movement had begun only fourteen years earlier. So swift had been the growth of cattle raising in this area roughly the size of Europe that local, state, and territorial governments were incapable of ministering to the business.[1]

The human volume of this exodus, often described as men who "didn't know a maverick from a mandamus," was matched by conversation in Great Britain. "Drawing rooms buzzed with stories of this last of bonanzas," said John Clay, and "staid old gentlemen who scarcely knew the difference betwixt a steer and a heifer discussed it over their port and nuts."[2] The resulting rash of cattle companies that broke out in the West characterized this reckless era of unfettered investment by Eastern and foreign capitalists.

The Scottish-born Prairie Cattle Company, launched at the end of 1880 with a million dollars in capital, set the pace. With range rights and 38,000 cattle scooped up in New Mexico's Cimarron Valley and southeastern Colorado, the Prairie was an instant success. First-year profits were equal to 26 percent on all paid-up capital, justifying its expansion to 2.5 million dollars. Within three years the Prairie had an almost unbroken range from the Canadian River in Texas to the Arkansas in Colorado.[3]

Nineteen other cattle companies appeared in 1881, and Denver and Cheyenne, each with different roles, became focal points of this frenzied activity. Anointed that year as Colorado's capital, Denver had some 36,000 persons, or 7 times its 1870 population. New silver strikes were large growth factors. With the coming of the rails to Cheyenne, Denver banks expanded enormously from draft sales to buy Texas cattle for southern Wyoming ranges. J. W. Iliff and Dennis Sheedy were among the host of wealthy ranchmen who invested cattle profits in Denver businesses and built palatial homes. The city's cattle trade now justified the merger of several shipping concerns into larger accommodations known as Denver Union Stock Yards Company.[4]

Cheyenne, although smaller than its sister city and almost ten years younger, had made spectacular progress from its roundhouse beginnings in 1867. The town was "possessed of 3,000 inhabitants" by 1875. In 1885, when five thousand citizens were counted,[5] it was the northern Plains center of the cow business and the capital of its social life. To oblige the "nouveau rich of the range" the fantastic Cheyenne Club went up along continental lines.[6] Verandaed and begabled, the plush wooden structure was the site of immense cattle transactions made in its lounge over champagne and caviar, in its restaurant with the finest cuisine, or on its spacious tennis court.[7] Cheyenne boasted electric lights by 1881, an Oscar Wilde billing at the new fifty-thousand-dollar opera house in 1882, and five newspapers the following year.[8]

A variety of causes generated and propelled the cattle boom. The cow business, which had started modestly with individual operators, had reached the point at which expenses no longer increased in direct ratio to herd size. Cheap beef production, then, was best achieved by large scale operations—the bigger the better. British reports stressed that large amounts of

ELEGANT EIGHTIES. *Denver's Capitol Hill, where Dennis Sheedy built his redstone mansion, claimed more millionaires in the 1880's than any other similar area of the world. Jobless until he rode night herd with trail cattle, Sheedy studied the country and saved. Knowing of water holes in the dry, panic year of 1873, he bought cheap cows for free range near Iliff's. Sheedy took in a defunct store on a debt, renamed it The Denver Dry Goods Company, and was its president for many years.*

money must be invested to secure the greatest returns. They noted the urgency of making these investments while low-cost cattle and free grass still were available.[9]

These elements were combining to move range management from individual ownership to corporate big business. Smaller ranchmen pooled their interests, sold out to giants called "cattle kings" or, more often, to speculative cattle companies managed by men unaccustomed to the cow. Almost six hundred of these concerns were formed from 1880 to 1886 in New Mexico, Colorado, Wyoming, and Montana alone. With the malignant influx of inexperience, fast but theoretical book count replaced the actual range count of cattle, both in trading and in company reports. And overnight the language of the range was one of stockholders, dividends, shares, and debentures.[10] Where earlier ranchmen scrimped in dugouts or cabins near their herds, several high-salaried managers now made occasional range visits from Kansas City or London offices, then relaxed at the Cheyenne Club. With a veneer of glamor and excitement, this once-frugal business now wore a saddle of pyramiding extravagance.[11]

Also, in 1880, barbed wire had begun its contraction of the range in earnest with eighty million spiny pounds manufactured and sold at half the cost of the first ten thousand pounds made in 1874.[12] But, happily for those who cherish the image of an unbridled range, two young adventurers with brush and pen came to Montana in 1880. While Missourian Charles Russell and New Yorker Frederic Remington never met, together they captured the color of the open range for future generations.[13]

Texas drives of almost 500,000 Longhorns ushered in this prosperous decade, swelling cattle numbers and greatly stimulating the growth of packing centers, corn-belt feeders, and the dressed-beef trade. Indeed, export figures of that product exceeded the tonnage of domestic barbed wire sales. From the 4,000 pounds of refrigerated beef that reached foreign shores in 1875, the trade jumped to nearly 85 million pounds in 1880.[14] Along with these markets, American housewives were demanding cheap beef, and reservation Indians were consuming 40 million pounds of it annually.[15]

It is doubtful whether any other aspect of western economic development held the same fascination for both Americans and Europeans as the range cattle industry of the eighties. Expanding operations were one gauge of magnetism; the flood of related literature was another.[16] This hypnotic period—the "beef bonanza" —takes its name from a book by James S. Brisbin, a Pennsylvania-born cavalry officer smitten with the West. Published in 1881, his *Beef Bonanza; or, How to Get Rich on the Plains* stressed what Western speculators wanted Easterners to believe and what eager Eastern and European speculators wanted to hear. "The beef business could not be overdone," Brisbin stated flatly.[17] Figuring hypothetically, he arrived at annual profits of at least twenty-five percent, and reasoned that "if $200,000 were invested in Texas cattle, it would double itself in four years and pay a semiannual dividend of 8 per cent."[18] A mirror of the idealism then hovering over the West, the horse soldier's work contributed little factual information about the industry but had far-reaching effects in luring foreign money.[19]

A deluge of range articles and books followed in the next four years with the recurrent theme of fortunes in a season. Drowned out were the few notes of warning that the western universe of grass might one day be exhausted and fatally vulnerable to a severe drouth or winter. Travelers, hunters, land speculators, and railroad and immigration promoters were among those who wrote alongside orthodox journalists.

Of the group, a red-bearded baron from Germany employed the pen with perhaps the most singular purpose—to win a wife. Walter Baron von Richthofen, arriving in Denver in the late seventies, was a playboy by profession. One day at the races he met a stunning widow. In their ensuing courtship, she agreed to marry the nobleman if he would show signs of settling down to a more stable career. A year later, in 1885, he proudly presented her with a copy of his efforts as an author: *Cattle Raising on the Plains of North America*. The beauteous blonde was soon a baroness, but there is no record that she ever became a cattle queen. While Richtho-

142

CASTLE IN COLORADO. *A book by a ranchless castle builder fanned the fable of quick cattle profits. In* Cattle Raising on the Plains of North America, *Walter Baron von Richthofen said an eighty-percent annual herd increase had not "the slightest element of uncertainty." The forty-room Denver replica of his German ancestral home includes his coat-of-arms above the entrance, and a three-foot head of Barbarossa on the structure's northwest corner.*

fen bred horses and had a dairy herd, his range knowledge was as theoretical as his book, dwelling on descendants a cow might expect in ten years and on the seeming success of Colorado cattle companies.[20]

The cattle boom continued unabated through the early 1880's under a set of virtually simultaneous circumstances. Investment money poured in, clamoring for ranches, range rights, and herds to be bought feverishly on book count. The national financial scene improved and these seasons on the range were good. By 1882, with range stock selling at thirty to thirty-five dollars a head, those who had purchased cattle three years earlier could realize a three hundred percent profit. Many large operators, alarmed at the rapid demise of free grass, overstocked their ranges, creating a buying demand that denuded the market supply and forced prices even higher.[21] Exuberant Texans increased the number and volume of their drives accordingly.

Selective breeding had made Longhorns a better quality cattle than those of earlier trail days, though little new blood stock had survived in South Texas. Panhandle ranchmen, however, had added fine Durhams and Herefords to the hardy strain. Having the shoe on the other foot had changed the outlook of these cowmen. Now they mortally feared fever-bearing herds from the south. Their leader—master trail blazer Charles Goodnight—enforced a Winchester quarantine on the ground and waged a warning campaign by mail. With characteristic clarity, in 1881 he wrote an old crony in the lower country:

I send Mr. Smith to turn your cattle so they will not pass through our range. . . .

I hope you will take this advice as yourselves and I have always been good friends, but even friendship will not protect you in the drive through here. . . .

My cattle are now dying of the fever contracted from cattle driven from Fort Worth, therefore do not have any hope that you can convince me that your cattle will not give mine the fever, this we will not speak of. I simply say to you that you will never pass through here in good health.

Yours truly,
C. Goodnight

The indignant friend, George T. Reynolds, asked the *Fort Griffin Echo* to print this notice so "that stock men generally may know how overbearing prosperity can make a man."[22]

Among a number of British cattle companies located in Texas by 1882 were two enormous corporations well under way and a third of staggering magnitude in the making.

Men of Dundee, Scotland, inspired by the Prairie Company's success, had formed the Texas Land and Cattle Company in December, 1881. With an authorized 2.1 million dollars they purchased Mifflin Kenedy's 236,000-acre fenced ranch in South Texas and 50,000 cattle. Then trebling its capital for more herds and 65,000 leased acres in the Texas Panhandle, the company paid a 15-percent dividend after the first season's cattle sales.[23]

In response to this good news, Scottish capitalists reached for more Texas lands and, late in 1882, registered the Matador Land and Cattle Company to purchase 100,000 acres in Motley, Dickens, Floyd, and Cottle counties. Ranch buildings and 40,000 cattle were included in the $1,250,000 package deal. An additional 73,000 acres were obtained from the state at 50 cents an acre. Within four months of its founding, the Matador had 60,000 cattle, more than 300,000 acres held in simple fee, and range privileges over 1.8 million acres. The speed of purchase proved wise, since Texas set a two-dollar-per-acre minimum on all unwatered lands soon after the Matador transaction.[24]

The biggest land swap in Texas history had taken place on January 1, 1882, when the building contract was let for the present state capitol. Contractors received 3 million acres of land in the Texas Panhandle. Their bid of 55½ cents an acre was an excellent price at the time. Ultimately the state realized almost twice that figure when building costs, estimated at 1.5 million dollars, more than doubled.[25] Development of the land with British money began in 1885.

Five years after the 1873 panic, western rail building had resumed. The railroads now rushed to install new cattle shipping facilities. Also, for the convenience of hundreds of trail hands returning home after the drives, railroads issued cowboy tickets at reduced rates.

'A FAIR REFLEX.' *Construction of the Texas Capitol at Austin was begun in the beef bonanza days by a Chicago syndicate and later refinanced in London. For the 3.7-million-dollar pink granite building the syndicate received 3,050,000 Panhandle acres that became the XIT Ranch. Taller than the nation's Capitol, the Texas statehouse, said its planners, combines all essential elements of proportion, dignity, and modern improvement, and is "a fair reflex of the enlightenment of our age."*

RAIL EXTENSION. *Post-panic railroad plans included a grand scheme for a narrow-gauge from Denver to Mexico. Dubbed the "baby road," the Denver & Rio Grande promised mountain branches to isolated ranchers, miners, and farmers. It had reached Trinidad and Durango, Colorado, by 1880. The "Cumbres," now Colorado's oldest locomotive, was built for the D.&R.G. in 1881, and pulled cattle and freight around Pueblo. The engine saw final use on a lumber road in 1948.*

145

The fare was twenty-five dollars from Dodge City to San Antonio—a week or ten-day train ride as against several months mounted or in a southbound chuck wagon.

Jack Potter, a cow waddie of sixteen, took advantage of the offer in 1882, and recorded with rollicking wit the first train trip for him and some of his peers. Reaching Dodge by rail from Greeley, Colorado, Potter found that "Dog Face" Smith of Cotulla, Texas, would be along on the rest of the journey, and was "all worked up" over having to go home in such a foreign manner:

I will never forget seeing that train come into Dodge City that night. Old "Dog Face" and his bunch were pretty badly frightened and we had considerable difficulty getting them aboard. It was about 12:30 when the train pulled out. . . . Old "Dog Face" was out of humor and was the last one to bed down.

At about three o'clock our train was sidetracked to let the westbound train pass . . . and just as it passed our coach the engineer blew the whistle. Talk about your stampedes! That bunch of sleeping cowboys rose as one man, and started on the run with old "Dog Face" Smith in the lead. . . .

I had not yet woke up, but thinking it was a genuine cattle stampede, yelled out, "Circle your leaders and keep up the drags." Just then the leaders circled and ran into the drags, knocking some of us down. They circled again and the news butcher crawled out from under foot and jumped through the window like a frog. Before they could circle again, the train crew pushed in the door and caught old "Dog Face" and the bunch quieted down. The conductor was pretty angry and threatened to have us transferred to the freight department and loaded into a stock car.[26]

In 1883, the year that Buffalo Bill organized his Wild West Show, "all the cattle in the world seemed to be coming up from Texas," a Montana cowboy observed.[27] This was also the year that Texas fever was recognized as a national problem and a government survey undertaken to locate northern limits of the infection.[28] It was another annum, too, of banner dividends from the big cattle companies with the Prairie leading the pack. Prairie's payment to shareholders equaled 20.5 percent on paid-up capital, and the clamor for such manna went on. That the dividend was paid out of

cattle sales capital rather than herd-increment profit was no deterrent.[29]

Largest of the corporations floated in 1883 was the Swan Land and Cattle Company, registered in Edinburgh and capitalized at 3 million dollars. Acquiring herds and ranches for the company in eastern Wyoming, Alexander Swan—the chief vendor and a charmer—became the company manager. John Clay recalled that it was fashionable in those days to throw in a lord (a duke was better) to give respectability to the board. The Swan had such a personage in Lord Douglas Gordon, M.P., of London.[30] Swan lands along the Laramie, Chug, and Sybille rivers extended 130 miles from east to west and the north-south line increased from 42 to 100 miles. Boosting capital to swell the holdings, half a million acres of railroad land were added to the empire in 1884.[31]

Meanwhile, the Northern Pacific Railroad, advancing westward from Bismarck, in Dakota Territory, had brought in a colorful entourage of passengers. Of note in 1883 was the Marquis de Mores, a resplendent Frenchman who, in quick order, built a range beef-packing plant, a twenty-six-room chateau, and the town of Medora, named for his lovely wife. A clubhouse for his cowboys and butchers had pool tables and bowling alleys.

The marquis established a newspaper and a stage line and purchased water rights over 45,000 acres that controlled several hundred thousand grazing acres. "That crazy Frenchman," Dakota cowmen called him when he brought in sheep. Fencing his range did not increase his popularity. The unusual tenderfoot killed a man for cutting his wire, then managed acquittal of the murder charge.

The packing plant was in operation by the 1883 fall, and eight thousand beeves were slaughtered the next year for transport east in his own refrigerated cars. The enterprises were spawned so swiftly that the 1884 government report on range cattle registered more wonderment than analysis: De Mores's ventures "have got beyond the experimental stage, and are evidently destined to farther development."[32] But range beef were ready for slaughter only in the fall, and the plant's enormous overhead could

BRUSH COUNTRY. *South of San Antonio in 1883, Teddy Blue tells of night thunder scaring cattle, and cowboys without chaps jumping up to chase them: "When daylight come . . . I was a bloody sight . . . a big hole in my forehead . . . my hands was cut to pieces . . . and my knees was worst of all. I was picking thorns out of them all the way to Kansas." Records show only clumps of South Texas brush prior to 1866. Sprouted mesquite beans in droppings of trail cattle soon made the area a thorny jungle.*

147

INTERNATIONAL VIEW. *From the porch of De Mores' chateau, the outlook was broad in late 1883. The cottonwood-filled valley of the Little Missouri drained extensive cattle holdings of Texas, Eastern, and foreign capital that had flocked to the area in the seven years since its opening. Included were Texas' big OX, 777, and "Hashknife"; Minnesota's Wadsworth and Hawley; Pennsylvania's Custer Trail properties; and the Neimmela Ranch backed by Sir John Pender of London.*

not justify once-a-year operations. De Mores departed in 1887, leaving behind the ruins of his investment and one of the most spectacular short chapters in the lore of the range.

Another 1883 sojourner to Dakota's Little Missouri was Theodore Roosevelt of New York, coming with the avowed purpose of a buffalo hunt. Within three weeks, however, the country's enchantment and the challenge of life in the open convinced him to add ranching to his growing political career. He spent a large part of the next four years in Dakota Territory, ranging between three thousand and five thousand cattle on two spreads around Medora. Roosevelt wanted desperately to master cowboy ways and threw himself wholeheartedly into the quest, after death in a single night took both his wife and his mother.

The cowboys did accept Teddy for dogged sportsmanship, although his leather-seated, corduroy riding breeches startled them into believing that he wore chaps backwards. The future "Rough Rider" never sat their kind of saddle rightly, roped well, or successfully wedded their vernacular to his Harvard accent. Accordingly, his major roundup task was hunting to provide fresh meat for the outfit. He shared their adventure, nonetheless, and proudly wrote his sister: "I have been on the roundup for a fortnight and really enjoy the work greatly. . . . We breakfast at three every morning and work from sixteen to eighteen hours a day, counting night guard; so I get pretty sleepy, but feel strong as a bear."

Later, he summarized these experiences more eloquently for publication: "We knew toil and hardship and hunger and thirst; and we saw men die violent deaths as they worked among the horses and cattle; but we felt the best of hardy life in our veins, and ours was the glory of work and the joy of living."

While Roosevelt was respected for leadership in Dakota and Montana stock growers' associations, he was not the region's largest ranchman, nor was he successful. Finally closing out his Badlands operations in 1898 with a loss, including interest, of about fifty thousand dollars, his contributions to cattle raising were small except for his vigorous writings. Yet he developed a love of the West and a philosophy of self-reliant action from which the nation as a whole would benefit. Here the future President came to appreciate the need for staying territorial wastes. When he exchanged his range for the White House, he championed conservation of America's scenic, natural, and historic resources.[33]

Although interest on cattle money rose from 1.5 to 2 per cent a month, there still was an abundance of borrowers in 1884. The heady demand for stock called in even farm cattle from the Midwest.[34] Since 1882 Texans had

FOR RANGE PACKING. *The Marquis de Mores began shipping processed beef direct from range to consumer late in 1883. He started the town of Medora with his huge packing plant, which had a blood-drying system and worked 150 men and as many cowboys on the range. The marquis formed a refrigerated rail car company, bought trail herds wholesale, and raised cabbages with the by-products. The chimney and boiler of his plant, which operated four years and burned in 1907, remain.*

driven well over half a million Longhorns into the seeming void of the Great Plains, and 300,000 more were on the way.

Six new British companies appeared in 1884, casting about for additional grazing with a capital aggregate of seven million dollars.[35] Much of this money was invested in Texas, where state-owned public domain, including school lands, totaled about eighty million acres early in the decade. More than a third of this area, heretofore dormant for lack of surface water, was taking on new import with the advent of deep wells, windmills, and man-made reservoirs.[36] Millions of these unwatered acres lay in the elevated plains of the Panhandle, where Goodnight and others had found excellent grasses for fattening cattle, and it was here that British interests centered.

Texas land was no longer Scot-free, however. In 1883 the state had passed leasing legislation that set nominal rentals for a ten-year period on alternate sections of school land.[37] While British newspapers continued to explain the wonders of plentiful land in the American West, they failed to note that the demand for grazing had forced Texas to up its land prices and to make the leasing provision. Despite this added expense to ranching, many investors, if apprised of the fact, probably welcomed some modicum of stability in land tenure, which was being questioned all over western America. Paid-up nominal capital of English and Scottish enterprises in Texas, including those concerned mainly with mortgage and land sales, was approximately 25 million dollars at the end of 1886. The land they owned, leased, occupied without title, or subjected to mortgage was estimated at 15 to 20 million acres. Texans did not like it.

A Dallas newspaper complained in January, 1884, of these growing monopolies that enabled foreign stockholders to "rule with the sway of lords that vast domain, gathering wealth without labor and without price. . . . Such open handed plunder has never been witnessed since William the Conqueror divided out the English farms among the Norman barons."[38]

Wily westerners were well aware that overseas capitalists were easily duped in their haste to become wealthy ranchers. With Colorado direction the 500,000-acre Spur Ranch in Texas was put together expressly for resale to the British. Two years later, in 1884, the ranch was sold to a London syndicate at more profit than the absentee owners would make in the next twenty years.[39]

A number of Britishers did come, however, for a first-hand sampling of the cattle business. To cowboys they were "remittance men" whose usefulness around a ranch was limited to allowances received from home. They, too, were easy prey. A practical education as cowmen was offered these young men of means by a "school for cowboys" that opened this same year at Van Raub, just north of San Antonio. The spread of a substantial house with large dining hall, parlor, and kitchen, and houses patterned after old range shacks was advertised in London papers. In this way the promoter, Byron Van Raub (or Van Raub Byron), secured a number of wealthy English boarders at twelve hundred dollars a year. The school founder was an Easterner whose get-rich-quick schemes had forced him to flee to Texas. His "practical" course was tested early by a neighboring farmer who took a small mare to be bred by Van Raub's Shetland stallion. When the little stud was led into the lot saddled and bridled, Van Raub explained the science to the speechless granger: The psychological influence on the mare would cause her colt to be born saddle- and bridle-wise without further training. The school was short-lived.[40]

Another national depression, set off in May, 1884, by the New York collapse of ex-President Grant's firm, did not gain velocity in the range country until the year end, but it added some concern to an industry already ailing. Barbed wire, sheep, and homesteaders were cutting into cattle ranges. Grazing leases were being questioned in Indian Territory, and the virulence of Texas fever on the northern Plains spread rumors that the Texas trails would be closed.[41] Yet the beef bonanza bubble continued its precarious increase.

Since 1880 cattle numbers had doubled in Montana and Wyoming, and almost so in Kansas and Nebraska for a four-state total exceeding 5 million.[42] Gains of 900,000 cattle in Colo-

DWINDLING BISON. *The only sizable buffalo herd left in the world was making its last stand in 1883, in the southwest corner of present North Dakota. About ten thousand head ranged south of newly built Northern Pacific tracks, which brought in an avalanche of Eastern hunters, including Theodore Roosevelt. Professional hide hunters were already at work. By early fall the herd numbered about twelve hundred, and the Sioux of Standing Rock Agency were allowed to join in the final kill that ended October 23.*

‘WONDERFUL REVOLUTION.’ *In his harbinger-of-change speech to national cattlemen, Missouri's governor said barbed wire and refrigerated rail cars had worked a "wonderful revolution." Cattle raising had been accelerated beyond any other enterprise. Incongruously, he also endorsed the National Cattle Trail, which the certain advance of wire and track made not only difficult but impractical.*

152

NO CATTALO! *With the cry for improved cattle, Goodnight began buffalo-Angus crosses in 1885. Starting a buffalo herd earlier, this cross idea came when his roundup caught a half-breed buffalo calf by the carcass of its Longhorn mother. That buffalo cooperated more readily than cattle in the plan is indicated by this heifer, peering nervously over her prickly pear rampart. Goodnight, who worked thirty years for a beef breed able to take hard winters, gave up "cattalo" because of expense and abortion.*

rado and New Mexico during that period pushed their combined figure to well over 2 million.[43] Another million had poured into Indian Territory.[44]

Goodnight, in Texas, and Granville Stuart, in Montana, were seeking legislation to regulate and protect the mushrooming business and, meanwhile, were cleaning out rustlers through grower organizations they had helped to form. Stuart's vigilance committee was known to have shot or hanged sixty-three outlaws and horse thieves.[45]

By far the largest and most successful banding of ranchmen was the Wyoming Stock Growers Association, formed in 1873 with ten men owning twenty thousand cattle. Colorado, Montana, Dakota, and Nebraska were represented in the membership of four hundred who were assessed for two million cattle in the mid-eighties. Stringent laws concerning roundups, branding, health, and transportation of cattle were enacted in Wyoming Territory through the influence of this powerful body. Association inspectors supervised the sale and transport by rails and trails of about one million cattle in 1884. The organization met in Cheyenne's opera house by day and in the Cheyenne Club by night.[46]

A Wyoming-dominated group of cattlemen had petitioned Congress in 1883 for a federal agency to cope with communicable stock diseases—pleuropneumonia, as well as Texas fever. The Bureau of Animal Industry, created in the Department of Agriculture, resulted in 1884.

Then in November that year, as the price of range cattle on the Chicago market dropped almost seven dollars per hundredweight from the 1882 peak, ranchmen from the farthest reaches of the cow country convened at St. Louis for a week-long meet.[47] A letter signed by prominent cattlemen and cattle-company representatives had called the thirteen hundred delegates to initiate "united action for general protection" that could be "secured only by National Organizations, such as we now propose." Thus the first annual convention of Cattle Growers of the United States—and the last for many years—got under way.

At issue were two major problems with a closely allied third. Ranchmen of the northern Plains sought desperately to long-term lease the public domain they ranged, and to control disease in their improved herds. Texans, on the other hand, were not so concerned with land matters, since their state owned its public lands and offered provision for lease and purchase. They were highly agitated, however, about continuance of the Texas trails and wanted a permanent "National Trail," which they believed would control the fever.

This historic assembly bespoke as nothing else the unbelievable spread of cattle ranching in a meager eighteen years. All the greats who had cradled the industry from a calf to a Bunyon-like bull were yet alive and present— from trail drivers to cattle kings, from cattle company spokesmen to bankers, packers, feeders, and government officials. Granville Stuart and Conrad Kohrs were there for Montana; and Joseph Carey, Thomas Sturgis, Alexander Swan, and John Clay for Wyoming. Joseph McCoy of Abilene fame represented a Kansas breeders' association. Ex-Governor John Routt of Colorado headed a very large delegation and presided over the convention. The beef bonanza phrase maker, James S. Brisbin, spoke for Idaho growers. Texans came en masse: Charles Goodnight, Shanghai Pierce, J. R. Blocker, Dillard Fant, the Driskills, the Days, the Snyders, and Richard King, with his son-in-law, Robert Kleberg. Congressman W. H. Crain, J. T. Lytle, Ike Pryor, J. F. Ellison, George Littlefield, C. C. Slaughter, and J. A. McFaddin also were among the three hundred Texans who advanced on Missouri.

It was clear from the outset that trail discussions would dominate the day and gain support from Eastern States seeking assured supplies of cheap beef. But extracts from the proceedings tell better the story of mounting problems and of near conflagration as these men espousing united action came together to wage verbal civil war within an industry.

The keynote address by Governor T. T. Crittenden of Missouri paid eloquent homage to the accomplishments of his audience but warned that more progress was necessary to protect their success:

Nothing has moved so rapidly as the great enterprise in which you are now engaged. . . . Hungry men, scientists, railway cars, refrigerated cars and barbed wire fencing have worked this wonderful revolution.

This business has awakened into life a new power—a new race of man—and made fruitful . . .

immense tracts of lands which had been given to desolation and waste. It has taken the frugal cowboy and made him a potential millionaire.

This is an age of greed, as well as progress. The cry is heard on farm and ranch, better blood, purer blood! Should not the cry of more care, better care, also be heard? I am aware . . . it is now quite impossible to shelter the large herds. . . . But, Sirs, the time will come when the herds will be smaller and their improved blood will demand such protection, else their carcasses will be found on every acre of land.

Governor Crittenden endorsed the national cattle trail and said Missouri would stand for this important measure. "The contest," he declared, was "between the railroads on the one side and the owners and consumers of beef on the other." It would be decided in favor of owners and consumers by the laws of trade and economy and by the appetites of humanity. A national trail, the governor said, not only would furnish cheaper means of transporting Texas cattle to the more nutritious grasses of the Northwest but would lessen greatly the danger of importing Texas fever to the northern herds.

Millions upon millions of acres of our public domain have been given to railroad corporations— enriching the few at the expense of the many—and now it is high time a few millions were donated in the interest of the people, as a means of supplying them cheaper food. . . . Cheap food is the desideratum of the age.

Kansas delegates vehemently opposed the trail and its attendant danger of Texas fever:

Mr. Russell of Kansas: "A burnt child shuns the fire and some of us from Kansas have been burned a good deal by the cattle trail from Texas. We are sick of it; we don't want any more of it.

"Our Texas friends often assert that Texas cattle do no harm. Some even go so far as to say there is no Texas fever; but when you have seen your cattle, that have not been in contact with Texas cattle, but have been either drinking water . . . or feeding on a range where Texas cattle have passed a week or two ago, and your cattle lie down and die by the dozen, by the hundred, then it touches your pockets and affects your interest."

Delegate from Texas: "How do you know that killed them?"

Mr. Russell: "Because we know what Texas fever

'EL RANCHO GRANDE.' *A. H. Pierce often stood on the second-story gallery of his rambling ranch house and shouted orders to men working cattle a mile away. With many things on his mind in 1884, his roar was louder than ever. Shanghai was busy with barbed wire to keep out an old enemy; he lobbied in Austin for a law making fence cutting a felony, was off to Denver discussions on Texas fever, and then to St. Louis as a National Cattle Trail advocate.*

155

is. When those cattle were cut open it was as clear as a pike-staff to any man who had ever lost any cattle from Texas disease. . . . It [the trail] goes today through the State of Kansas, but I tell you it won't go through the State of Kansas next year.

"This business has grown up in a certain way by reason of the profit on cattle. All southwest Kansas is filled with improved and improving herds.

"You may pass a thousand resolutions, but you will find that there are other things which are going to settle this matter," Russell said. "You can scarcely find a section of land along the present trail that has no squatters upon it south of Dodge City, and settlers necessarily destroy a cattle trail."

Colonel Stuart of Montana: "The greater part of our herds in Montana were originally from Texas. They have been importing into Montana every year for fifteen years from the great State of Texas, but I come here to protest against the wording of the resolution. It speaks about "the breeding grounds of Texas;" giving them a trail . . . to "the maturing grounds of the North." It is not right. The strip of country on both sides of the Rocky Mountains, from Texas to the British possessions, is as much breeding ground for cattle as the great State of Texas.

"Why, then, should they come with their propositions asking government aid to make a cattle trail from Texas which seeks an outlet for its surplus stock . . . ?

"We in Montana, are in many localities absolutely overstocked today. This very year thousands of cattle have been shipped to market from Montana because we were overstocked."

Stuart, protesting federal aid to "bring in more cattle and overwhelm us," put Montana's delegation on record as voting solidly against the trail.

General Curtis of New York said the question was of national importance, stressing that the East was the consumer of Western beef. The conditions referred to by Russell of Kansas existed because no regulated system or law existed. "That is, in itself, a reason why there should be some such provision by the Federal Government in establishing a great highway upon which these animals may go," the general said. He concluded that exotic cattle diseases had obtained a foothold in the country because of government carelessness and neglect, and that all sections of the country should bring this to the attention of Congress.

Wyoming, speaking first for the leasing of public lands, opposed the trail but offered a compromise.

Mr. Babbitt of Wyoming: "It [leasing] is a proposition to pay for something for which we now pay nothing. It is a proposition to bring order out of chaos. The history of the cattle business is that we have all made money; why isn't that good enough? As long as ranges were available the business was good; but in Texas they have reached their limit; they have reached their limit in the Northwest. Our ranges . . . are too heavily stocked, and from this year forward every head that is put on them is that much in excess of the grazing capacity of that Territory. That is why we object to the trail. . . . Our investments are at stake. We have made our money on Texas cattle more than on any others, and we can double the capacity of grazing grounds if we can have long tenure to justify improvements."

In return for Texas support on long-term leasing of public lands, Babbitt said Wyoming would vote for a national cattle trail.

General J. S. Brisbin of Idaho: "I think there are nearly 400 people here who would not have come to this Convention if it had not been for the purpose of securing the passing of this land lease request. . . . Every herdsman today is a trespasser upon the public land, within the eyes of the law; he is a criminal to a certain extent, and something should be done for his relief from that onus."

As General Brisbin's remarks indicated, Northern men were impatient to get on with the leasing issue, but so much time was given to the trail that other business received scant attention. The minority report against long-term leases was read by Joseph McCoy, one of the signers. Leasing, he said, would repeal provisions of the homestead and preemption laws and would be in the interest of wealthy cattle corporations and owners. It was but another way to fence the public domain.

A number of speakers dwelled on the tragic effects of Texas fever, but admitted that knowledge of the cause belonged to the future:

Address of Professor S. Waterhouse: "Texas fever perplexes the pathologist with mysteries that elude explanation. It is surpassingly strange that only cattle in apparently perfect health transmit

156

the disease, while animals sick with the fever do not spread the contagion. . . . The losses of stockmen are aggravated by the fact that the contagion selects the most valuable animals for destruction. . . . These facts are enigmas for which science has no present solution to offer. Meanwhile, according to the United States Department of Agriculture, the plague is spreading."

Dr. E. A. Carothers, a San Antonio physician and ranchman, provided the meeting's only comic relief with sarcastic debunking of the "newly discovered germ theory" of Texas fever as enunciated by Department of Agriculture veterinarians. He quoted Dr. D. E. Salmon's report that pastures in infected districts were "covered by immense numbers of disease germs." These bacteria were taken into stomachs of Texas cattle and deposited on northern ranges, causing a highly mortal disease among northern cattle. The theory needs only to be proved, Dr. Carothers continued:

I have nowhere, in all of the literature of the subject, found a single description of any germ claimed to have been found upon Texas grasses, or in Texas cattle. Where are they? . . . these "immense numbers" of germs, spores, diplococci, bacteria, bacilli, schizophytae, or "varmints" . . . for which a Greek name has never been invented that has the remotest relation to Texas fever. Gentlemen, they have never been seen, because they have no existence except in the vivid imagination . . . of these learned scientists.

The report caused the British Privy Council to prohibit the introduction of our beef into Great Britain, and has taken more money out of the pockets of the stockmen on this floor than would have supported an affluence of a dozen scientists for the rest of their lives. It is a cheap way of obtaining notoriety, but it is "death to the frogs."

Carothers told of systematic checks by medical officers on all cattle slaughtered at Texas military posts. After four years they were convinced that Texas cattle were free from disease at home. Northern ranges were not the first to suffer the ravages of *"murrain,"* which had threatened in the sixteenth century to exterminate the bovine race in Europe.

"Murrain" was, and is a popular term meaning *"a highly infectious and mortal disease among cattle,"* . . . and its use is as old as history, being referred to in the Bible, Exodus 9:3:

"There shall be a very grievous murrain."

. . . many causes were assigned to it from the anger of Deity down. The Scots in the 17th century found that *witches did it.* This important discovery engaged the earnest attention of all classes, and even of the King. . . . Along with causing an accepted translation of the Bible to be made, he wrote a very learned treatise proving incontestibly the existence of the witches.

Carothers said witches were as tangible as nonexistent germs on Texas grass and cattle.

Again, if we believe, as is almost universally conceded . . . that no living organism exists that did not have a parent similar . . . where did the first germ come from? Was there a Texas steer in the ark or in the Garden of Eden with these diplococci in his spleen? The accepted theory of Texas fever fits nothing in the whole realm of pathology.

We are as sincere as you are in trying to unravel the apparent mystery. Whether it be a contagion or a ferment, whether it is something generated or carried by our cattle, or is of local origin . . . whether the ticks are the cause of it, or it is generated from the feet of the cattle made sore by excessive travel in wet weather . . . and whether it is the same disease that kills the northern fine stock when taken to Texas . . . the fact that a disease known by the name of Spanish or Texas fever does kill your cattle, remains a very serious one; and that it is injuring both our interests and yours is indisputable.

We are willing to meet you full half way in adopting any precautionary measures to prevent the spread of the disease while determining its true character and modes of prevention; but do not ask us to take leave of our senses . . . by believing the monstrous theory promulgated by . . . the Agricultural Department.[48]

Reluctantly, the divided and thinning ranks adopted resolutions for The National Cattle Trail and for long-term leases of public land. These measures would be presented to Congress as the official wishes of the National Cattle Growers Association. But when the call was made to elect officers of this permanent organization, Wyoming and Montana failed to answer; their delegates were aboard the train for home.[49] This association of cattlemen would not meet again. As the distraught year of 1884 drew to a close, foreign companies that had rushed into the "brilliant gamble in wild cattle" were realizing for the first time some of the odds against them.[50] Calf crops were short of anticipation, cattle on the books were far in excess of those on the range, and unexpected losses and expenses were rising. The Prairie, "mother of British cattle companies,"[51] halved its dividend; those of the sprawling Matador, and the Texas Land and Cattle were cut, some corporations passed dividends entirely, and many smaller concerns folded.[52]

This was clearly the beginning of the end of an era in the cattle business; another closed in December with the death of John Chisum. He was the last of the really feudal lords of the open range and there would be no more. Because of his ruthless sway over southern New Mexico, Chisum was not particularly mourned —but he did know cattle. "He was a great trail man," appraised Goodnight in retrospect, "and the best counter I ever knew. He could count three grades of cattle at once . . . even if they were going in a trot."[53]

A blue norther howled in Austin as the Texas Live Stock Association convened in mid-January, 1885, and members raised to their favorite mission the toast printed on their programs:

To a National Cattle Trail
May Congress establish it as a measure of justice to Texas Stockmen.[54]

Two days later Texas Representative James F. Miller gave Congress that opportunity, introducing a bill to establish a quarantined trail capable of regulating livestock commerce between the states. With an average width of three miles, the route from the southern border of Colorado to Canada would be 690 miles long and contain 2,070 square miles or 1,324,000 acres.[55] But the National Cattle Trail as a controlled throughfare died aborning and never led past the congressional halls.

However, the general course of the Western, or Texas, Trail did follow the route described in the bill after March, 1885, when Kansas quarantined the whole state against through trail traffic. Nebraska in the same month also passed quarantine legislation which, coupled with the Kansas action, forced the trail westward beyond their boundaries and thus did away with Dodge and Ogallala as cowtowns.

The new route up from Texas sliced horizontally across the Oklahoma Panhandle—then "No Man's Land"—and entered Colorado's southeast corner. Keeping east and bearing north, it emerged in a broad concourse with the Goodnight Trail at Pine Bluffs, in southeastern Wyoming. Farther north the trail was not altered.

Richard King, pointing to the great value this land would have when no longer needed as a trail, had urged cattlemen at the St. Louis convention to purchase outright this vertical swath up the nation's heartland.[56] His faith in future land values already was being justified when he died in April, 1885, leaving his heirs the 600,000-acre Santa Gertrudis, which he valued at 6.5 million dollars. He had bought a tenth of this South Texas land 30 years before at less than 10 cents per acre.[57]

While Captain King was successful in upgrading horse stock with fine Kentucky blood, his Durham imports that survived Texas fever produced no such effect on Longhorns during his lifetime. But from culling, even as to color, King Ranch cattle were mightier and heavier than average range animals. After King's death there were no more of the long, matched herds on the trail—bay horses with red cattle, black horses with black cattle, and brown horses with brown cattle. From then on the ranch could ship its livestock on nearby rails.[58]

Steers not under contract were scarce in Texas that drouthy 1885 summer, and old Shang Pierce ranged far in their quest. He also was greasing his cattle to clear them of ticks and said it worked like a charm. Pierce was one of the few who believed tick infestation had anything to do with Texas fever, and he was finding that Brahman cattle were more fever resistant than most breeds. Any imported bull "that has no Brahma in him, or has not been greased, will die, even though I pour a double dose of Epsom salts down him every morning," the sage South Texan said.[59]

Dry as it was, there was frenzied activity on the state's high plains where, since 1882, the 3 million acres of Capitol Syndicate land had lain like a sleeping giant stretched out on the western Panhandle. The holdings now were surveyed. Fencing was begun on the north end

CHISUM'S PLANTINGS. *Giant trees that line the South Springs Ranch approach near Roswell, New Mexico, were switches from the mountains planted by John Chisum in the 1870's. Trailing cattle from Texas to this headquarters, he earmarked 100,000 with his famous "jinglebob" and ruled the Pecos Valley from Fort Sumner to the Texas line. Cowboy gunmen, including Billy the Kid, guarded Chisum's empire until his death in 1884 made way for a new era of smaller ranches and diversified farming.*

159

CAPTAIN KING'S LEGACY. *The dinner bell tower and early kitchen, erected during Richard King's lifetime, are among many reminders on the King Ranch that its founder built wisely and well. When he died in 1885, cattle ranching generally was on the brink of mammoth change. Yet the change was to precepts he had practiced: clear-title land, permanent improvements, and constant upgrading and experimenting for quality livestock. In this tradition his descendants continue King Ranch expansion.*

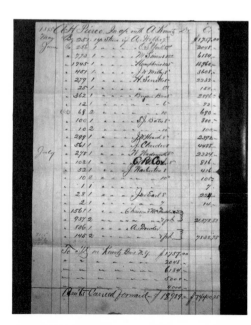

LONGHORN ROUNDUP. *In July, 1885, Shanghai Pierce completed the buying of twelve thousand one- and two-year-old steers to stock the ranch of his new neighbor, Augustus Kountz. The Longhorns were hard to find. While Texas had as many cattle as when the trails began, the unbranded ones were gone and their descendants were under contract to now-plentiful markets. Pierce fanned out two hundred miles to purchase these inferior "Eastern Texas devills, swamp angels, and saddlepocket dogies."*

160

BARBS THAT FENCED A BORDER. *Ribbon wire in Panhandle-Plains Museum, Canyon, Texas, is from the XIT fence that began at Texas' northwest corner and ran 150 straight miles down the New Mexico line. The XIT enclosed 3 million acres in 1885–1886. Unless stock reached through the strands, the three-eighths-inch flat metal with vertical sheet metal barbs was kind. "Brinks Flat" also was popular in Colorado and Kansas and on the coast, where its heavy galvanize resisted salt corrosion.*

while contracts were made for 65,000 cattle.[60]

Controlling the syndicate were Chicagoans John V. and Charles B. Farwell, men dedicated to the highest improvement of the land. But their extravagant bent, plus doubling costs and delays in building the Texas statehouse, caused them to seek quick foreign money to finish the projects. Hurrying off to London, they had no difficulty in finding backers to form the fifteen-million-dollar Capitol Freehold Land and Investment Company. In the unusual arrangement made in June, 1885, the company did not buy the land, which was put up as security, but merely loaned funds for its development and for completion of the capitol.

The unfavorable and false impression was created, nevertheless, that this was another British-owned-and-operated spread. Ab Blocker thought so, too, as he trailed in the first cattle on July 1 and sized up the outfit. How like the English, he mused disgustedly, to have the "damnedest ranch in the world" with *no brand*! Leaving his remedy—XIT—scratched in the sand, Ab refused a job offer and rode back to the trail.[61]

In other parts of the West, ranchmen and cattle companies were edgy over what stand the new President might take in regard to fencing on the public lands and grass leasing in Indian Territory. They had not long to wait. Both issues were subjects of federal investigations. Grover Cleveland, taking office in March, marked time only until congressional fact finders reported on grazing leases from the Indians.

By proclamation on July 23, he declared all leases void on the Cheyenne-Arapaho reservation and ordered ranchmen to remove their cattle within 40 days. General Philip Sheridan was there with troops to expedite the roundup

of more than 200,000 head on the 3 million acres.

Two weeks later, with another proclamation, Cleveland delivered a second blow to men on the open range: all fences would come down on the public lands. Government officials in the West were called upon to execute the order.[62] The fences came down, but not without much effort and litigation, particularly in Colorado, where the excess of illegal fencing had drawn attention of the General Land Office as early as 1882.[63]

Cattle forced from the Cheyenne-Arapaho lands were distributed to already overstocked and overgrazed ranges in Kansas and Texas, where any remaining grass was seared by the exceptionally hot season. Ranchmen north of the reservation in the Cherokee Strip and those in abutting Kansas fought this influx to the point that trail herds had to have military escorts to get through.[64]

If that summer in the Southwest was severe, the winter was even worse. Cattle losses would have been high without the sudden thrust of thousands more upon its range; with them, it was tragic. Ranchmen would curse Cleveland the rest of their days, dating the decline of range-cattle raising to the summer of 1885.[65]

Neither freezing weather nor slumping markets hindered the XIT's progress or plans, as contracts were let to fence the west side of the ranch early in 1886. By the end of the year this largest fencing project in history was almost complete, and the three million acres were enclosed. Despite the enormous cost, the Farwells' London connections allowed them financial room to look toward a Montana fattening range almost as large as their Panhandle holdings.[66]

This was not so of most other cattle syndi-

161

cates dependent upon a supply of British sterling. The big Powder River Cattle Company in Wyoming went into voluntary liquidation. The much larger Swan was in trouble.[67] In March, 1886, its cagey manager presented shareholders with an apology for poor prices and expectations of increasing values. He did not mention that their ranges were overstocked, but added carefully that three thousand steers had been removed from the books because they could not be found. So the Swan went on buying cattle and cut its dividend to six percent.[68]

These companies, Eastern and foreign, built on inflated values and, shrinking with the price of cattle, were rapidly destroying confidence in the cow business, said veteran trailman D. H. Snyder.[69] This destruction of faith extended to individual operators of large ranches and rose to harsh resentment of their image. "The livestock men of the plains made a gigantic mistake when they failed to kill the first toadying editor who called them cattle kings," observed the *New Mexico Stock Grower*.[70]

Cattle-swollen northern ranges stewed in a summer heat reminiscent of the year before on grazing lands to the south. Still overstocking continued. As more money was borrowed to increase the herds held covetously for better prices, estimates of the 1886 Texas drives rose to 350,000 head.[71] And those cattle, placed unacclimated on the northern Plains, became the first casualties of the winter that followed.

The initial blast in mid-November drifted six inches of fine, hard snow and dropped temperatures below zero from the Canadian border to southern Colorado. Three weeks later a second onslaught of greater intensity, longer duration, and lower thermometer readings drove cattle into piles against the nearest fence. Suffocating and freezing, they died miserably.

The weather moderated before Christmas, and ranchmen, optimistic that the worst was over, congratulated themselves that overall cattle losses probably did not exceed ten percent.[72] But the reprieve for their hopes and fortunes ended on January 9, 1887, with a snow that fell an inch an hour for sixteen hours. The mercury plunged to forty-six degrees below zero on the fifteenth over much of the mountain West. The storm did not abate for ten days. Another great

blizzard of seventy-two hours' duration swept the Northwest late in January, terminating with a warm chinook wind that cast the die for the shrunken survivors of cow kind. The welcome melting of top snow had "played the Judas" by morning, when more arctic temperatures froze the range into an ice cake that would hold a steer.[73]

Hunger-mad cattle staggered into Great Falls, Montana, uprooting trees and devouring the roots and branches. In Dakota, gaunt drifts of steers struggling for existence chewed tar paper from the sides of Medora shacks until the animals dropped—a repast for buzzards and the big gray wolves.[74]

Over a million head of cattle, horses, mules, and sheep perished in that still-unsurpassed winter on the northern Plains.[75] Now the beef bonanza was a broken reed. Weakened with one disaster heaped upon another, this golden brick of cattle crumbled under nature's protest of greed and mismanagement and melted with the snow in the long-coming spring.[76]

Some herds were wiped out completely. Most cattle companies reported losses of thirty-five to sixty percent, and many ranchmen, like Granville Stuart, quit the business.[77] "I never wanted to own again an animal that I couldn't feed or shelter," he wrote in remorse.[78] Symbolically, the whole range cattle industry was aboard the last stagecoach that left Cheyenne for the Black Hills on February 20, 1887.[79] Open range practices of the past were discontinued rapidly by cattle outfits that had managed to stay afloat, and none dared thereafter to be without emergency means of caring for livestock.[80]

The need for these changes was brought more sharply into focus with the bombshell announcement in May that Alexander Swan had failed. The industry's superstructure tottered as bankers rushed to Cheyenne on the hopeless errand of salvaging something from utter ruin.[81] Effects of the wretched winter were demanding cash that Swan neither had nor could procure and revealed his practice of trading beyond his means.[82] Swan was deposed as manager of the British company, which he took for some $800,000, and an investigating committee of shareholders summarized their

162

FIRE DRAGS. *To fight prairie fires the XIT made drags of heavy chains, interlaced to resemble huge fish nets. Cowboys attached these to their saddle horns and took off, cutting the fire away from the grass. Other hands followed on foot with anything to beat out embers. Few human lives were lost in these blazes, but land and cattle were devastated. Confining the Indians reduced only one fire danger; retaliators against fencing fired many ranges, and there was always lightning.*

SCANTY FORAGE. *On November 16, 1886, the thermometer fell below zero over the Rockies. A northwest wind shattered the icy silence and drifted six inches of fine hard snow across the dry ranges. Native stock and double-wintered Texas steers stood this first storm well, but cattle trailed recently from Texas wandered aimlessly in circles. Before the ghastly winter was over, ninety percent of these newcomers were dead.*

163

plight: "If more attention had been paid to erecting shelter . . . and providing a supply of hay for winter feed, instead of expending so much on extravagant purchases of land and cattle, the company would have been in a different financial position today."[83] Cheyenne's largest bank also went under, as did the Niobrara Cattle Company of Nebraska, carrying with it the major St. Louis Stock Yards banking house.[84]

The beginning break-up of large cattle companies saw the liquidation of mutilated herd remnants that somehow survived the "big die-up." Many cattle were shipped to Chicago at a dollar per hundredweight—almost ninety percent under prices commanded in 1882.[85]

Obviously, the Texas trails as a means of supplying cheap beef had outlived their usefulness; yet abandonment was not immediate. The Trail had become an institution with a philosophy, tradition, and practice not easily discarded. The mass movement of trail cattle was done, however, and the long drives that continued for a decade were mainly operations of large ranches from the southern to the northern grasslands they controlled. The trickle of Longhorns into Colorado in the 1887 summer was but a shadow of former years. It came despite rumors that herds were being turned back, that Texas fever again was rampant, and that the trail was closed.

Exploring these allegations, the *Rocky Mountain News* seemed dedicated to preserving the trail awhile longer. The Texas representative of the Bureau of Animal Industry was interviewed at Denver's Windsor Hotel in July to "ascertain facts" about the turning back of trail herds. He said a few herds had turned back to Indian Territory to be wintered or sold, but that 35,000 cattle—a major portion of the season's drive—were being held for sale in Colorado, and a number of these were going to Kansas feeders.

It was untrue, the story continued, that Colonel John Simpson's forty thousand trail cattle had been forced back to Texas. These herds already had passed out of Colorado on their way to his Montana ranch and were never on the open market. Furthermore, due to precautions taken by veterinary inspectors, not a single case of Texas fever had appeared.[86]

In answer to talk that the Texas Trail was closed, the *News* printed a letter from a Colorado stockman who sized up the situation accurately, but with the nostalgic glow that already surrounded the trails. Several papers, he wrote, had called the attention of cattle and rangemen "to the astonishing fact that the Texas cattle trail is closed forever. This will be news assuredly for hundreds of us who make the range our dwelling place and who have driven up the old trail many a dusty time and are in expectancy of driving many more times.

"The Texas Trail is not closed," he maintained, and the stories were the "same old funeral reports . . . that have been fired at the public every year that range has become scarce." Many herds were being held for better prices and the calf crop was unequaled, "so, having cattle to sell it isn't strange that this year should be a light one on imports from Texas."

Just as long as Texas can breed two or three calves to our one, just so long as the Northern ranges can turn yearlings into heavier beeves than the Texas country can possibly do, just so long will the Texas Trail continue to exist. And when the time comes that railroads will consent to transfer cattle as cheaply as the old trail did for years, then . . . the curtain will be indeed rung down upon the old footpath, only to rise upon the greater exports and immigrations of the iron trail.

When the trail really dies, however, it will die so quietly and naturally that people will hardly know 'tis dead.[87]

And that's the way it happened.

Years later, the son of a pioneer ranchman in Wyoming realized that he had witnessed the end of the trail. "I was on hand," he said, "when the last herd ever trailed from Texas to Montana. It passed Raw Hide Ranch and JM Creek, June 17, 1897. The boss was Scanlous John."[88]

'LAST OF THE FIVE THOUSAND.' *Like the Charles Russell drawing of the Great Blizzard's toll in 1886–1887, this cow study reflects the agony of her kind in extreme weather conditions. After the "big die-up" in which animals perished by the millions on Northern ranges, big cattle companies either withdrew or retrenched in smaller units. In a better but less picturesque business, the open range vanished entirely and emergency means of livestock shelter and feed became the order of the day.*

END OF THE TRAIL. *Like all chuck wagons used on the trail, this gear of Charles Goodnight's is now at ease. It rests with him near his last home at Goodnight, Texas. These wagons fed cowboys on roundups long after the trail had passed, and some are restored for service in parades and celebrations when the ranch country recalls the days of its youth.*

165

HISTORIC DEVELOPMENTS. *The trail survives in "Cowtown,"
Wichita, Kansas, in the way that history begins with fact and ends with
symbol. Original track and a unit of Wichita's first stockyards date to
1872, when the Santa Fe fingered into town to make it the new end of
the Chisholm Trail. Then as wooden windmills advanced on the Plains
and sped fencing of land without surface water, rails penetrated the
Longhorns' homeland and relegated their trails to memory.*

166

Epilogue

The trails passed into history with a legacy of problems as well as lore. Left unsolved was the mystery of Texas fever, the recourse of tottering cattle companies, and the question of long-term leases on the public lands.

In 1889 the cause of Texas fever was found: a blood parasite transmitted by the bite of the southern cattle tick, *Boophilus annulatus*. This startling discovery by Dr. Theobald Smith of the Bureau of Animal Industry was the first medical knowledge of disease by protozoan transmission. Smith succeeded where others had failed when he matched up these strange organisms present in ticks with those in red corpuscles of a cow that had died of Texas fever. About this time the bureau's Dr. Cooper Curtice determined the tick's life cycle. His work and that of Smith paved the way for man's triumph over such diseases as malaria, typhus, and yellow fever. Scientists theorize that the Panama Canal would not have been built if these animal experimentations had failed to reveal the etiology of yellow fever.

The first order for a national quarantine defining areas of tick infestation in the Southern and Southwestern States was issued in July, 1889. Strict railroad shipping regulations also helped with control in the North, but did little to improve conditions in the South. So long as one tick remained alive, Texas fever would persist. The problem seemed insuperable, since one tick could produce up to five thousand eggs, and larvae hatched in the grasses could survive starvation more than eight months.

Robert J. Kleberg, administrator of the Santa Gertrudis Ranch after the death of his father-in-law, Richard King, had begun to dip cattle for mange and itch in 1890. Finding that some ticks were killed in the process, Kleberg offered his facilities for government experiments. These, and later efforts by the Fort Worth Stock Yards and by paint and chemical manufacturers, resulted in 1914 in a standard dip strong enough to kill ticks, yet mild enough to leave cattle unharmed.

It became apparent that the bite of this tick, which lived on cattle blood, immunized southern bovines without ill effects shortly after birth. These cattle in turn were the hosts that carried the tick and its devastating fever to susceptible northern herds. Imitating nature's mode of transmission, Dr. Mark Francis of Texas A and M College developed a means of pre-immunization by injecting a blood serum from infected cattle into calves. This method in time reduced Texas fever mortality and made possible the importation of quality breeding stock to Texas and other tick areas.

In the seventeen years from discovery of the fever's cause to 1906, losses from all sources related to the disease exceeded one billion dollars. In that year when parts of fifteen states—one-fourth of the nation—were under quarantine, the Bureau of Animal Industry, state officials, and cattlemen united in an all-out war of tick extermination. Compulsory dipping was enforced and became as much a part of ranch work as branding in the long years before 1942, when the cattle fever tick was declared eradicated in the United States. Government inspectors continue, nonetheless, to patrol a safety zone along the Rio Grande in southern Texas, where the ticks are found occasionally because of stray or smuggled cattle from Mexico.[1]

The liquidation of cattle companies formed hastily at the height of trail activity likewise extended into the mid-twentieth century. Corporations that dissolved shortly before or after

167

the great blizzard of 1886-1887 suffered financial ruin. Others that continued operations, passing or issuing scanty dividends, made profits for heirs of original stockholders as land values increased and cattle prices reached erratic peaks.

At the end of the nineteenth century, English losses in the American range cattle industry were estimated at 10 million dollars, Scottish mark-offs at almost 8 million. Some sources place the aggregate red figure as high as 25 million dollars.

A majority of the English companies succumbed before 1900, and mortality was high in the next two decades among all big cattle corporations. After many management changes, the Swan reorganized in 1905 and switched to sheep; yet this company never was successful, with either cattle or sheep. The Capitol Freehold Company sold off the XIT cattle in 1912 and passed out of existence in 1918, yielding no dividends but recovering investments. The Prairie closed its books between 1914 and 1916 and recouped its capital with some to spare. American Pastoral, the one remaining English company, also continued until World War I, when its land sales recovered only investments.

Western Ranches, making a final tally in 1921, paid original stockholders double their capital after averaging more than nine percent annual dividends for 37 years. Only the Matador Land and Cattle Company, with average annual dividends of 11.8 percent for the 49 years dating from 1901, could claim more profit on comparable investments. Selling its 800,000 Texas acres for 20 million dollars in 1951, and returning $23.70 for each of its 70-cent shares, this last giant of the foreign cattle companies went into voluntary liquidation.[2]

In the matter of long-term public land leases, Congress maintained the view that ranching was a temporary pursuit occupying country that ultimately would be cultivated. Countless attempts were thwarted for laws to permit extended grazing leases on the public domain, or public land sales in tracts large enough for profitable ranches.

With precarious tenure on many pasture lands outside of Texas, ranchmen overstocked to reap quickly what they could. This short-sighted practice also reaped the whirlwind. Whole regions were grazed bare before winter, and subsequent cattle losses brought bankruptcy to their owners. In the industry's transitory condition permanent improvements were not feasible on public and Indian lands, and few families came to live in the range camps or shacks. As a result, ranching developed as a rough occupation devoid of stabilizing influences rooted in the home. The uncertain tenure further prevented scientific study of the land's carrying capacity, the ratio of breeding animals, and the financing and credit required over a period of years.

The ranch business reached a low ebb at the end of World War I, but an upswing was indicated. Beyond the Lone Star State enormous tracts in private hands had continued as grazing lands, and much of the vacant and unreserved public domain was used for pasturage. It was clear that cattle and sheep ranching were here to stay and that little of the existing public lands ever would feel the plow.

Finally in 1934, the industry as a whole was put on a more firm and permanent basis by provisions of the Taylor Grazing Act. This act gave governmental authority to administer eighty million acres of public domain, allowing long-term leases, but controlling grazing and other uses of the land for the benefit of the country at large.[3]

The American public, however, never regarded ranching as a passing trade. The trail-born image of the cowboy at home on the range was in movie form by 1910. With his range extended to television, the theme by the 1950's netted the entertainment world annually more than the total price of cattle driven to northern markets.

The popularity of dude ranches and rodeos in recent years has drawn visitors to the West with the zeal of those in the 1880's, clamoring to sample this legendary way of life. The West works at keeping its old spirit alive in reconstructed trail towns at Ogallala, Nebraska, and Dodge City, Abilene, and Wichita, Kansas; and much of its story is recounted in the Cowboy

168

INTO TOMORROW. *Though the trails died of progress as they came of age—twenty-one years after 1866—they rise again in the minds of men to thunder forever the "bold, restless freedom" that pioneered the American continent.*

Hall of Fame at Oklahoma City. Interested individuals in the 1960's formed a Longhorn breeders association in Texas and a Mustang protection society in California to perpetuate these foundation strains that started the ranch and its everlasting appeal. And a mighty factor of this appeal remains in the vast expanses of western landscape where climate and soil have conspired to keep it cattle country. Though the view be from a four-lane highway, these silent, uncluttered reaches of earth and sky still impart the feeling Charles Goodnight described as he summed up his days on the trail: "We were solitary adventurers in a great land as fresh and new as a spring morning, and we were free and full of the zest of darers."[4]

169

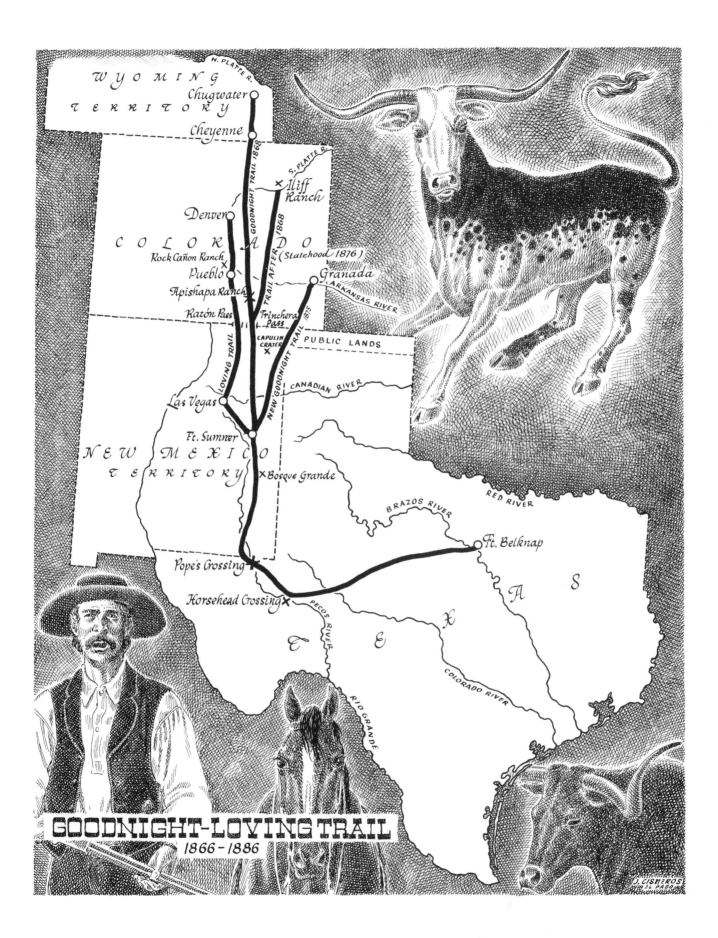

GOODNIGHT-LOVING TRAIL
1866-1886

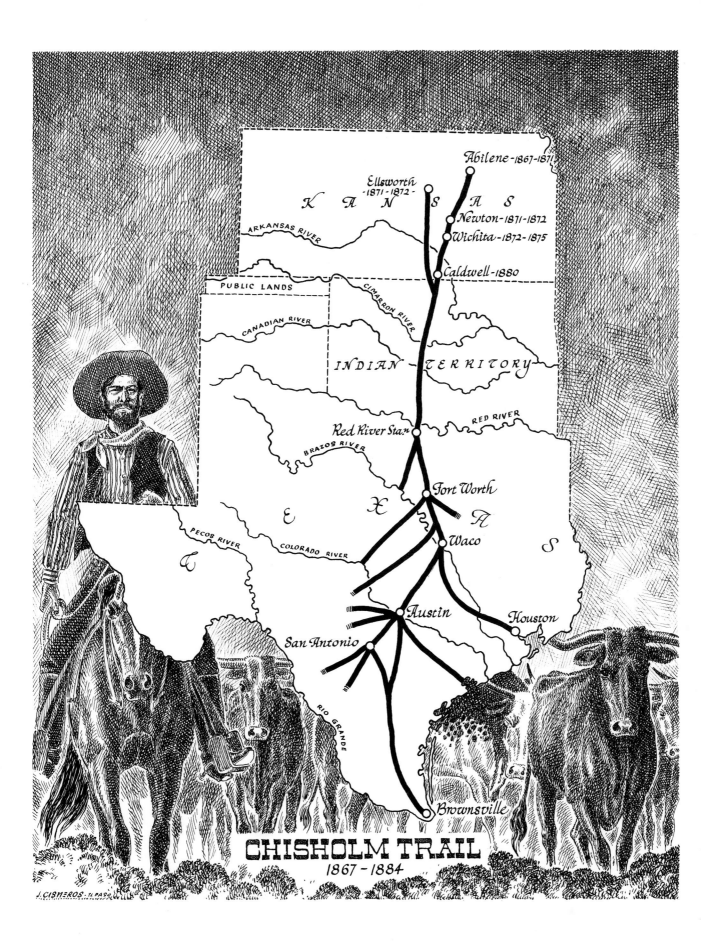

Abilene -1867-1871

Ellsworth -1871-1872

K A N S A S

ARKANSAS RIVER

Newton -1871-1872
Wichita -1872-1875

Caldwell -1880

PUBLIC LANDS

CIMARRON RIVER

CANADIAN RIVER

INDIAN - TERRITORY

RED RIVER

Red River Star.

BRAZOS RIVER

T E X A S

PECOS RIVER

COLORADO RIVER

Fort Worth

Waco

Austin

Houston

San Antonio

RIO GRANDE

Brownsville

CHISHOLM TRAIL
1867-1884

J. CISNEROS - EL PASO

WESTERN TRAIL 1876
Sections above southern Colorado line in use until
1897

Notes to Text

'THAT COW OUT THERE'

[1] Harbert Davenport to Holland McCombs, November 17, 1952, letter in McCombs research file, King Ranch.

[2] Bernard DeVoto, "Horizon Land (I)," *Saturday Review of Literature* 14, no. 25 (October 17, 1936), p. 8.

[3] Walter Prescott Webb, *The Great Plains*, pp. 207, 240; J. Frank Dobie, *The Mustangs*, p. 315.

[4] Frederick Jackson Turner, *The Significance of the Frontier*, p. 37.

[5] Dee Brown and Martin F. Schmitt, *Trail Driving Days*, p. 231.

[6] Joe B. Frantz and Julian Ernest Choate, Jr., *The American Cowboy: The Myth and the Reality*, p. 70.

[7] Ibid., pp. 33-34, 47, 53, 73-74, 139; Wayne Gard, *The Chisholm Trail*, p. 11.

[8] *Texas Longhorn Centennial Booklet*, 1966, p. 14.

[9] Gard, *Chisholm Trail*, p. 13.

[10] Frantz and Choate, *The American Cowboy*, p. 35.

[11] Ibid., p. 145.

[12] J. Marvin Hunter (ed.), *The Trail Drivers of Texas*. This 1000-page volume of firsthand accounts is the largest single source of information about the drovers. It is considered here as a cross section though the 282 sketches of actual trail men represent less than one percent of the approximately 35,000 drovers. Of the 282 men included, 111 were born outside Texas, 102 in Texas. Since 59 did not indicate a place of birth, accurate percentages break down. But obviously 40 percent, and perhaps half, were not native Texans.

[13] Dobie, *Mustangs*, pp. 6, 22; Garnet M. and Herbert O. Brayer, *American Cattle Trails, 1540-1900*, p. 5; Douglas Branch, *The Cowboy and His Interpreters*, pp. 2-3.

[14] William Dusenberry, "Constitutions of Early and Modern American Stock Growers' Associations," *Southwestern Historical Quarterly* 53, no. 3 (January, 1950) pp. 255-256, 262.

[15] Dobie, *Mustangs*, pp. 24-25.

[16] Sandra L. Myres, "The Spanish Cattle Kingdom of the Province of Texas," *Texana* 4, no. 3 (Fall, 1966), pp. 233-246.

[17] J. Frank Dobie, *The Longhorns*, p. 9.

[18] Dobie, *Mustangs*, pp. 99-100.

[19] William H. Oberste, *Remember Goliad*, p. 91.

[20] Dobie, *Longhorns*, pp. 11-12, 23-25, 20.

[21] Ibid., pp. 30, 32, 33.

[22] A. Fiske, *A Visit to Texas*, pp. 118, 23.

[23] Dobie, *Longhorns*, pp. 25, 22, 33, 29-30, 36-38.

[24] *Beaumont: A Guide to the City and Its Environs*, pp. 49, 53.

[25] *Houston: A History and Guide*, p. 60.

[26] Walter Prescott Webb (ed.), *The Handbook of Texas*, II, p. 54.

[27] Gail Bordon, Jr., Papers. D.R.T. Library, San Antonio.

[28] J. Evetts Haley, "A Survey of Texas Cattle Drives to the North, 1866-1895" (thesis), pp. 63, 74.

[29] Dobie, *Mustangs*, p. 107.

[30] Harry Sinclair Drago, *Great American Cattle Trails*, p. 220.

[31] Gard, *Chisholm Trail*, pp. 23-24.

[32] W. M. MacKellar, "Cattle Tick Fever," *The Cattleman*, February, 1943, pp. 63, 61.

[33] *Third Annual Report of the Metropolitan Board of Health of the Metroplitan Sanitary District*, 1869, pp. 187, 186, 190, 196, 207.

[34] Dr. D. E. Salmon, *USDA Bureau of Animal Industry Special Report on Diseases of Cattle and on Cattle Feeding, 1896*, pp. 431-432.

[35] T. R. Havins, "Texas Fever," *Southwestern Historical Quarterly* 52, no. 2 (October, 1948), p. 147.

[36] Tom Lea, *The King Ranch*, I, pp. 103-104, 108-110.

[37] Gard, *Chisholm Trail*, p. 32.

[38] T. C. Richardson, "Cattle Trails," in Webb, *Handbook of Texas*, I, p. 316.

[39] Gard, *Chiholm Trail*, pp. 32, 35-36.

[40] Haley, "Survey," p. 63.

[41] Dobie, *Longhorns*, pp. 33-34, 41.

[42] Andy Adams, *Log of a Cowboy*, p. 201; Hunter, *Trail Drivers*, p. 924.

[43] Chris Emmett, *Shanghai Pierce: A Fair Likeness*, pp. 10-27, 37-38.

[44] Hunter, *Trail Drivers*, pp. 923-924.

[45] Emmett, *Shanghai Pierce*, p. 12.

GOODNIGHT-LOVING TRAIL

AUTHOR'S NOTE: The basic source for this section is J. Evetts Haley of Canyon, Texas, who as Goodnight's neighbor and biographer interviewed the colorful cowman almost daily for several years. Haley accompanied me to several points on the trail that Goodnight personally had pointed out to him. I gratefully acknowledge his help and permission to quote.

[1] Charles Kenner, "The Origins of the 'Goodnight' Trail Reconsidered," *Southwestern Historical Quarterly* 77, no. 3 (January, 1974), pp. 392-394.

[2] J. Evetts Haley, *Charles Goodnight: Cowman and Plainsman*, p. 121; Wayne Gard, *The Chisholm Trail*, p. 54.

[3] Haley, *Charles Goodnight*, pp. 15-20.

[4] Ibid., pp. 35, 36, 40-42.

[5] Ibid., p. 68.

[6] Ibid., pp. 100, 102.

[7] Ibid., pp. 111-112.

[8] Ibid., pp. 126-127.

[9] Ibid., pp. 122, 402.

[10] Willie Clytes Cullar, *The Loving Family in Texas*, pp. 43-49.

[11] Grace Miller White, "Oliver Loving, the First Trail Driver," *Frontier Times* 19, no. 7 (April, 1942), p. 271.

[12] Charles Goodnight, "Managing a Trail Herd in the Early Days," *Frontier Times* 6, no. 5 (March, 1929), p. 250.

[13] *San Angelo Standard-Times*, Seventieth Anniversary Edition, August 29, 1954.

[14] Haley, *Charles Goodnight*, pp. 128-139.

[15] Ibid., pp. 140, 145, 147.

[16] Ibid., pp. 155, 162, 166, 168.

[17] Ibid., pp. 169-182.

[18] Ibid., pp. 193, 198.

[19] Ibid., pp. 199, 200; Baca House Museum Files, Trinidad, Colorado.

[20] Haley, *Charles Goodnight*, pp. 201, 205, 260, 264.

[21] Ibid., p. 204.

[22] Ibid., p. 184; White, "Oliver Loving," *Frontier Times*, April, 1942, p. 274.

[23] "Goodnight Sets Out upon 'New Adventure,'" *Frontier Times* 5, no. 1 (October, 1927), p. 30.

[24] Haley, *Charles Goodnight*, pp. 185, 225-226; Colorado Territory Legislative Assembly, *An Act to Prohibit the Introduction of Texas Cattle into Colorado Territory*, Sixth Session, 1867, pp. 86-87.

CHISHOLM TRAIL

[1] Wayne Gard, *The Chisholm Trail*, pp. 44-45; J. Marvin Hunter, *The Trail Drivers of Texas*, p. 417; Graves Peeler to S. F., interview, 1966. Peeler, who in 1966 had raised Longhorns for more than thirty years, pinpointed the early calving age. He noted also that steers grew longer horns if not castrated too young. This finding may account for the lengthier horns of early days, when cattle were not dislodged from the brush at any particular age.

[2] Lewis Atherton, *The Cattle Kings*, pp. 20-21.

[3] *Galveston News*, August 16, 1866.

[4] James D. Otis, "Jesse Chisholm: A Pioneer Who Never Carried a Gun," *Wichita Falls Times* feature magazine, December 19, 1965, p. 14; Jerry Lockett,

"Longhorns Not Long Gone," *Houston Post*, August 15, 1965.

[5] Gard, *Chisholm Trail*, p. 68; Wayne Gard, "Retracing the Chisholm Trail," *Southwestern Historical Quarterly*, Extra Number, May 1, 1956, p. 15.

[6] Gard, *Chisholm Trail*, pp. 61-66.

[7] Gard, "Retracing," p. 9; *Old Trail Drivers of Texas Program*.

[8] T. C. Richardson, "Cattle Trails of Texas," *Texas Geographic Magazine* 1, no. 2 (November, 1937). p. 17.

[9] Gard, "Retracing," pp. 11-13.

[10] Glenn O. Wilson, "The Texas County of Trails," *100 Years in Montague County, Texas* (booklet); Bob Gray, "Chisholm Trail," *The Texas and Southwestern Horseman*, July, 1965, p. 37.

[11] Gard, "Retracing," p. 13; Fred Grove, "The Chisholm Trail," *Oklahoma Today* 16, no. 4 (Autumn, 1966), p. 27.

[12] H. S. Tennant, "The Two Cattle Trails," *Chronicles of Oklahoma* 15, no. 1 (March, 1936), p. 117.

[13] James W. Cloud, "The Surveyed Route of the Chisholm Trail" (manuscript).

[14] Hunter, *Trail Drivers*, p. 118.

[15] Gard, "Retracing," p. 14; Glen French to S. F., interview, May 30, 1966.

[16] J. Frank Dobie, *The Longhorns*, pp. xv-xvi.

[17] *Old Trail Drivers of Texas Program*, 1931.

CHANGING TIMES AND TRAILS

[1] Edward Everett Dale, *The Range Cattle Industry*, pp. 20-21; Joe B. Frantz and Julian Ernest Choate, Jr., *The American Cowboy: The Myth and the Reality*, pp. 135-136.

[2] Maurice Frink, W. Turrentine Jackson, and Agnes Wright Spring, *When Grass Was King*, pp. 38-39; J. Evetts Haley, *Charles Goodnight: Cowman and Plainsman*, p. 228.

[3] Dale, *Range Cattle Industry*, p. xiii.

[4] Wayne Gard, *The Chisholm Trail*, pp. 55, 92-96; *Prose and Poetry of the Livestock Industry of the United States*, p. 437.

[5] Haley, *Charles Goodnight*, pp. 225-228. Arapahoe County, Colorado, is spelled with an ending "e"; Oklahoma usage generally is Arapaho.

[6] Frink, and others, *When Grass Was King*, pp. 358-359.

[7] Haley, *Charles Goodnight*, p. 206.

[8] See Iliff photographs in Frink and others, *When Grass Was King*, following p. 242; Dee Brown and Martin Schmitt, *Trail Driving Days*, p. 197; Lewis Atherton, *The Cattle Kings*, facing p. 107. Goodnight pictures are in Haley, *Charles Goodnight*, p. 122; Brown and Schmitt, *Trail Driving Days*, p. 133; and Mari Sandoz, *The Cattlemen: From the Rio Grande Across the Far Marias*, following p. 274.

[9] Atherton, *The Cattle Kings*, pp. 111-112; Henry T. Williams (ed.), *The Pacific Tourist and Guide*, pp. 52-54.

[10] Richard E. Leach, "John W. Iliff," *The Trail* 4, no. 9 (March, 1912), p. 15.

[11] Frink and others, *When Grass Was King*, pp. 316-320.

[12] Atherton, *Cattle Kings*, pp. 132-133, 144-145; Frink and others, *When Grass Was King*, p. 424. At his wife's solicitation, Goodnight joined a church shortly before his death, "but when someone asked him what church . . ., he answered . . .: 'I don't know, but it's a damned good one.' " (Haley, *Charles Goodnight*, pp. 461-462).

[13] Atherton, *The Cattle Kings*, pp. 220, 241; Edward W. Milligan, "John Wesley Iliff," *Westerners Brand Book* 6 (1950), p. 59.

[14] Haley, *Charles Goodnight*, pp. 207-209.

[15] Ibid., p. 210; J. Evetts Haley to S. F., interview, September 2, 1965.

[16] Haley, *Charles Goodnight*, pp. 228-229. The New Goodnight Trail in 1875 again bore east of former routes in New Mexico, passing the Rabbit Ears, near present Clayton, and the Cimarron Seco near Robbers' Roost. Into Colorado, it headed northwest to Freeze Out, Two Butte, and Granada.

[17] Ibid., pp. 215, 261.

[18] Ibid., pp. 220-222; Charles Goodnight, "Managing a Trail Herd in the Early Days," *Frontier Times* 6, no. 5 (March, 1929), p. 250; *Prose and Poetry of the Livestock Industry*, p. 535.

[19] Charles Goodnight to LeRoy R. Hafen, September 29, 1927, Library, State Historical Society of Colorado, Denver.

[20] Haley, *Charles Goodnight*, p. 260.

[21] Ibid., pp. 261-262.

[22] Ibid., p. 265.

[23] Goodnight to Hafen.

[24] Phil K. Hudspeth, owner of the Goodnight ranch in 1965, can attest, as the barn then was in use. Always a showplace, the ranch is destined to remain so. Plans for the 18,000-acre Frying Pan–Arkansas Project include the barn in a vast recreation and game preserve area. Goodnight Avenue in Pueblo leads to the ranch, and Goodnight Elementary School is nearby.

[25] Atherton, *Cattle Kings*, p. 467; Robert G. Athearn, "The Denver & Rio Grande Railway, Colorado's 'Baby Road,' " *The Colorado Magazine* 35 (January, 1958), p. 46.

[26] Haley, *Charles Goodnight*, p. 266.

[27] Charles Goodnight, Las Animas County Records, Trinidad, Colorado.

[28] J. Marvin Hunter, *The Trail Drivers of Texas*, pp. 1030, 657; Roger N. Conger, "The Waco Suspension Bridge," *Texana* 1, no. 3 (Summer, 1963), pp. 180-224.

[29] Muriel H. Wright and George H. Shirk, *Mark of Heritage* (booklet); Robert A. Weinstein and Russell E. Belous, "Indian Portraits: Fort Sill, 1869," *The American West* 3, no. 1 (Winter, 1966), p. 61.

[30] Dale, *Range Cattle Industry*, pp. 28, 64; Robert G. Athearn, *High Country Empire*, p. 123.

[31] E. E. White, *Experiences of a Special Indian Agent*, p. 246.

[32] Dale, *Range Cattle Industry*, p. 25; Robert K. Heiman, *Nation's Heritage*, I, no. 5, pp. 108-112.

[33] Carl Coke Rister, *The Southwestern Frontier, 1865-1881*, pp. 270-274.

[34] Hunter, *Trail Drivers*, pp. 1030, 823.

[35] Dale, *Range Cattle Industry*, p. 25; B. A. Botkin (ed.), *A Treasury of Western Folklore*, p. 214.

[36] Dale, *Range Cattle Industry*, pp. 26-27.

[37] Hunter, *Trail Drivers*, p. 1030; Rister, *Southwestern Frontier*, p. 283.

[38] *San Antonio Daily Herald*, July 12, 1871.

[39] Gard, *Chisholm Trail*, p. 151.

[40] Rister, *Southwestern Frontier*, p. 283.

[41] Hunter, *Trail Drivers*, p. 137.

[42] *San Antonio Daily Herald*, July 12, 1871.

[43] Gard, *Chisholm Trail*, p. 157.

[44] Hunter, *Trail Drivers*, p. 807.

[45] *Texas, A Guide to the Lone Star State*, p. 59.

[46] J. Frank Dobie, *A Vaquero of the Brush Country*, pp. 24-26.

[47] *Rockport Pilot*, Centennial Edition, March 27, 1969.

[48] *San Antonio Express*, June 17, 1934.

[49] Dobie, *Vaquero*, pp. 24-27.

[50] *1869 Texas Almanac*, p. 171; Gard, *Chisholm Trail*, p. 193.

[51] H. P. N. Gammel, *The Laws of Texas*, VI, p. 832; *San Antonio Express*, August 17, 1870.

[52] *San Antonio Weekly Herald*, June 24, 1871.

[53] Gard, *Chisholm Trail*, pp. 263, 209.

[54] James P. Baughman, *Charles Morgan and the Development of Southern Transportation*, p. 129.

[55] *1870 Texas Almanac*, pp. 163-164.

[56] A. Ray Stephens, *The Taft Ranch*, pp. 10-12.

[57] Gard, *Chisholm Trail*, pp. 158-160; Brown and Schmitt, *Trail Driving Days*, pp. 66-67.

[58] Gard, *Chisholm Trail*, pp. 160, 188.

[59] *Ellsworth Reporter*, July 25, 1873.

[60] Brown and Schmitt, *Trail Driving Days*, pp. 68-69.

[61] Gard, *Chisholm Trail*, pp. 182-184; Brown and Schmitt, *Trail Driving Days*, p. 70.

[62] *Wichita City Eagle*, July 5 and 19, 1872.

[63] Gard, *Chisholm Trail*, pp. 190-191.

[64] Brown and Schmitt, *Trail Driving Days*, p. 93.

[65] Gard, *Chisholm Trail*, pp. 160-161.

[66] *Rocky Mountain News*, April 5, 1872.

[67] Hunter, *Trail Drivers*, pp. 575, 761.

[68] Dobie, *Vaquero*, pp. 23-24.

[69] *Wichita City Eagle*, August 2, 1872.

[70] Gard, *Chisholm Trail*, p. 223; Tom Lea, *The King Ranch*, I, p. 299.

[71] H. P. N. Gammel, *The Laws of Texas*, III, p. 17; Walter Prescott Webb (ed.), *The Handbook of Texas*, I, p. 312; Gard, *Chisholm Trail*, pp. 141-142; *San Antonio Daily Herald*, July 12, 1871.

[72] American Tobacco Company, "Bull Durham Fact Sheet"; J. Frank Dobie, Introduction to Eugene Man-

love Rhodes, *The Little World Waddies*, pp. xvii-xviii; Hunter, *Trail Drivers*, pp. 147, 138.

[73] Victor M. Rose, *History of Victoria County*, pp. 130-132, 118; Leopold Morris, *Pictorial History of Victoria County*; Corinne Wood and Sidney R. Weisiger to S. F., interview, November, 1966; *Wichita City Eagle*, July 10, 1873; Mrs. Thomas O'Connor, Sr., to S. F., letter, May 11, 1966.

[74] Garnet M. and Herbert O. Brayer, *American Cattle Trails, 1540-1900*, p. 105; Gard, *Chisholm Trail*, pp. 156-157; "Mrs. Holmsby Went Up the Chisholm Trail," *Frontier Times* 4, no. 10 (July, 1927), p. 28; Mary Taylor Bunton, *A Bride on the Chisholm Trail in 1886*.

[75] Gard, *Chisholm Trail*, p. 211.

[76] T. U. Taylor, "An Airplane Trip over the Chisholm Trail," *Frontier Times*, August, 1939, pp. 467-471.

[77] Emily Jones Shelton, "Lizzie E. Johnson, a Cattle Queen of Texas," *Southwestern Historical Quarterly* 50, no. 3 (January, 1947), pp. 348-360.

[78] Hunter, *Trail Drivers*, pp. 75-77.

[79] *Ibid.*, p. 151.

[80] Gard, *Chisholm Trail*, pp. 203-204.

[81] Joseph G. McCoy, *Historic Sketches of the Cattle Trade of the West and Southwest*, p. 251.

[82] Henry D. and Frances T. McCallum, *The Wire That Fenced The West*, pp. 26-27, 38, 240, 66, 11, 226, 138; Walter Prescott Webb, *The Great Plains*, pp. 300-318; James D. Horan, *The Great American West*, pp. 184, 194.

[83] Webb, *Great Plains*, pp. 330-348; Terry G. Jordan, "Windmills in Texas," *Agricultural History* 37, no. 2 (1961), pp. 80-85; Lynn White, Jr., "The Legacy of the Middle Ages in the American Wild West," *The American West* 2, no. 4 (Fall, 1965), p. 76; *1870 Texas Almanac*, p. 154.

[84] *Dedication of the Cyrus K. Holliday Plaque* (booklet), pp. 31-32; Webb, *Great Plains*, pp. 273-280.

[85] *Missouri Pacific Lines: The First 112 Years* (pamphlet), p. viii; Tom Lea, *The King Ranch*, I, p. 461 n. 12.

[86] Lea, *King Ranch*, I, pp. 299, 301.

[87] *Corpus Christi Gazette*, February 7, 1874.

[88] Weinstein and Belous, "Indian Portraits," pp. 55-62; Wright and Shirk, *Mark of Heritage*.

[89] David Lavender, *The American Heritage History of the Great West*, pp. 354-355.

[90] Robert Hogarth to S. F., interview, September 21, 1965; John J. Gering, "Deadwood," *Lawrence County Dakota Territory Centennial, 1861-1961* (booklet).

[91] Joseph Nimmo, Jr., *The Range and Ranch Cattle Traffic of the United States* (House document), pp. 66-67.

[92] Dale, *Range Cattle Industry*, pp. 47-48.

[93] Harry Sinclair Drago, *Great American Cattle Trails*, pp. 98-99; Hunter, *Trail Drivers*, pp. 438, 199.

[94] W. S. Adair, "3 Cows Paid for Clock by Early Texans," *Dallas Morning News*, March 17, 1929.

[95] Gard, *Chisholm Trail*, pp. 217-218, p. 228; Hunter, *Trail Drivers*, pp. 322, 361-362.

[96] James C. Olson, *Red Cloud and the Sioux Problem*, p. 208.

THE WESTERN TRAIL

[1] J. Marvin Hunter, *The Trail Drivers of Texas*, p. 434.

[2] Jack Potter, *Cattle Trails of the Old West*, p. 17.

[3] "Hige Nail, an Early Trail Driver," *Frontier Times* 4, no. 2 (November, 1926), p. 16; H. S. Tennant, "The Two Cattle Trails," *Chronicles of Oklahoma* 15, no. 1 (March, 1937), pp. 88, 101; Frank Collinson, *Life in the Saddle*, p. 31; James H. Cook, "The Texas Trail," *Nebraska History Magazine* 26, no. 4 (October-December, 1935), pp. 228-240; Hunter, *Trail Drivers*, p. 469.

[4] Collinson, *Life in the Saddle*, p. 35.

[5] Potter, *Cattle Trails of the Old West*, pp. 17-18.

[6] Robert T. Hill, "Old-Time Texas Roads and Trails," *Dallas Morning News*, D.R.T. Library clipping file, San Antonio .

[7] "Jack Potter's Famous Map," *The Texas Longhorn* 1, no. 1, (September, 1965), p. 16; Andy Adams, *The Log of a Cowboy*, pp. 30-31; Robert S. Weddle, "Pegleg Station on the San Saba" (manuscript); Wayne Gard, *The Chisholm Trail*, p. 277.

[8] *Fort Worth Democrat*, August 25 and October 27, 1876.

[9] Hunter, *Trail Drivers*, pp. 772-779, 699, 665.

[10] *Ibid.*, pp. 419, 313-314.

[11] Garnet M. and Herbert O. Brayer, *American Cattle Trails, 1540-1900*, pp. 89, 95, 98.

[12] Hunter, *Trail Drivers*, p. 573.

[13] "Goodnight Sets Out upon 'New Adventure,'" *Frontier Times* 5, no. 1 (October, 1927), p. 29.

[14] J. Frank Dobie, *The Longhorns*, p. 178.

[15] Hunter, *Trail Drivers*, p. 742.

[16] James Cox, *Historical and Biographical Record of the Cattle Industry and the Cattlemen of Texas and Adjacent Territory*, pp. 89-91.

[17] Dee Brown and Martin Schmitt, *Trail Driving Days*, pp. 97-98.

[18] Jesse James Benton, *Cow by the Tail*, pp. 72, 49-54.

[19] Joe B. Frantz and Julian E. Choate, Jr., *The American Cowboy: The Myth and the Reality*, p. 144.

[20] Brown and Schmitt, *Trail Driving Days*, p. 121; J. Evetts Haley, *Charles Goodnight: Cowman and Plainsman*, pp. 275, 281-282, 296.

[21] Brayer, *American Cattle Trails*, p. 60.

[22] "Early Nebraska History along the Canals and Lakes of the Central Nebraska Public Power and Irrigation District" (pamphlet).

[23] Hunter, *Trail Drivers*, p. 539; Gard, *Chisholm Trail*, p. 228.

[24] Ogallala Chamber of Commerce Fact Sheet.

[25] Fort Robinson Museum Files.

[26] Louis Pelzer, *The Cattleman's Frontier*, p. 47.

[27] C. W. Brandon Collection, Western Research Center, University of Wyoming, Laramie; Leopold Morris, *Pictorial History of Victoria County*. Kendrick,

born in Texas in 1857, married a half niece of the Snyder Brothers. He twice drove the Western Trail, was Wyoming Stock Growers president in 1912-1913, governor of Wyoming in 1915, and elected to the U.S. Senate from that state in 1916 and 1922.

[28] John B. Kendrick, "The Texas Trail," *Wyoming Tribune*, September 16, 1916; Brayer, *American Cattle Trails*, pp. 63-64.

[29] Brayer, *American Cattle Trails*, pp. 63-64.

[30] Russell Thorp, "Early Cowboy Days in Wyoming," *Westerners Brand Book*, October 1, 1945.

[31] Mark H. Brown and W. R. Felton, *Before Barbed Wire*, p. 163; Brayer, *American Cattle Trails*, pp. 64-65.

[32] Edward Everett Dale, *The Range Cattle Industry*, p. 77; Joseph Nimmo, Jr., *Range and Ranch Cattle Traffic of the United States* (House document), p. 170; Maurice Frink, W. Turrentine Jackson, and Agnes Wright Spring, *When Grass Was King*, p. 139n.

[33] Frink and others, *When Grass Was King*, pp. 141-142, 69.

BONANZA TO BLIZZARD

[1] Louis Pelzer, *The Cattleman's Frontier*, p. 88.

[2] Maurice Frink, W. Turrentine Jackson, and Agnes Wright Spring, *When Grass Was King*, p. 74.

[3] Jackson, in ibid., pp. 146-147; Dee Brown and Martin Schmitt, *Trail Driving Days*, p. 127.

[4] Louisa Ward Arps, *Denver in Slices*, p. 49; Edward Everett Dale, *The Range Cattle Industry*, p. 68; Spring, in Frink and others, *When Grass Was King*, p. 422; Frink, *When Grass Was King*, pp. 73-74.

[5] *Cheyenne Daily Leader*, March 27, 1875; April 29, 1882.

[6] Frink, *When Grass Was King*, p. 72.

[7] John Clay, *My Life on the Range*, p. 76. The Cheyenne Club building was destroyed by fire in the mid-twentieth century.

[8] *Cheyenne Daily Leader*, February 24, 1881; January 4, 1882; May 24, 1882; December 29, 1883.

[9] Jackson, in Frink and others, *When Grass Was King*, pp. 142-143; Dale, *Range Cattle Industry*, p. 59.

[10] Pelzer, *Cattleman's Frontier*, pp. 162-163; Frink, *When Grass Was King*, p. 73.

[11] Clay, *My Life on the Range*, p. 165.

[12] Walter Prescott Webb, *The Great Plains*, pp. 309-310.

[13] Frink, *When Grass Was King*, pp. 70-71.

[14] Dale, *Range Cattle Industry*, pp. 58, 75; Joseph Nimmo, Jr., *The Range and Ranch Cattle Traffic of the United States* (House document), pp. 28, 175, 170. Nimmo estimates 1880 drives to Kansas at 394,784 head. The Goodnight Trail, according to Dale, carried 20 to 25 percent as many cattle, or 98,696, that year.

[15] Dale, *Range Cattle Industry*, p. 64.

[16] James S. Brisbin, *The Beef Bonanza; or, How to Get Rich on the Plains*, p. viii.

[17] Ibid., pp. xi, 194.

[18] Ibid., p. 191.

[19] Ibid., pp. xii, xiii.

[20] Arps, *Denver in Slices*, pp. 155-168.

[21] Webb, *Great Plains*, pp. 234-235; Frink, *When Grass Was King*, pp. 72-73; Pelzer, *Cattleman's Frontier*, p. 120.

[22] J. Evetts Haley, *Charles Goodnight: Cowman and Plainsman*, pp. 361-362.

[23] Jackson, in Frink and others, *When Grass Was King*, pp. 148-149.

[24] Ibid., p. 150.

[25] J. Evetts Haley, *The XIT Ranch of Texas and the Early Days of the Llano Estacado*, pp. 55, 52.

[26] J. Marvin Hunter, *The Trail Drivers of Texas*, pp. 62-68.

[27] E. C. Abbott and Helen Huntington Smith, *We Pointed Them North*, p. 64.

[28] United States Department of Agriculture, *Keeping Livestock Healthy, Yearbook of Agriculture, 1942*, p. 573.

[29] Clay, *My Life on the Range*, p. 128.

[30] Ibid., pp. 196-197.

[31] Jackson, in Frink and others, *When Grass Was King*, pp. 166-167, 205.

[32] Brown and Schmitt, *Trail Driving Days*, pp. 185-187; Nimmo, *Range and Ranch Cattle*, p. 64.

[33] Chester L. Brooks and Ray H. Mattison, *Theodore Roosevelt and the Dakota Badlands* (booklet), pp. 30, 27, 44; United States Department of the Interior, *Theodore Roosevelt National Memorial Park, North Dakota* (pamphlet); Brown and Felton, *Before Barbed Wire*, p. 57.

[34] Webb, *Great Plains*, p. 325.

[35] Jackson, in Frink and others, *When Grass Was King*, p. 222.

[36] Dale, *Range Cattle Industry*, pp. 84-85.

[37] Ibid., pp. 110, 112; Jackson, in Frink and others, *When Grass Was King*, pp. 163-164, 197-198; J. Fred Rippy, "British Investments in Texas Lands and Livestock," *Southwestern Historical Quarterly* 59, no. 3 (January, 1955), pp. 331-332.

[38] Rippy, "British Investments in Texas Land and Livestock," pp. 333-335.

[39] Brown and Schmitt, *Trail Driving Days*, p. 127.

[40] Julius H. Matthey, "The Reminiscences of Fifty Years—1872-1922" (manuscript), p. 53; Walter Prescott Webb (ed.), *The Handbook of Texas*, II, p. 832.

[41] Frink, *When Grass Was King*, pp. 90-91; Clay, *My Life on the Range*, p. 177; Dale, *Range Cattle Industry*, p. 132.

[42] Dale, *Range Cattle Industry*, p. 76; Nimmo, *Range and Ranch Cattle*, p. 54.

[43] Frink, *When Grass Was King*, p. 26.

[44] Nimmo, *Range and Ranch Cattle*, p. 54.

[45] Haley, *Charles Goodnight*, pp. 357-380; Brown and Schmitt, *Trail Driving Days*, pp. 112-119.

[46] Pelzer, *Cattleman's Frontier*, pp. 87, 93; Clay, *My Life on the Range*, pp. 112, 114-115.

[47] Pelzer, *Cattleman's Frontier*, p. 139; Frink, *When Grass Was King*, p. 101.

[48] *Proceedings of the First National Convention of*

Cattlemen and of the First Annual Meeting of the National Cattle and Horse Growers of the United States, November 17-22, 1884.

⁴⁹ Clay, *My Life on the Range*, p. 177; Mrs. Augustus Wilson, Report on 1884 National Cattleman's Convention in St. Louis, *Parson's Memorial and Historical Magazine.*

⁵⁰ Jackson, in Frink and others, *When Grass Was King*, p. 208.

⁵¹ Clay, *My Life on the Range*, p. 126.

⁵² Jackson, in Frink and others, *When Grass Was King*, pp. 187, 224.

⁵³ Haley, *Charles Goodnight*, p. 235.

⁵⁴ *Texas Live Stock Association Program, January 15, 1885.*

⁵⁵ Nimmo, *Range and Ranch Cattle*, pp. 160, 32.

⁵⁶ Paul Wellman, *The Trampling Herd*, pp. 225-226.

⁵⁷ Tom Lea, *The King Ranch*, I, pp. 138, 370, 356.

⁵⁸ Ibid., II, p. 484, I, p. 462.

⁵⁹ Chris Emmett, *Shanghai Pierce: A Fair Likeness*, p. 174.

⁶⁰ Haley, *XIT*, p. 79.

⁶¹ Lewis Nordyke, *Cattle Empire*, pp. 73-76, 13, 83.

⁶² Dale, *Range Cattle Industry*, pp. 92-93, 127, 132-134.

⁶³ Pelzer, *Cattleman's Frontier*, pp. 172, 187.

⁶⁴ Hunter, *Trail Drivers*, p. 321.

⁶⁵ Dale, *Range Cattle Industry*, pp. 92-93.

⁶⁶ Haley, *XIT*, pp. 87-88.

⁶⁷ Jackson, in Frink and others, *When Grass Was King*, p. 256.

⁶⁸ Pelzer, *Cattleman's Frontier*, p. 143; Clay, *My Life on the Range*, p. 199.

⁶⁹ Webb, *Great Plains*, p. 236.

⁷⁰ Frink, *When Grass Was King*, p. 37 n.

⁷¹ Wayne Gard, *The Chisholm Trail*, p. 260.

⁷² Abbott and Smith, *We Pointed Them North*, p. 176.

⁷³ Harry Sinclair Drago, *Great American Cattle Trails*, p. 251.

⁷⁴ Brown and Schmitt, *Trail Driving Days*, p. 225; Clay, *My Life on the Range*, p. 200.

⁷⁵ Drago, *Great American Cattle Trails*, p. 250.

⁷⁶ Clay, *My Life on the Range*, pp. 218, 311, 175, 200.

⁷⁷ Drago, *Great American Cattle Trails*, p. 173.

⁷⁸ Brown and Schmitt, *Trail Driving Days*, p. 226.

⁷⁹ *Cheyenne Daily Leader*, February 20, 1887.

⁸⁰ Frink, *When Grass Was King*, p. 100.

⁸¹ Clay, *My Life on the Range*, p. 202.

⁸² Jackson, in Frink and others, *When Grass Was King*, p. 258.

⁸³ Pelzer, *Cattleman's Frontier*, p. 147.

⁸⁴ Dale, *Range Cattle Industry*, p. 97.

⁸⁵ Frink, *When Grass Was King*, p. 101.

⁸⁶ *Rocky Mountain News*, July 27, 1887.

⁸⁷ Ibid., July 25, 1887.

⁸⁸ J. T. Coffee to Harry B. Coffee, September 29, 1948, Charles F. Coffee Collection, Western Research Center, University of Wyoming. Scanlous John McCanless was trail boss for the XIT. (Nordyke, *Cattle Empire*, p. 241).

EPILOGUE

¹ W. M. MacKellar, "Cattle Tick Fever," *The Cattleman*, February, 1942; Lewis Nordyke, *Great Roundup*, p. 117; T. R. Havins, "Texas Fever," *Southwestern Historical Quarterly* 52, no. 2 (October 1948); United States Department of Agriculture, *Manual on Livestock Ticks*, June, 1965, p. 53; Hubert Schmidt, *Eighty Years of Veterinary Medicine at the Agricultural and Mechanical College of Texas* (booklet), pp. 2-6, 36; R. D. Turk to Sue Flanagan, interview, December, 1970; *San Antonio Light*, February 11, 1971.

² W. Turrentine Jackson, in Maurice Frink and others, *When Grass Was King*, pp. 297-315; J. Fred Rippy, "British Investments in Texas Lands and Livestock," *Southwestern Historical Quarterly* 59, no. 3 (January, 1955); Lewis Nordyke, *Cattle Empire*, p. 252; W. M. Pearce, *The Matador Land and Cattle Company*, pp. 220, 223.

³ Edward Everett Dale, *The Range Cattle Industry*, pp. 175-180; Maurice Frink, *When Grass Was King*, pp. 110-111.

⁴ Douglas Branch, *The Cowboy and His Interpreters*, p. 228; Jimmy Walker, "The Last of the Longhorns," *Texas Parade*, September, 1956; J. Evetts Haley, *Charles Goodnight: Cowman and Plainsman*, p. 259.

Notes to Photograph Captions

'THAT COW OUT THERE'

Rascality of the Rio Grande (Frontispiece): A. A. Champion and P. J. Vivier, Jr., of Brownsville were guides to this Texas-side location near an old cattle crossing on San Ygnacio (now Gavito) Ranch, some fifteen miles from the river's mouth.

'That Cow Out There' (p. 2): Chris Emmett, *Shanghai Pierce: A Fair Likeness*, p. 52; Walter Prescott Webb, *The Great Plains*, pp. 213, 263; Douglas Branch, *The Cowboy and His Interpreters*, p. 14. "That cow" is on the brush country ranch of Graves Peeler, near Pleasanton, Texas.

Home on the Open Range (p. 5): Chester L. Brooks and Ray H. Mattison, *Theodore Roosevelt and the Dakota Badlands* (booklet), pp. 17, 60; Dee Brown and Martin F. Schmitt, *Trail Driving Days*, p. 231.

Mission Ranching (p. 7): William H. Oberste, *Remember Goliad*, pp. 21–23, 25; J. Frank Dobie, *The Longhorns*, pp. 8–9; Sandra L. Myres, "The Spanish Cattle Kingdom in the Province of Texas," *Texana* 4, no. 3 (Fall, 1966), p. 235; Walter Prescott Webb, *The Handbook of Texas*, II, pp. 215–216.

On Wild Horse Desert (p. 8): Tom Lea, *The King Ranch*, I, pp. 11–12. Elvie Turner, Jr., to S.F., Interview, March, 1966.

Armed for Freedom (p. 8): Longhorn on Graves Peeler Ranch, near Pleasanton, Texas; J. Evetts Haley, *F. Reaugh: Man and Artist* (booklet).

First Anglo-Texan Ranch House (p. 9): M. Fiske, *A Visit to Texas*, p. 10; Dobie, *Longhorns*, pp. 29, 359; William Seale to S.F., letter, December 24, 1966.

Official 'Cow Paper' (p. 10): Two-dollar bill of 1841, Daughters of the Republic of Texas Library, San Antonio.

Early Marketing Attempt (p. 11): Meat Biscuits prospectus, Gail Borden Papers, Daughters of the Republic of Texas Library, San Antonio.

Cattle Ticks (p. 12): Dr. R. D. Turk to S.F., interview, December 5, 1966, The Texas A and M College of Veterinary Medicine was begun in 1888 to cope with the Texas fever problem. In 1889, federal researchers discovered the disease was tick-transmitted, and Dr. Mark Francis, at A and M, developed a fever immunization.

Santa Gertrudis Creek (p. 13): Lea, *King Ranch*, I, pp. 94–95, 110, 104, 108–109, 122; John A. Cypher, Jr., to S.F., interview, November 9, 1965.

Sea of Horns (p. 15): Photo made on Longhorn Centennial Trail Drive, 1966.

GOODNIGHT-LOVING TRAIL

Inventiveness (p. 18): Boone McClure to S.F., interview, September 3, 1965; J. Evetts Haley, *Charles Goodnight: Cowman and Plainsmen*, p. 122.

Loving's Valley (p. 20): Willie Clytes Cullar, *The Loving Family in Texas*, pp. 43–49. Loving descendant Joe H. McCracken, III, of Dallas guided the author to Loving's home place.

Experience (p. 21): Haley, *Charles Goodnight*, p. 20; Cullar, *The Loving Family*, pp. 9, 47–48; Joe H. McCracken, III, to S.F., interview, June 28, 1966. The loving home place is nine miles north of Mineral Wells in Loving's Valley. A West Texas county also is named for him.

Fort Phantom Hill (p. 22): *San Angelo Standard-Times*, Seventieth Anniversary Edition, August 29, 1954.

Ninety-six Miles to Water (p. 23): Charles Goodnight, "Managing a Trail Herd in the Early Days," *Frontier Times* 6, no. 5 (March, 1929), p. 251. Photo was made on the Longhorn Centennial Trail Drive in June, 1966.

Castle Canyon (p. 23): Haley, *Charles Goodnight*, pp. 128–139; *San Angelo Standard-Times*, Seventieth Anniversary Edition. Charles Stroder, Fred Wilkinson, and Mrs. J. L. Damron of Crane, Texas, were guides to the gap on the Shilling Estate in 1966.

Horsehead Crossing on the Pecos (p. 24): Haley, *Charles Goodnight*, pp. 128–139. A proposal was made in 1965 to establish a state park in the historic Castle Gap-Horsehead area.

Juan Cordona Salt Lake (p. 25): *San Angelo Standard-Times*, Seventieth Anniversary Edition.

Bosque Grande (p. 27): Roswell artist Sidney C. Redfield was one of the few persons who knew the way to the still-remote Bosque in 1965.

Fort Union (p. 28); Robert M. Utley, *Fort Union* (booklet), p. 1; Haley, *Charles Goodnight*, p. 198; *The Westerners Brand Book* 6 (1950), p. 47; J. Marvin Hunter, *The Trail Drivers of Texas*, pp. 725–726, 1030.

'The Only Bank' (p. 27): Haley, *Charles Goodnight*, p. 242; Agnes Wright Spring, *The First National Bank of Denver: The Formative Years*, 1860–65 (booklet); Maurice Frink and others, *When Grass Was King*, pp. 7–8; Dr. Harry Kelsey to S.F., interview, September 8, 1965.

Capulin Crater (p. 30): Haley, *Charles Goodnight*, pp. 155, 209.

Raton Range (p. 30): Haley, *Charles Goodnight*, pp. 198–199.

Wootton's Roadhouse (p. 31): The Wootton house, eleven miles south of Trinidad, was the private residence of Mr. and Mrs. Don Berg in 1965. Baca House Museum files, Trinidad, Colorado; Haley, *Charles Goodnight*, pp. 199, 238.

Apishapa Range (p. 32): Haley, *Charles Goodnight*, pp. 201, 205, 206, 246. While Goodnight's Apishapa claim, filed May 3, 1869, in Trinidad, Colorado, was never proved up, it is believed to be the only homestead claim he ever staked. The claim was located in 1965 by Baca House Director Arthur R. Mitchell and veteran rancher Carl Taylor of Trinidad.

Trail Fatality (p. 33): A detailed account of Loving's death is found in Haley, *Charles Goodnight*, pp. 169–184.

CHISHOLM TRAIL

Jesse Chisholm, 'Good Samaritan' (p. 34): Kent Ruth to S.F., interview, January 24, 1966; James Cloud to S.F., letter, February 13, 1967; T. U. Taylor, "An Airplane Trip Over the Chisholm Trail," *Frontier Times* 16, no. 11 (August, 1939), pp. 467–471. Taylor located Chisholm's grave and set the present marker. The spring, called "Raven's Spring" in Chisholm's day, was given to Chief Left Hand in the 1869 Arapaho land grants.

South Texas Prairies (p. 37): T. C. Richardson, "Cattle Trails of Texas," *Texas Geographic Magazine* 1, no. 2 (November, 1937), p. 17.

Cattle Buyer's Home (p. 37): J. Marvin Hunter, *The Trail Drivers of Texas*, pp. 515–518; Mrs. William Wheeler Pettus and Mrs. Frances Johnston to S.F., interviews, April 13, 1966.

Brushy Creek on a Rise (p. 38): Ken England to S.F., interview, May 19, 1966; Hunter, *Trail Drivers*, p. 626.

Chisholm's Pool (p. 39): Mrs. Ray Hyer Brown to S.F., interview, May 19, 1946; D.H. Snyder in Hunter, *Trail Drivers*, p. 1031.

Muttering Thunder (p. 40): Dr. J. B. Cranfill, *Dr. J. B. Cranfill's Chronicle*, pp. 154–158. Photo was made about five miles southwest of Moody, Texas. In 1967 the family of Miss Margaret Munz of Moody owned land on the creek near the famous stampede site.

Perpetuated History (p. 41): Edwin B. Dow to S.F., interview, May 23, 1966; James E. Vance, "He Wants Longhorns," *The Texas Longhorn*, no. 1 (September, 1965), p. 26.

Panther Creek (p. 43): Hunter, *Trail Drivers*, pp. 231–233, 689.

Crossing at Red River Station: (p. 44): Glenn O. Wilson, "The Texas County of Trails," in *100 Years in Montague County, Texas* (booklet); "T. C. Richardson on the Trail," *Frontier Times* 16, no. 12 (September, 1939), p. 546.

Monument Rocks (p. 45): Gard, *Chisholm Trail*, p. 79; H. S. Tennant, "The Two Cattle Trails," *Chron-*

icles of Oklahoma 15, no. 1 (March, 1937), pp. 110–111; Hunter, *Trail Drivers*, pp. 659, 577.

Ruts of the Trail (p. 46): The trail-rutted land, originally part of the old Addington Ranch, was owned by Price Cattle Company in 1966.

The Icy Washita (p. 47): Hunter, *Trail Drivers*, pp. 129–131, 704, 211.

Salt Fork of the Arkansas (p. 48): Fred Grove, "The Old Chisholm Trail," *Oklahoma Today* 16, no. 4 (Autumn, 1966), p. 27.

Buffalo Range (p. 49): It should be noted that this picture site is not in Oklahoma, but on the John Mecom Ranch southeast of Laredo, Texas. The photo is inserted here because it fits drover descriptions in Hunter, *Trail Drivers*, pp. 118, 432, 1023.

Box Canyon and Elm Springs (p. 52): Glen French, a native of Abilene who herded Longhorns himself in the 1920's, was the guide to the Elm Springs country in 1966.

Trail's End—Abilene (p. 53): Dee Brown and Martin F. Schmitt, *Trail Driving Days*, pp. 9–10; A.T. Andreas, *History of the State of Kansas*, pp. 688–689. Merchant's Hotel is the only original building related to the trail in Old Abilene Town, a popular tourist attraction in Abilene, Kansas. Harvard Goodrich was Old Abilene's manager in 1966.

CHANGING TIMES AND TRAILS

Moving to Market (p. 54): Edward Everett Dale, *The Range Cattle Industry*, p. 43; Walter Prescott Webb, *The Great Plains*, p. 223.

Beginning at the Apishapa (p. 56): Maurice Frink, W. Turrentine Jackson, and Agnes Wright Spring, *When Grass Was King*, pp. 358–359; David Lavender, *The Great West*, p. 352.

The Platte and the Crow (p. 57): J. Evetts Haley, *Charles Goodnight: Cowman and Plainsman*, p. 206.

Chalk Bluffs (p. 59): Frink and others, *When Grass Was King*, pp. 374, 390. Chalk Bluffs Ranch in 1965 was owned by Dean Prosser, Jr.

'Hoodoo on the Horizon' (p. 59): Haley, *Charles Goodnight*, p. 206; John Clay, *My Life on the Range*, pp. 193, 202, 222; Clarice Whittenburg, *Wyoming, Prelude to Statehood* (booklet), p. 36.

Goodnight Hill (p. 60): Haley, *Charles Goodnight*, p. 208.

Cimarron Seco (p. 60): Haley, *Charles Goodnight*, p. 209.

Historic Valley (p. 61): J. Evetts Haley to S.F., interview, September 2, 1965; Haley, *Charles Goodnight*, p. 209; "Trinchera Named" (typescript).

Trinchera Pass (p. 61): Haley, *Charles Goodnight*, pp. 209–210.

Rock Cañon Ranch (p. 62): Charles Goodnight to Leroy Hafen, September 29, 1927, Library, State Historical Society of Colorado. Haley, *Charles Goodnight*, pp. 260, 265; Phil K. Hudspeth to S.F., interview, September 24, 1965. The Pueblo Reservoir Dam, part of the Frying Pan-Arkansas Project, will cross Rock Cañon at the site of Goodnight's bridge.

Built to Stay (p. 65): Goodnight to Hafen, September 29, 1927; Haley, *Charles Goodnight*, pp. 272, 266; Hudspeth to S.F.

Snyders' Trail Office (p. 66): Hunter, *Trail Drivers*, pp. 1029–1031. Mrs. Ray Hyer Brown to S. F., interview, May 19, 1966.

Trail Endowments (p. 67): Methodist acquisition of Southwestern was with the condition that the church not be involved in school debt. The Snyder Brothers guaranteed this provision. Lewis Atherton, *The Cattle Kings*, pp. 145–146; Agnes Wright Spring in Frink and others, *When Grass Was King*, p. 427 and n. 15; Mrs. Brown to S.F.; Dedication, *The Sou'wester*, 1909, Hunter, *Trail Drivers*, p. 729; Walter Prescott Webb (ed.), *The Handbook of Texas*, II, p. 647; Edward W. Milligan, "John Wesley Iliff," *Westerners Brand Book* 6 (1950), pp. 57–58.

Waco Suspension Bridge (p. 68): Roger N. Conger, "The Waco Suspension Bridge," *Texana* 1, no. 3 (Summer, 1963), pp. 181–224; J. Marvin Hunter, *The Trail Drivers of Texas*, p. 657.

Mail on the Trail (p. 68): Mrs. Johnnie Stubbs to S.F., interview, May 22, 1966.

Cheyenne-Arapaho Agency (p. 69): Muriel H. Wright and George H. Shirk, *Mark of Heritage* (booklet); George Wint to S.F., interview, May 26, 1966.

Margin of the Bays (p. 71): A. Ray Stephens, *The Taft Ranch*, pp. 8–12; J. L. Baughman, "A History of the Meat Packing Industry at Fulton, Texas" (pamphlet); W. R. Woolrich, "Mechanical Refrigeration—Its American Birthright," *Refrigeration Engineering* 53, no. 3 (March, 1964), and 53, no. 4 (April, 1947).

Coastal Show Place (p. 72): Stephens, *Taft Ranch*, pp. 37–39; Dorothy Louis Nims, "A History of the Village of Rockport" (thesis), pp. 55, 57, 60; Mrs. Wills W. Wood, "History of Rockport, Fulton, St. Mary's, Lamar, the El Copano" (manuscript).

For Hide and Tallow (p. 74): J. L. Baughman to S.F., interview, April 19, 1966; *San Antonio Express*, June 17, 1934; *Texas: A Guide to the Lone Star State*, p. 59.

Big Business (p. 74): The Four-foot by six-foot canvas, owned by Arthur Bracht of Fulton, was in Aransas County Junior High School cafeteria in 1966; J. L. Baughman, "A History of the Meat Packing Industry at Fulton, Texas" (pamphlet); *San Antonio Express*, June 17, 1934.

Ellsworth Jail (p. 76): *Ellsworth Reporter*, July 25, 1873.

Welcomed Cowcatcher (p. 78): Wayne Gard, *The Chisholm Trail*, pp. 183–185, 190; *Santa Fe Railroad's Cyrus K. Holliday* (pamphlet); *Dedication of the Cyrus K. Holliday Plaque* (pamphlet), pp. 30–31. The locomotive, named *Cyrus K. Holliday* for the railroad's founder, stays at company headquarters in Topeka, Kansas, when not on tour.

New End of the Line (p. 78): R. M. Long, *Historic Wichita Cowtown* (pamphlet); Gard, *Chisholm Trail*, pp. 190–191. The station is in Wichita's "Cowtown," a twenty-three-acre area with original and reconstructed buildings devoted entirely to re-creating the atmosphere of the 1870's.

For Wichita Worship (p. 79): Long, *Historic Wichita Cowtown*; Gard, *Chisholm Trail*, p. 182. The church is now in Wichita's "Cowtown."

For Law and Order (p. 79): Long, *Historic Wichita Cowtown*. The jail and house are part of Wichita's "Cowtown."

Fort Hays (p. 81): Dee Brown and Martin Schmitt, *Trail Driving Days*, p. 93.

More Civilized (p. 82): *Wichita City Eagle*, August 2, 1872; Gard, *Chisholm Trail*, p. 191; Tom Lea, *The King Ranch*, pp. 299, 362. In 1966, this heavy Longhorn steer was one of the few kept on the King Ranch in Texas, where a new breed—the Santa Gertrudis—has been developed.

Woman's Marker on the Trails (p. 84): Victor M. Rose, *History of Victoria County*, pp. 130–132; Mrs. Thomas O'Connor, Sr., to S.F., letter, May 11, 1966.

Goodnights' Gear (p. 84): "Mrs. Goodnight's Saddle," *Frontier Times* 4, no. 4 (January, 1927), p. 8; J. Evetts Haley and Boone McClure to S.F., interview, September 3, 1965. The saddles are in the Panhandle-Plains Museum at Canyon.

'The Winner' (p. 86): Henry D. and Frances T. Mc-Callum, *The Wire That Fenced The West*, pp. 110–111, 117–118, 129. Boone McClure to S.F., interview, 1966.

A Vanishing American (p. 87): This windmill, photographed at its original Harrell Ranch location, has been preserved through the efforts of Henry Hertner of Amarillo, longtime chairman of the Potter County Historical Survey Committee. Terry G. Jordan, "Windmills in Texas," *Agricultural History* 37, no. 2 (1961), pp. 80–85.

Wheat Threshing Stone (p. 88): *Dedication of the Cyrus K. Holiday Plaque*, pp. 31–32.

'So Large a Rancho' (p. 89): *Corpus Christi Weekly Gazette*, February 7, 1874.

Fort Reno (p. 91): Frank Dalton, "Military Escort for a Trail Herd," *The Cattleman* 31, no. 1 (June, 1944), pp. 13–14; Hunter, *Trail Drivers*, pp. 108, 872. Fort Reno in 1966 was an agricultural station.

French Creek (p. 92): David Lavender, *The American Heritage History of the Great West*, pp. 354–355.

Red Cloud Buttes (p. 93): James C. Olson, *Red Cloud and the Sioux Problem*, pp. 206–210, 337–338.

WESTERN TRAIL

Up from the Rio Grande (p. 94): Walter Prescott Webb, *The Great Plains*, p. 215.

Arroyo Colorado (p. 96): Andy Adams, *The Log of a Cowboy*, p. 30; Tom Lea, *The King Ranch*, I, p. 94; A. A. Champion to S.F., interview, April, 1966.

The Coast Route (p. 96): Adams, *Log of a Cowboy*, pp. 30–31, 40.

The Nueces (p. 97): "Jack Potter's Famous Map,"

The Texas Longhorn 1, no. 1 (September, 1965), p. 16.

Proved on the Plaza (p. 98): Charles Ramsdell, *San Antonio: A Historical and Pictorial Guide*, pp. 110–111; R. Henderson Shuffler, "'Bet-a-Million' Gates," *Texas Magazine* (*Houston Post-Houston Chronicle*), May 29, 1966.

Bandera's Jail (p. 99): Mrs. John V. Saul to S.F., interview, August, 1966; *Frontier News & Dude Wrangler*, June 23, 1966.

Long-time Longhorn Range (p. 100): J. Marvin Hunter, *The Trail Drivers of Texas*, pp. 361–362. Charles Schreiner, III, was the moving power behind formation of the Texas Longhorn Breeders Association of America in 1964 to insure American posterity a look at the antlered cattle.

Coleman's Oldest House (p. 100): J. M. Skaggs, "The Cowtown's Vest Pocket Economy," *Old West* 5, no. 2 (Winter, 1968), p. 58; Mrs. R. Bailey to S.F., interview, June, 1966. The stone house, built by Mrs. Bailey's father, was at the back of her residence on West Pecan Street in 1966.

Albany's Courthouse (p. 101): Skaggs, "The Cowtown's Vest Pocket Economy," p. 58; Hunter, *Trail Drivers*, p. 636.

Fort Griffin Bakery (p. 101): *Wichita Falls Times Feature Magazine*, February 1, 1959, p. 7; Frank Collinson, *Life in the Saddle*, p. 35.

'The Flat' (p. 102): T. P. Fincher to S.F., interview, June 30, 1966; Dee Brown and Martin Schmitt, *Trail Driving Days*, p. 95; Hunter, *Trail Drivers*, p. 109; Collinson, *Life in the Saddle*, p. 84.

Clear Fork of the Brazos (p. 102): Hunter, *Trail Drivers*, pp. 655, 109; Brown and Schmitt, *Trail Driving Days*, p. 96.

Seymour Center (p. 103): Skaggs, "The Cowtown's Vest Pocket Economy," p. 58; Mrs. Sid Perryman to S.F., interview, April 11, 1966; Walter Prescott Webb (ed.), *The Handbook of Texas*, II, p. 594.

Edith's Point (p. 104): Edith's Point is in the background of Harold Bugbee's trail-drive painting, reproduced in bronze on the Doan's Crossing monument.

Doan's (p. 104): Hunter, *Trail Drivers*, pp. 772–779; Mrs. Bertha Doan Ross to S.F., interview, September 1, 1965.

'Oh, Bury Me Not on the Lone Prairie' (p. 105): Mrs. Bertha Doan Ross to S.F., interview, September 1, 1965; W. B. Alderman, "Oh, Bury Me Not . . . ," *Texas Parade*, February, 1966, pp. 36–38; E. C. Abbott and Helen Huntington Smith, *We Pointed Them North*, p. 223. Conflicting dates and places of origin will be found for the song set to an old sailor tune, "Oh, Bury Me Not in the Deep Blue Sea." Alfred I. Moye (in Hunter, *Trail Drivers*, p. 458) says it was sung in 1874 in northwestern Kansas.

Sundown at Doan's Crossing (p. 105): Adams, *Log of a Cowboy*, p. 121.

Into Red River (p. 106): Photo made at Doan's Crossing during the 1966 Longhorn Centennial Trail Drive.

Trail Break (p. 107): Garnet M. and Herbert O. Brayer, *American Cattle Trails, 1540–1900*, p. 109. This photo was made at Doan's Crossing during the 1966 Longhorn Centennial Trail Drive.

Moving 'Em Out (p. 107): Brayer, *American Cattle Trails*, p. 109. Photo made at Doan's Crossing during the 1966 Longhorn Centennial Trail Drive.

Wichita Mountains (p. 108): Hunter, *Trail Drivers*, pp. 165, 193, 222.

The Grassy Way (p. 108): Dr. Robert T. Hill, "Old-Time Texas Roads and Trails," *Dallas Morning News*, Daughters of the Republic of Texas clipping file.

Indian Territory (p. 109): Hunter, *Trail Drivers*, pp. 688, 690.

Camp Supply (p. 110): Brown and Schmitt, *Trail Driving Days*, p. 96; "Western State Hospital on the Site of Old Fort Supply" (fact sheet). The camp's name was changed to Fort Supply in 1889, and the post was abandoned four years later. Since 1908, when it was turned over to the state, the installation has been enlarged as Oklahoma's Western State Hospital.

The Cimarron (p. 111): Hunter, *Trail Drivers*, pp. 237–238, 254, 71; Oklahoma State Highway Engineering Department, *Map of a Portion of Oklahoma Showing the Location of the Old Texas Cattle Trail*.

The Trouble with Calves (p. 113): Hunter, *Trail Drivers*, pp. 666, 534–535. The Longhorn cow and calf were in Edwin Dow's herd near Fort Worth in 1966.

Unsteady Steps (p. 113): "Goodnight Sets Out upon 'New Adventure,'" *Frontier Times* 5, no. 1 (October, 1927), p. 29.

Bedgrounds (p. 114): Hunter, *Trail Drivers*, pp. 239–240.

Fort Dodge (p. 114): Arthur Rose to S.F., interview, June 13, 1966; Hunter, *Trail Drivers*, pp. 239–240; Brown and Schmitt, *Trail Driving Days*, p. 71. Fort Dodge became the state soldiers' home in 1889.

The Arkansas at Dodge City (p. 115): George Henrichs to S.F., interview, June 14, 1966.

Wine, Winnings, and Chance (p. 116): Henrichs to S.F.

Over the Bar (p. 116): The painting is one of the originals. Henrichs to S.F.

'A Credit to the Town' (p. 117): Henrichs to S.F.; Robert A. Dykstra, *The Cattle Towns*, pp. 90–91, photo 30, following p. 210. The old Mueller house, built in 1881, is at 112 East Vine Street.

Canyon Trails (p. 119): J. Evetts Haley, *Charles Goodnight: Cowman and Plainsman*, pp. 275, 281–282, 296. Haley showed this place to the author as Goodnight had done for him.

Early Development (p. 119): Haley, *Charles Goodnight*, pp. 314, 303, 313; J. Evetts Haley to S.F., interview, September 3, 1965. Goodnight's dugout has been faithfully restored in Palo Duro Canyon. The Dyer cabin, now owned by West Texas State University's experiment station, is located near its original site north of Canyon, Texas.

Limestone Fenceposts (p. 120): Grace Muilenburg, *The Land of the Post Rock or Fencepost Limestone Country*, pp. 3–6; Les Beitz, *Treasury of Frontier Relics: A Collector's Guide*, pp. 216–217. Average post length was 6 feet, with each post set 2 feet in the ground; a mile of fence required 160 to 175 posts. The uniform stratum from which they came —8 or 9 inches thick—has been named Fencepost Limestone. With wedges inserted in hand-drilled holes, light pounding caused the rock to split into desired widths. The practice was discontinued many years ago when the cost of wooden and steel posts was reduced.

Sodbusters (p. 120): Baylis John Fletcher, *Up the Trail in '79*, p. 47; V. A. Kear to S.F., interview, June 2, 1966.

Wild Horse Spring (p. 121): Adams, *Log of a Cowboy*, p. 258; Hunter, *Trail Drivers*, pp. 238, 861. Nebraska has marked the spring about fifteen highway miles south of Ogallala on State Highway 61.

Boot Hill (p. 122): Badger Clark, *Sun and Saddle Leather*, p. 103.

North of Ogallala (p. 123): Louis Pelzer, *The Cattleman's Frontier*, p. 47.

Hazardous Holes (p. 123): Abbott and Smith, *We Pointed Them North*, p. 37. Abbott (Teddy Blue) was with the John Lytle herd near Blue River, Nebraska. The prairie dog pictured is in southern South Dakota.

Approach to Pine Ridge (p. 124): James C. Olson, *Red Cloud and the Sioux Problem*, p. 263.

Fort Robinson (p. 125): Fort Robinson Museum File. In 1956 the Nebraska State Historical Society opened at the old fort a museum in which the story of the Indian wars is graphically portrayed.

Scalp Shirt of Crazy Horse (p. 127): Fort Robinson Museum File. The scalp shirt is in Nebraska's Fort Robinson Museum.

Beef Flats (p. 127): Western Collection notes, Denver Public Library; Hunter, *Trail Drivers*, p. 82; Dale, *Range Cattle Industry*, p. 64. Pens at Pine Ridge are of the same construction as those of the 1870's and 1880's, but such pens last only about ten years.

Pine Ridge Church (p. 128): Edward Everett Dale, *The Range Cattle Industry*, p. 24; Will Spindler to Ben Irving and Irving to Spindler, exchange letter, June 16, 1966; Hunter, *Trail Drivers*, p. 82; Olson, *Red Cloud and the Sioux Problem*, p. 263. The church, although remodeled, is the original structure.

The Broad North Platte (p. 129): Hunter, *Trail Drivers*, pp. 79–80.

Court House and Jail Rocks (p. 130): "A Drive from Texas to North Dakota," *Frontier Times* 3, no. 7 (April, 1926), p. 4; Hunter, *Trail Drivers*, p. 79.

Chimney Rock (p. 130): Hunter, *Trail Drivers*, p. 170.

Pine Bluffs (p. 131): Russell Thorp address, Texas Trail Markers Dedication at Pine Bluffs and Torrington, Wyoming, August 1, 1948, Russell Thorp Collection.

September Snow (p. 131): Hunter, *Trail Drivers*, p. 824; Russell Thorp address. Photo made September 16, 1965.

Fort Laramie (p. 131): Robert A. Murray to S.F., interview, September 17, 1965.

'Squaw Winter' (p. 133): Adams, *Log of a Cowboy*, p. 361; Murray to S.F. The cabin, about seventeen miles north of Lingle, was owned in 1965 by Bryan Patrick, whose grandfather built it.

Hat Creek Station (p. 134): The house is two miles east and one mile south of U.S. Highway 85, fourteen miles north of Lusk.

The Big Powder (p. 135): Ramon Adams, *Western Words: A Dictionary of the Range, Cow Camp, and Trail*, pp. 118–119.

Powder River Valley (p. 136): Brown and Schmitt, *Trail Driving Days*, p. 198; Hunter, *Trail Drivers*, p. 170.

Fort Keogh (p. 137): *Miles City Star*, May 19, 1963; Abbott and Smith, *We Pointed Them North*, p. 100. Fort Keogh was active through World War I and, in 1924, was converted to a U.S. Range Livestock Experiment Station.

Sunday Creek (p. 138): Mark H. Brown and W. R. Felton, *Before Barbed Wire*, p. 163; Frederic G. Renner, *Charles M. Russell: Paintings, Drawings, and Sculpture in the Amon G. Carter Collection. A descriptive catalogue* (brochure on book).

Hotel in Caldwell (p. 139): Dykstra, *The Cattle Towns*, p. 212; Dowell Stiles to S.F., interview, May 12, 1966; Adams, *Log of a Cowboy*, p. 134. In 1966 the Southwestern Hotel was being used as a hospital.

Bound for New Markets (p. 139): Abbott and Smith, *We Pointed Them North*, p. 62. Photo made on the Oklahoma side of Doan's Crossing during the 1966 Longhorn Centennial Trail Drive.

BONANZA TO BLIZZARD

Elegant Eighties (p. 141): Edith Eudora Kohl, *Denver's Historic Mansions*, pp. 58–62; Agnes Wright Spring, in Maurice Frink and others, *When Grass Was King*, p. 394. With ranches in four states or territories, Sheedy was a Wyoming Stock Growers' director. His Denver mansion at 1115 Grant Street was a fine-arts studio in 1966.

Castle in Colorado (p. 143): Walter Baron von Richthofen, *Cattle Raising on the Plains of North America*, p. 54; Frink, *When Grass Was King*, p. 25; Louisa Ward Arps, *Denver in Slices*, pp. 155–171; Kohl, *Denver's Historic Mansions*, pp. 193–201; Mrs. Etienne Perenyi to S.F., interview, 1966.

'A Fair Reflex' (p. 145): Texas agreed to pay $520,-037.15 in addition to the three million acres for the building. Syndicate construction costs were $3,224,-593.45. J. Evetts Haley, *The XIT Ranch of Texas and the Early Days of the Llano Estacado*, pp. 3, 72, 53, 54, 56.

Rail Extension (p. 145): Brit Allen Storey, "William Jackson Palmer, Promoter," *The Colorado Magazine* 43, no. 1 (Winter, 1966), pp. 42–55; Robert

G. Athearn, "The Denver & Rio Grande Railway, Colorado's 'Baby Road,'" *The Colorado Magazine* 35 (January, 1958), p. 46; Bob Richardson to S.F. interview, September 11, 1965.

Brush Country (p. 147): E. C. Abbott and Helen Huntington Smith, *We Pointed Them North*, pp. 60–61; *San Antonio Light*, August 22, 1965; Tom Lea, *The King Ranch*, I, pp. 499–500; *Corpus Christi Gazette*, May 24, 1873. Brush infestation increased until about 1940, when eradication methods improved.

For Range Packing (p. 148): Brown and Schmitt, *Trail Driving Days*, pp. 185–187; "Chateau de Mores" (pamphlet).

International View (p. 149): Chester L. Brooks and Ray H. Mattison, *Theodore Roosevelt and the Dakota Badlands* (booklet), pp. 12–13.

Dwindling Bison (p. 151): Brooks and Mattison, *Theodore Roosevelt*, p. 19. Buffalo are in Custer Park, South Dakota, about a hundred miles south of the last wild herd's range.

'Wonderful Revolution' (p. 152): This "experimental" barbed-wire fence, erected by the Texas Panhandle's Frying Pan Ranch in 1881, remained in 1970.

No Cattalo! (p. 153): J. Evetts Haley, *Charles Goodnight: Cowman and Plainsman*, pp. 439, 443–445. Longhorn and buffalo are on John Mecom Ranch near Laredo, Texas.

'El Rancho Grande' (p. 155): Henry D. and Frances T. McCallum, *The Wire That Fenced the West*, p. 141; Chris Emmett, *Shanghai Pierce: A Fair Likeness*, pp. 143, 174. The old Pierce ranch house is near Blessing, Texas.

Chisum's Plantings (p. 159): Mrs. Bert Aston to S.F., interview, September 27, 1965. Harry Sinclair Drago, *Great American Cattle Trails*, p. 224; Harry E. Chrisman, *Lost Trails of the Cimarron*, pp. 181–182.

Captain King's Legacy (p. 160): John A. Cypher Jr., to S.F., interview, November 5, 1965. The peafowl above the bell is one of many that roamed the King Ranch headquarters in 1970.

Longhorn Roundup (p. 160): Emmett, *Shanghai Pierce*, pp. 108–109. Bill of sale owned by Mrs. Charles Herring, Austin, Texas.

Barbs That Fenced a Border (p. 161): Haley, *XIT*, pp. 87, 88, 46; Panhandle–Plains Museum staff; McCallum, *The Wire That Fenced the West*, pp. 258–259.

Fire Drags (p. 163): Haley, *XIT*, pp. 170, 179–180. This fire drag, stored with hitching gear in the Range Riders Museum, Miles City, Montana, was used on XIT ranges.

Scanty Forage (p. 163): Brown and Schmitt, *Trail Driving Days*, p. 225; Abbott, *We Pointed Them North*, pp. 184–185. This photo was made in January, 1966—almost eighty years after the storm described—in an unusually heavy snow on the Charles Schreiner Ranch near Kerrville, Texas.

'Last of the Five Thousand' (p. 165): Photo made in January, 1966, on Charles Schreiner's ranch near Kerrville, Texas.

End of the Trail (p. 165): Mrs. Lee Palmer to S.F., interview, September 2, 1965. In 1965 Mrs. Palmer's husband managed the ranch that was part of Goodnight's last holdings, and their private residence was the home he built in 1887.

Into Tomorrow (p. 169): Longhorns on the 1966 Centennial Trail Drive, San Antonio to Dodge City.

Bibliography

Unpublished Sources

Bass, Stirling W. "The History of Kleberg County." Thesis, The University of Texas at Austin, 1931.

Bennett, Rossie Beth. "History of the Cattle Trade in Fort Worth, Texas." Master's thesis, Texas Technological College, Lubbock, 1931.

Cloud, James W. (Oklahoma City). "The Surveyed Route of the Chisholm Trail." Manuscript.

Devinoy, M. L. "History of South Texas." Manuscript, Daughters of the Republic of Texas Library, San Antonio.

Graf, LeRoy P. "Economic History of the Lower Rio Grande Valley." Doctoral thesis, two volumes, Harvard University, Cambridge, 1942.

Haley, J. Evetts. "A Survey of Texas Cattle Drives to the North, 1866-1895." Thesis, The University of Texas at Austin, 1936.

Huson, Hobart, editor and annotator (Refugio, Texas). "Two Sea-Captains Johnson and Some of Their Friends, as told by Peter A. Johnson." Manuscript.

McCombs, Holland (Dallas). King Ranch research file.

Matthey, Julius H. "The Reminiscences of Fifty Years, 1872-1922." Manuscript, Daughters of the Republic of Texas Library, San Antonio.

Nims, Dorothy Louise. "A History of the Village of Rockport." Thesis, Southwest Texas State Teachers College, San Marcos, 1939.

Weddle, Robert S. (Austin). "Pegleg Station on the San Saba." Manuscript.

Wood, Mrs. Wills W. "History of Rockport, Fulton, St. Mary's, Lamar, and El Copano." Manuscript, Aransas County Schools.

Special Collections

Anglo American Cattle Company draft, July 8, 1883. Sutler Records, Fort Laramie National Historic Site, Wyoming.

Baca House Museum Files. Trinidad, Colorado.

Barnes, Joseph N. Interviewed by E. R. Barkey, "Driving Cattle from Texas for Hittson, Earnest & Iliff." Manuscript 23, 47a. Library, State Historical Society of Colorado, Denver.

"Beef." Golden, Colorado, Transcript, Manuscripts 23, 41. Library, State Historical Society of Colorado, Denver.

Bill of Sale, April 10, 1872. Texas Hall of State, Dallas.

Borland, Margaret. Papers. The University of Texas Archives, Austin.

Borden, Gail, Jr. Papers. Daughters of the Republic of Texas Library, San Antonio.

Brandon, C. W. Collection. Western History Research Center, University of Wyoming, Laramie.

"Bureau of American Ethnology," Bulletin 30, part 2, N-Z (typescript). Hebard Collection. Western History Research Center, University of Wyoming, Laramie.

Coffee, Charles F. Collection. Western History Research Center, University of Wyoming, Laramie.

Colorado. Collected Interviews, 1933-1934. Pamphlet 344, no. 43. Library, State Historical Society of Colorado, Denver.

————. "Trinchera Named." Typescript. Library, State Historical Society of Colorado, Denver.

Daughters of the Republic of Texas Library. Clipping File. San Antonio.

Dobie, J. Frank. Collection. Texana Department, The University of Texas at Austin.

Ford, John S. Memoirs. Manuscript. The University of Texas Archives, Austin.

Fort Robinson. Museum Files. Fort Robinson, Nebraska.

Goodnight, Charles. Letters to LeRoy Hafen, September 20 and 29, 1927. Copies in Library, State Historical Society of Colorado, Denver.

McCombs, Holland. King Ranch Research File. Volumes 14-16. Holland McCombs, Dallas.

Pierce, Abel Head. Bill of Sale, 1885. Mrs. Charles Herring, Austin.

Reid, G. O. Letter to M. J. Mattes, December 20, 1945. Sutler Records, Fort Laramie National Historic Site, Wyoming.

Republic of Texas. Two-dollar Bill, 1841. Daughters of the Republic of Texas Library, San Antonio.

Stoddard, General H. B. Papers. Daughters of the Republic of Texas Library, San Antonio.

189

Texas A and M University. Cattle Tick and Tick Fever Files. Veterinary Library, College of Veterinary Medicine, Texas A and M University, College Station.

Thorp, Russell. Address. Texas Trail Markers Dedication at Pine Bluffs and Torrington, Wyoming, August 1, 1948. Russell Thorp Collection, Western History Research Center, University of Wyoming, Laramie.

Wells-Fargo. Waybill Ledgers, 1870-1872. Wyoming State Archives and Historical Department, Cheyenne.

Western Collection. Denver Public Library, Denver.

Western Range Cattle Industry Study. Library, State Historical Society of Colorado, Denver.

Wyoming. Historical Name Derivations. Western History Research Center, University of Wyoming, Laramie.

Newspapers

Brownsville Herald (Texas), April 21, 1935.

Cheyenne Daily Leader, January 3, 1870; February 8, 1872; September 25, 1874; March 27, October 29 and December 31, 1875; February 2 and August 31, 1876; December 16, 1877; February 13 and 14, 1878; February 24, 1881; January 4, April 29 and May 24, 1882; December 29, 1883; July 29, 1884; February 20, 1887.

Cheyenne Sun, August 23, 1885.

Corpus Christi Caller-Times, April 6, 1930; January 18, 1959.

Corpus Christi Gazette, May 24 and June 7, 1873; February 7, 1874.

Denver Tribune-Republican, July 19, 1884; July 9, 1886; June 15, 1891.

Ellsworth Reporter (Kansas), July 25, 1873.

Fort Worth Democrat, August 25 and October 27, 1876.

Frontier News & Dude Wrangler (Bandera, Texas), June 23, 1966.

Galveston News, August 16, 1866.

Lamar Daily News (Colorado), November 17, 1930.

Lusk Herald (Wyoming), August 6, 1886; August 15, 1940.

Miles City Star (Montana), May 19, 1963.

Pikes Peak Journal (Manitou Springs, Colorado), June 20, 1940.

Pueblo Chieftain, October 25, 1908.

Rockport Pilot (Texas), Centennial Edition, March 27, 1969.

Rocky Mountain News (Denver), August 13, 1870; April 5, 1872; January 4, 1874; July 11, 1877;

February 19, 1878; August 4, 1880; April 1, 5 and 22, June 23, July 11, August 16 and 18, November 14, 1884; January 10 and March 18, 1885; July 25 and 27, 1887.

San Angelo Standard-Times (Texas), Seventieth Anniversary Edition, August 29, 1954.

San Antonio Daily Herald, July 12, 1871.

San Antonio Express, August 17, 1870; June 17, 1934.

San Antonio Light, April 20, 1958; August 22, 1965; February 11, 1971.

San Antonio Weekly Herald, August 17, 1870; June 24, 1871.

Victoria Advocate (Texas), 88th Anniversary Number, September 28, 1934.

Wichita City Eagle (Kansas), July 5 and 19, August 2, 1872; July 10, 1873.

Wichita Falls Times (Texas), February 1, 1959.

Maps

Many books cited here contain general maps on the cattle trails, but no two maps are identical. Shifting quarantine lines, advancing rails and fences, and the drovers' search for grass and water in times of drouth or heavy trail traffic, altered the route in any given year. Other sources consulted include:

Colorado Apishapa Quadrangle. Washington, D.C., U.S. Geological Survey, 1897. Baca House Museum, Trinidad, Colorado.

Indian Territory (1875). First Lieutenant E. H. Ruffner, engineer. Collection of James Cloud, Oklahoma City.

Indian Territory (1879). Department of the Interior. Collection of James Cloud, Oklahoma City.

"Jack Potter's Famous Map," *The Texas Longhorn* 1, no. 1 (September, 1965), p. 16. (Original in Old Trail Drivers' Museum, San Antonio.)

Kansas Pacific Railway, The Best and Shortest Cattle Trail from Texas, 1875. The University of Texas Archives, Austin.

Map of a Portion of Oklahoma Showing the Location of the Chisholm Trail. Oklahoma State Highway Engineering Department, 1933. Authorized by H.B. 149, 13th Session, Oklahoma Legislature.

Map of a Portion of Oklahoma Showing the Location of the Old Texas Cattle Trail, also Called the Western Cattle Trail, Abilene & Ft. Dodge Trail, Ft. Griffin-Ft. Dodge Trail, Dodge City Trail. Oklahoma State Highway Engineering Department, 1933. Authorized by H.B. 149, 13th Session, Oklahoma Legislature.

Map of the County of Cameron, Texas. J. J. Cocke, County Surveyor, October 25, 1884. Collection of A. A. Champion, Brownsville, Texas.

Rollinson, J. K. Map. W. M. Fitzhugh Collection, Western History Research Center, University of Wyoming, Laramie.

Public Documents

Best, Charles. "Texas Frontier Troubles," *Report No. 343, House of Representatives*, Forty-fourth Congress, First Session, 1877.

Colorado Territory Legislative Assembly. *An Act to Prohibit the Introduction of Texas Cattle into Colorado Territory.* Sixth Session, 1867, pp. 86-87.

Goodnight, Charles. Las Animas County Records: Apishapa homestead claim, May 3, 1869. Las Animas County Courthouse, Trinidad, Colorado.

———. PAT and PAT M cattle brands registered July 20, 1872. Las Animas County Courthouse, Trinidad, Colorado.

Graybill, H. W. *Methods of Exterminating the Texas-Fever Tick.* Farmers' Bulletin 378. Washington, D.C.: United States Department of Agriculture, 1909.

Nimmo, Joseph, Jr. *The Range and Ranch Cattle Traffic of the United States.* Forty-eighth Congress, Second Session, *House Executive Document No. 267.* Washington, D.C.: 1885.

Report of the Commissioner of Agriculture for the Year, 1869. Washington, D.C.: Government Printing Office, 1870.

Salmon, Dr. D. E. *Special Report on Diseases of Cattle and on Cattle Feeding.* Washington, D.C.: Bureau of Animal Industry, United States Department of Agriculture, 1896.

Third Annual Report of the Metropolitan Board of Health of the Metropolitan Sanitary District. Albany, New York: Argus Company (printers), 1869.

United States Department of Agriculture. *Contagious Diseases of Swine and Other Domestic Animals.* Washington, D.C.: Government Printing Office, 1880.

———. *Manual on Livestock Ticks.* Washington, D.C.: Agricultural Research Service, 1965.

———. *Yearbook of Agriculture. Keeping Livestock Healthy.* Washington, D.C.: Government Printing Office, 1942.

War of Rebellion, The: A Compilation of the Official Records of the Union and Confederate Armies. Ser. I, XLVIII, part 2. Washington, D.C. Government Printing Office, 1894.

Books

Abbott, E. C. (Teddy Blue) and Helen Huntington Smith. *We Pointed Them North.* New York: Farrar and Rinehart, 1939.

Abernathy, Jack. *In Camp with Theodore Roosevelt.* Oklahoma City: Times Journal Publishing Company, 1933.

Adams, Andy. *The Log of a Cowboy.* Boston and New York: Houghton Mifflin Company, 1903.

Adams, Ramon F. *From the Pecos to the Powder.* Norman: University of Oklahoma Press, 1965.

———. *Western Words: A Dictionary of the Range, Cow Camp, and Trail.* Norman: University of Oklahoma Press, 1946.

Andreas, A. T. *History of the State of Kansas.* Chicago: privately printed, 1883.

Arps, Louisa Ward. *Denver in Slices.* Denver: Sage Books, 1959.

Athearn, Robert G. *High Country Empire.* Lincoln: University of Nebraska Press, 1960.

Atherton, Lewis. *The Cattle Kings.* Bloomington: Indiana University Press, 1961.

Baughman, James P. *Charles Morgan and the Development of Southern Transportation.* Nashville: Vanderbilt University Press, 1968.

Beaumont: A Guide to the City and Its Environs. Writers' Program of the Work Projects Administration in Texas. American Guide Series. Houston: Anson Jones Press, 1940.

Beitz, Les. *Treasury of Frontier Relics: A Collector's Guide.* New York: Edwin House, 1966.

Benton, Jesse James. *Cow by the Tail.* Boston: Houghton Mifflin Company, 1943.

Boethel, Paul C. *On the Headwaters of the Lavaca and the Navidad.* Austin, Texas: Von Boeckmann-Jones Company, 1967.

———. *Sand in Your Craw.* Austin: Von Boeckmann-Jones Company, 1959.

Botkin, B. A., ed. *A Treasury of Western Folklore.* New York: Crown Publishers, Inc., 1951.

Bourke, John Gregory. *On the Border with Crook.* Chicago: Rio Grande Press, Inc., 1962.

Branch, Douglas. *The Cowboy and His Interpreters.* New York: Cooper Square Publishers, Inc., 1961.

Brayer, Garnet M. and Herbert O. *American Cattle Trails, 1540-1900.* Bayside, New York: American Pioneer Trails Association, 1952.

Brisbin, James S. *The Beef Bonanza; or, How to Get Rich on the Plains.* Philadelphia: J. B. Lippincott Company, 1881 (reprinted, Norman: University of Oklahoma Press, 1959).

Brown, Dee, and Martin F. Schmitt. *Trail Driving Days.* New York: Charles Scribner's Sons, 1952.

Brown, John Henry. *The Indian Wars and Pioneers of Texas.* Austin: L. E. Daniell, n.d.

Brown, Mark H. *The Plainsmen of the Yellowstone.* New York: G. P. Putnam's Sons, 1961.

Brown, Mark H., and W. R. Felton. *Before Barbed Wire.* New York: Henry Holt and Company, 1956.

Bunton, Mary Taylor. *A Bride on the Chisholm Trail in 1886.* San Antonio: The Naylor Company, 1939.

Bye, John O. *Back Trailing in the Short Grass Country.* Everett, Washington: Alexander Printing Company, 1956.

Chrisman, Harry E. *Lost Trails of the Cimarron.* Denver: Sage Books, 1964.

Clark, Badger. *Sun and Saddle Leather.* Boston: Chapman and Grimes, 1936.

Clark, C. M. *A Trip to Pike's Peak and Notes by the Way.* Chicago: Steam Book and Job Printing House, 1861.

Clay, John. *My Life on the Range.* Norman: University of Oklahoma Press, 1960.

Collinson, Frank. *Life in the Saddle.* Norman: University of Oklahoma Press, 1963.

Conkling, Roscoe P. and Margaret B. *The Butterfield Overland Mail, 1857-1869.* Three volumes. Glendale, California: Arthur H. Clark Company, 1947.

Cook, J. H. *Fifty Years on the Old Frontier.* New Haven: Yale University Press, 1923.

Cox, James. *Historical and Biographical Record of the Cattle Industry and the Cattlemen of Texas and Adjacent Territory.* Saint Louis: Woodward and Tiernan Printing Company, 1895.

Cranfill, Dr. J. B. *Dr. J. B. Cranfill's Chronicle.* New York: Fleming H. Revell Company, 1916.

Cullar, Willie Clytes. *The Loving Family in Texas.* Privately printed, n.d.

Dale, Edward Everett. *Frontier Ways: Sketches of Life in the Old West.* Austin: University of Texas Press, 1959.

————. *The Range Cattle Industry.* Norman: University of Oklahoma Press, 1930.

Dobie, J. Frank. *A Vaquero of the Brush Country.* Dallas: Southwest Press, 1929.

————. Introduction to *The Little World Waddies* by Eugene Manlove Rhodes. El Paso: Carl Hertzog, 1946.

————. *The Longhorns.* Boston: Little, Brown and Company, 1941.

————. *The Mustangs.* New York: Bramhall House, 1952.

Drago, Harry Sinclair. *Great American Cattle Trails.* New York: Dodd, Mead and Company, 1965.

Dykstra, Robert K. *The Cattle Towns.* New York: Alfred A. Knopf, Inc., 1968.

Emmett, Chris. *Shanghai Pierce: A Fair Likeness.* Norman: University of Oklahoma Press, 1953.

Emrich, Duncan. *It's an Old Wild West Custom.* New York: Vanguard Press, 1949.

Farber, James. *Fort Worth in the Civil War.* Belton, Texas: Peter Hansbrough Bell Press, 1960.

Fiske, A. *A Visit to Texas.* New York: Goodrich and Wiley, 1834 (reprinted, Austin: The Steck Company, 1952).

Fletcher, Baylis John. *Up the Trail in '79.* Norman: University of Oklahoma Press, 1968.

Fletcher, Ernest W. *The Wayward Horseman.* Denver: Sage Books, 1958.

Frantz, Joe B., and Julian Ernest Choate, Jr. *The American Cowboy: The Myth and the Reality.* Norman: University of Oklahoma Press, 1955.

Friedrichs, Irene Holmann. *History of Goliad.* Victoria, Texas: Regal Printers, 1961.

Frink, Maurice, W. Turrentine Jackson, and Agnes Wright Spring. *When Grass Was King.* Boulder: University of Colorado Press, 1956.

Gammel, H. P. N. *The Laws of Texas.* Ten volumes. Austin: The Gammel Book Company, 1898.

Gard, Wayne. *The Chisholm Trail.* Norman: University of Oklahoma Press, 1954.

Gressley, Gene M. *Bankers and Cattlemen.* New York: Alfred A. Knopf, Inc. 1966.

Haley, J. Evetts. *Charles Goodnight: Cowman and Plainsman.* Norman: University of Oklahoma Press, 1949.

————. *The XIT Ranch of Texas and the Early Days of the Llano Estacado.* Second Edition. Norman: University of Oklahoma Press, 1954.

Hamner, Laura. *Short Grass and Longhorns.* Norman: University of Oklahoma Press, 1943.

Heimann, Robert K. *Nation's Heritage.* I, no. 5. New York: Heritage Magazine, Inc. (division of B. C. Forbes & Sons Publishing Company, Inc.), 1949.

————. *Tobacco and Americans.* New York: McGraw-Hill, 1960.

Holden, William Curry. *Alkali Trails.* Dallas: Southwest Press, 1930.

Holland, G. A. *History of Parker County and the Double Log Cabin.* Weatherford, Texas: Herald Publishing Company, 1937.

Horan, James D. *The Great American West.* New York: Crown Publishers, Inc., 1959.

Horgan, Paul. *Great River: The Rio Grande in North American History.* Two volumes. New York and Toronto: Rinehart and Company, Inc., 1954.

192

Hough, Emerson. *The Passing of the Frontier*. New Haven: Yale University Press, 1918.

Houston: A History and Guide. Writers' Program of the Work Projects Administration in Texas, American Guide Series. Houston: Anson Jones Press, 1942.

Howard, Joseph Kinsey. *Montana, High, Wide and Handsome*. New Haven: Yale University Press, 1943.

Hunter, J. Marvin, ed. *The Trail Drivers of Texas*. Nashville: Cokesbury Press, 1925.

Huson, Hobart. *Refugio*. Two volumes. Houston: Guardsman Publishing Company for Rooke Foundation, Inc., Woodsboro, Texas, 1953.

Kohl, Edith Eudora. *Denver's Historic Mansions*. Denver: Sage Books, 1957.

Krakel, Dean. *South Platte Country, A History of Old Weld County*. Laramie, Wyoming: Powder River Publishers, 1954.

Lapage, Geoffrey. *Monnig's Veterinary Helminthology and Entomology*. Fourth Edition. Baltimore: Williams and Wilkins Company, 1956.

Lavender, David. *The American Heritage History of the Great West*. New York: American Heritage Publishing Company, 1965.

Lea, Tom. *The King Ranch*. Two volumes. Boston and Toronto: Little, Brown and Company, 1957.

Lomax, John A. *Cowboy Songs and Other Frontier Ballads*. New York: The Macmillan Company, 1938.

McCallum, Henry D. and Frances T. *The Wire that Fenced the West*. Norman: University of Oklahoma Press, 1965.

McCoy, Joseph G. *Historic Sketches of the Cattle Trade of the West and Southwest*. Introduction and notes by Ralph P. Bieber. Glendale, California: Arthur H. Clark Company, 1940.

Miles, Nelson A. *Personal Recollections and Observations*. Chicago: Werner and Company, 1897.

Morris, Leopold. *Pictorial History of Victoria and Victoria County*. San Antonio: Clemens Printing Company, 1953.

Muilenberg, Grace. *The Land of the Post Rock or Fencepost Limestone Country*. State Geological Survey, second edition. Lawrence: University of Kansas, 1958.

Nebraska. American Guide Series. New York: Viking Press, 1939.

New Mexico, A Guide to the Colorful State. Writers' Program of the Work Projects Administration in New Mexico, American Guide Series. Albuquerque: University of New Mexico Press, 1945.

Nordyke, Lewis. *Cattle Empire*. New York: William Morrow and Company, 1949.

———. *Great Roundup*. New York: William Morrow and Company, 1955.

Oberste, William H. *Remember Goliad*. Second edition. Austin: Von Boeckmann-Jones Company, 1949.

Olson, James C. *Red Cloud and the Sioux Problem*. Lincoln: University of Nebraska Press, 1965.

Peake, Ora Brooks. *The Colorado Range Cattle Industry*. Glendale, California: Arthur H. Clark Company, 1937.

Pearce, W. M. *The Matador Land and Cattle Company*. Norman: University of Oklahoma Press, 1964.

Pelzer, Louis. *The Cattleman's Frontier*. Glendale, California: Arthur H. Clark Company, 1936.

Potter, Jack. *Cattle Trails of the Old West*. Clayton, New Mexico. Laura R. Krehbiel (editor and publisher), 1939.

Powell, Cuthbert. *Twenty Years of Kansas City's Live-Stock Trade and Traders*. Kansas City, Missouri: Pearl Printing Company, 1893.

Prose and Poetry of the Live Stock Industry of the United States. Denver and Kansas City: National Live Stock Historical Association, 1905.

Ramsdell, Charles. *San Antonio: A Historical and Pictorial Guide*. Austin: University of Texas Press, 1959.

Richardson, Rupert N., and Carl Coke Rister. *The Greater Southwest*. Glendale, California: Arthur H. Clark Company, 1934.

Richthofen, Walter Baron von. *Cattle Raising on the Plains of North America*. New York: D. Appleton and Company, 1885.

Rister, Carl Coke. *The Southwestern Frontier, 1865-1881*. Cleveland: Arthur H. Clark Company, 1928.

Roosevelt, Theodore. *Ranch Life and the Hunting Trail*. New York: G. P. Putnam's Sons (n.d.).

Rose, Victor M. *History of Victoria County*, Victoria, Texas: Book Mart, 1961.

Ross, Charles P. and T. L. Rouse, *Early Day History of Wilbarger County*. Vernon, Texas: *Vernon Times*, 1933.

Sandoz, Mari. *The Cattlemen: From the Rio Grande across the Far Marias*. New York: Hastings House, 1958.

South Dakota. American Guide Series. New York: Hastings House, 1952.

Shaw, James C. *North from Texas*. Evanston, Illinois: Branding Iron Press, 1952.

Sou'wester, The. Yearbook, Southwestern University, Georgetown, Texas, 1909.

Stanley, F. *One Half Mile from Heaven*. Denver: World Press Publishing Company, 1949.

Steinel, Alvin T. *History of Colorado Agriculture*,

1858-1926. Fort Collins: Colorado A and M College, 1926.

Stephens, A. Ray. *The Taft Ranch*. Austin: University of Texas Press, 1964.

Streeter, Floyd Benjamin. *Prairie Trails and Cow Towns*. Boston: Chapman and Grimes, 1936.

Taylor, I. T. *Cavalcade of Jackson County*. San Antonio: The Naylor Company, 1938.

Taylor, T. U. *The Chisholm Trail and Other Routes*. San Antonio: The Naylor Company, 1936.

Texas Almanac, 1869, 1870. Galveston: Richardson and Company.

Texas: A Guide to the Lone Star State. Workers of the Writers' Program of the Work Projects Administration in the State of Texas. American Guide Series. New York: Hastings House, 1940.

Thorp, N. Howard. *Songs of the Cowboys*. Boston and New York: Houghton Mifflin Company, 1921.

Turner, Frederick Jackson. *The Significance of the Frontier*. Academic Reprints, Inc. El Paso: Texas Western Press, 1960.

United States Department of Agriculture. *Keeping Livestock Healthy, Yearbook of Agriculture, 1942*. Washington, D.C.: Government Printing Office.

Vestal, Stanley. *Queen of the Cowtowns: Dodge City*. New York: Harper and Brothers, 1952.

Veterinary Journal and Annals of Comparative Pathology. Volume II. New York: W. R. Jenkins, 1880.

Wallis, George A. *Cattle Kings of the Staked Plains*. Second edition. Denver: Sage Books, 1964.

Webb, Walter Prescott. *The Great Plains*. New York: Ginn and Company, 1931.

————, ed. *The Handbook of Texas*. Two volumes. Austin: The Texas State Historical Association, 1952.

Wellman, Paul. *The Trampling Herd*. Garden City, New York: Doubleday and Company, 1951.

White, E. E. *Experiences of a Special Indian Agent*. Norman: University of Oklahoma Press, 1965.

Williams, Amelia, and Eugene C. Barker, eds. *The Writings of Sam Houston*. Eight volumes. Austin: University of Texas Press, 1938-1943.

Williams, Henry T., ed. *The Pacific Tourist and Guide*. New York: Henry T. Williams, 1879.

Wolfenstine, Manfred R. *Manual of Brands and Marks*. Norman: University of Oklahoma Press, 1970.

Wright, Robert. *Dodge City, the Cowboy Capital*. Wichita, Kansas: Wichita Eagle Press, 1913.

Wyoming: A Guide to Its History, Highways and People. New York: Oxford University Press, 1941.

Articles

Adair, W. S. "3 Cows Paid for Clock by Early Texans." *Dallas Morning News*, March 17, 1929.

"A Drive from Texas to North Dakota." *Frontier Times* 3, no. 7 (April, 1926), pp. 1-4.

Alderman, W. B. "Oh, Bury Me Not. . . ." *Texas Parade*, February, 1966, pp. 36-38.

"An Old Time Cattle Inspector." *Frontier Times* 3, no. 6 (March, 1926), pp. 44-45.

"An Old Trail Driver Talks About Early Texas." *Frontier Times* 1, no. 8 (May, 1924) pp. 26-27.

"Arnold Capt, Trail Driver." *Frontier Times* 4, no. 5 (February, 1927), p. 3.

Ashton, John. "Texas Cattle Trade in 1870," *The Cattleman* 38, no. 2 (July, 1951), pp. 74-75.

"A Texas Boy's First Experience on the Trail," *Frontier Times* 5, no. 1 (October, 1927), pp. 10-13.

Athearn, Robert G. "The Denver & Rio Grande Railway, Colorado's 'Baby Road.'" *The Colorado Magazine* 35 (January, 1958), pp. 37-47.

"A Vivid Story of Trail Driving Days." *Frontier Times* 2, no. 10 (July, 1925), pp. 20-23.

"Barbed Wire Has Its Place in History." *Frontier Times* 16, no. 12 (September, 1939), pp. 534-535.

Bernstein, Harry. "Spanish Influence in the United States: Economic Aspects." *The Hispanic American Historical Review* 18, no. 1 (February, 1938), pp. 43-65.

"Bob Glasscock Tells of Cow-Punching Days." *Frontier Times* 4, no. 8 (May, 1927), pp. 41-43.

Carpenter, Clifford D. "The Early Cattle Industry in Missouri." *Missouri Historical Review*, April, 1953, pp. 201-215.

"Chisholm Cattle Trails in Texas Preserved by Writers." *Frontier Times* 7, no. 12 (September, 1930), pp. 554-555.

Conger, Roger N. "Fencing in McLennan County, Texas." *Southwestern Historical Quarterly* 59, no. 2 (October, 1955), pp. 215-221.

————, ed. "Journal of a Saddle Trip Through Central Texas in 1871." by G. C. McGregor. *Southwestern Historical Quarterly* 55, no. 2 (October, 1951), pp. 262-266.

————. "The Waco Suspension Bridge." *Texana* 1, no. 3 (Summer, 1963), pp. 180-224.

Cook, James H. "The Texas Trail." Edited by E. S. Ricker. *Nebraska History Magazine* 26, no. 4 (October-December, 1935), pp. 228-240.

Cranfill, J. B. "The Romance of the Old Texas Cattle Trail." *Frontier Times* 7, no. 2 (November, 1929), pp. 89-96.

Dalton, Frank. "Military Escort for a Trail Herd." *The Cattleman* 31, no. 1 (June, 1944), pp. 13-14.

DeVoto, Bernard. "Horizon Land (I)." *Saturday Review of Literature* 14, no. 25 (October 17, 1936), p. 8.

"Doan's Store on Red River." *Frontier Times* 5, no. 1 (October, 1927), p. 2.

"Dudley Tom." *Frontier Times* 6, no. 6 (March, 1929), pp. 237-240.

Dusenberry, William. "Constitutions of Early and Modern American Stock Growers' Associations." *Southwestern Historical Quarterly* 53, no. 3 (January, 1950), pp. 255-275.

Dykstra, Robert. "Ellsworth, 1869-1875: The Rise and Fall of a Kansas Cowtown." *Kansas Historical Quarterly* 28, no. 2 (Summer, 1961), pp. 161-192.

"Early Texas Cattle Industry." *Frontier Times* 5, no. 12 (September, 1928), pp. 476-481.

"Epic of Cattle Trails." *Frontier Times* 8, no. 8 (May, 1931), p. 338.

"First Cattle Ranch in Texas." *Frontier Times* 13, no. 6 (March, 1936), pp. 304-308.

Frenzny and Tavanier. "The Texas Cattle Trade." *The Cattleman* 17, no. 5 (October, 1930), pp. 24-25 (reprinted from *Harper's Weekly*, May 2, 1874).

Gard, Wayne. "Retracing the Chisholm Trail." *Southwestern Historical Quarterly*, Extra Number, May 1, 1956, pp. 7-24.

Gay, Will. "Open Range Sketches." *Frontier Times* 15, no. 5 (February, 1937), pp. 211-212.

Gillett, James B. "Beef Gathering in '71 Was Thrilling." *Frontier Times* 3, no. 7 (April, 1926), pp. 6-7.

Goodnight, Charles. "Managing a Trail Herd in the Early Days." *Frontier Times* 6, no. 6 (March, 1929), pp. 250-252.

"Goodnight Sets Out Upon 'New Adventure.'" *Frontier Times* 5, no. 1 (October, 1927), pp. 28-30.

Grange, Roger T., Jr. "Fort Robinson, Outpost on the Plains." *Nebraska History Magazine* 39 (September, 1958), pp. 191-240.

Gray, Bob. "Chisholm Trail." *The Texas and Southwestern Horseman*, July, 1965, pp. 33-35, 38-41.

Grove, Fred. "The Chisholm Trail." *Oklahoma Today* 16, no. 4 (Autumn, 1966), pp. 24-27.

Havins, T. R. "Texas Fever." *Southwestern Historical Quarterly* 52, no. 2 (October, 1948), pp. 147-162.

Heard, W. E. "Going Up the Trail." *Frontier Times* 9, no. 9 (June, 1932), pp. 419-424.

Herring, Mrs. Clark, and Grace Smith. "Hide and Tallow Played Important Role in Early Days." *Rockport Pilot*, August 31, 1939.

"Hige Nail, An Early Trail Driver." *Frontier Times* 4, no. 2 (November, 1926), p. 16.

Hill, Dr. Robert T. "Old-Time Texas Roads and Trails." *Dallas Morning News*, n.d., Daughters of the Republic of Texas Library clipping file, San Antonio.

Huffmeyer, Adolph. "A Long Dry Drive on the Cattle Trail." *Frontier Times* 17, no. 8 (May, 1940), pp. 335-336.

"Introducing Barbed Wire in Texas." *Frontier Times* 9, no. 1 (November, 1931), pp. 90-92.

"John S. Chisum." *True West* 2, no. 3 (February, 1964), pp. 66-70.

Jordan, Terry G. "The Origin of Anglo-American Cattle Ranching in Texas: A Documentation of Diffusion from the Lower South." *Economic Geography* 45, no. 1 (January, 1969), pp. 63-87.

————. "Windmills in Texas." *Agricultural History* 37, no. 2 (1961), pp. 80-85.

Kenner, Charles. "The Origins of the 'Goodnight' Trail Reconsidered." *Southwestern Historical Quarterly* 77, no. 3 (January, 1974), pp. 390-394.

"Kept a Diary on Old Cow Trail." *Frontier Times* 5, no. 7 (April, 1928), pp. 317-318.

Kendrick, John B. "The Texas Trail." *Wyoming Tribune*, September 16, 1916.

Leach, Richard E. "John W. Iliff." *The Trail* 4, no. 9 (March, 1912), pp. 14-17.

Lockett, Jerry. "Longhorns Not Long Gone." *Houston Post*, August 15, 1965.

MacKeller, W. M. "Cattle Tick Fever." *The Cattleman* 29, no. 9 (February, 1943), pp. 33, 61-63.

McKee, W. M. "Reminiscences of Old Chisholm Trail." *Frontier Times* 4, no. 9 (June, 1927), p. 7.

"Made Trip to North with Cattle Herds." *Frontier Times* 7, no. 12 (September, 1930), pp. 529-531.

Martin, Tom. "The Livestock Cavalcade of Texas." *Frontier Times* 17, no. 3 (December, 1939), pp. 85-96.

Menn, Alfred E. "Texan's Diary Reports Cattle Drive in 1871." *Kansas City Star*, November 21, 1952.

Milligan, Edward W. "John Wesley Iliff." *Westerners Brand Book* 6 (1950), pp. 44-59.

Moore, W. C. "Chivalry and Romance of the Open Range." *Frontier Times* 17, no. 6 (March, 1940), pp. 235-244.

"More Lore of Cattle Trails." *Frontier Times* 4, no. 1 (October, 1926), pp. 42-43.

Morris, W. J. "Over the Old Chisholm Trail." *Frontier Times* 2, no. 7 (April, 1925), pp. 41-43.

"Mrs. Goodnight's Saddle." *Frontier Times* 4, no. 4 (January, 1927), p. 8.

"Mrs. Holmsby Went Up the Chisholm Trail." *Frontier Times* 4, no. 10 (July, 1927), pp. 28-30.

Myres, Sandra L. "The Spanish Cattle Kingdom in the Province of Texas." *Texana* 4, no. 3 (Fall, 1966), pp. 233-246.

Nunn, Annie. "Over the Goodnight and Loving Trail." *Frontier Times* 2, no. 2 (November, 1924), pp. 4-7.

Otis, James D. "Jesse Chisholm: A Pioneer Who Never Carried a Gun." *Wichita Falls Times* feature magazine, *December* 19, 1965.

Richardson, T. C. "Cattle Trails of Texas." *Texas Geographic Magazine* 1, no. 2 (November, 1937), pp. 16-29.

Rippy, Fred J. "British Investments in Texas Lands and Livestock." *Southwestern Historical Quarterly* 59, no. 3 (January, 1955), pp. 331-341.

Salmon, D. E. "Texas Cattle Fever: Is It a Chimera or a Reality?" *Journal of Comparative Medicine and Surgery* 5, no. 3 (July, 1884), pp. 213-235.

Sanders, A. Collett. "Adventures on the Old Cattle Trail—Brownsville to Dodge City." *Frontier Times* 3, no. 10 (July, 1926), pp. 1-3.

Shelton, Emily Jones. "Lizzie E. Johnson, a Cattle Queen of Texas." *Southwestern Historical Quarterly* 50, no. 3 (January, 1947), pp. 348-360.

Shuffler, R. Henderson. "Bet-a-Million Gates." *Texas Magazine (Houston Post-Houston Chronicle)*, May 29, 1966.

Skaggs, J. M. "The Cowtown's Vest Pocket Economy." *Old West* 5, no. 2 (Winter, 1968), pp. 18-19, 58, 60.

Storey, Brit Allan. "William Jackson Palmer, Promoter." *The Colorado Magazine* 43, no. 1 (Winter, 1966), pp. 42-55.

Taylor, T. U. "An Airplane Trip over the Chisholm Trail." *Frontier Times* 16, no. 11 (August, 1939), pp. 467-471.

———. "A Reunion of the Chisholm Family." *Frontier Times* 16, no. 12 (September, 1939), pp. 508-511.

———. "Granite Monument to Jesse Chisholm." *Frontier Times* 16, no. 10 (July, 1939), pp. 435-439.

———. "Old Red River Station." *Frontier Times* 16, no. 11 (August, 1939), pp. 502-504.

———. "Original Chisholm Trail." *Frontier Times* 6, no. 5 (February, 1929), pp. 195-199.

"T. C. Richardson on the Trail." *Frontier Times* 16, no. 12 (September, 1939), pp. 546-548.

Tennant, H. S. "The Two Cattle Trails." *Chronicles of Oklahoma* 15, no. 1 (March, 1937), pp. 84-122.

"Texas First to Manufacture Ice." *Frontier Times* 7, no. 2 (November, 1929), p. 63.

Thomson, Frank. "The Thoen Stone." *Lawrence County Dakota Territory Centennial, 1861-1961*. Lead, South Dakota: Suton Publishing Company, 1960.

Thorp, Russell. "Early Cowboy Days in Wyoming." *Westerners Brand Book*, October 1, 1945, pp. 2-10.

"Up the Cattle Trail in 1867." *Frontier Times* 8, no. 5 (February, 1931), pp. 194-195.

Vance, James E. "He Wants Longhorns." *The Texas Longhorn* 1, no. 1 (September, 1965) p. 26.

"Veteran Cowboy in Brownsville Seeks to Mark Old Trail." *Frontier Times* 6, no. 9 (June, 1929), p. 355.

Walker, Jimmy. "The Last of the Great Horns." *Texas Parade*, September, 1956, pp. 8-12.

Ward, Hortense Warner. "Hide and Tallow Factories." *The Cattleman* 34, no. 9 (February, 1948), p. 21.

"Was Among First to Go Up the Trail." *Frontier Times* 6, no. 8 (May, 1929), pp. 319-320.

Watson, Elmo Scott. "The Old Chisholm Trail." *Frontier Times* 17, no. 9 (June, 1940), pp. 393-395.

Weinstein, Robert A. and Russell E. Belous. "Indian Portraits: Fort Sill, 1869." *The American West* 3, no. 1 (Winter, 1966), pp. 55-62.

White, Grace Miller. "Oliver Loving, the First Trail Driver." *Frontier Times* 19, no. 7 (April, 1942), pp. 269-276.

White, Lynn, Jr. "The Legacy of the Middle Ages in the American Wild West." *The American West* 2, no. 4 (Fall, 1965), pp. 73-95.

Wilson, Mrs. Augustus. Report on 1884 National Cattlemen's Convention in St. Louis, *Parson's Memorial and Historical Magazine*. Daughters of the Republic of Texas Library clipping file, San Antonio.

Wilson, Glenn O. "Red River Station—An Address." *Southwestern Historical Quarterly* 60, no. 1 (July, 1956), pp. 76-79.

Woolford, Sam. "Zip Along Now, Little Dogie!" *San Antonio Express*, July 24, 1966.

Woolrich, W. R. "Mechanical Refrigeration—Its American Birthright." *Refrigerating Engineering* 53, no. 3 (March, 1947), and 53, no. 4 (April, 1947), pp. 196 ff. and pp. 304 ff.

Booklets, Pamphlets, Etc.

Baughman, J. L. *A History of the Meat Packing Industry at Fulton, Texas.* Pamphlet printed for Arthur Bracht, Rockport, Texas, n.d.

Brooks, Chester L. and Ray H. Mattison. *Theodore Roosevelt and the Dakota Badlands.* Booklet. Washington, D.C.: National Park Service, 1958.

"Bull Durham Fact Sheet." New York: American Tobacco Company, n.d.

Central Colorado Improvement Company, First Annual Directors Report, December 31, 1872.

Chateau de Mores. State Historical Society of North Dakota, n.d.

Dedication of the Cyrus K. Holliday Plaque. Topeka, Kansas: Santa Fe Station, April 3, 1949.

Directions for Cooking Borden's Meat Biscuit, or the Extract of Beef Dried in Flour. New York: D. Fanshaw (printer), 1855.

"Early Nebraska History along the Canals and Lakes of the Central Nebraska Public Power and Irrigation District." Fact sheet, n.d.

Fanning, Leonard M. *Gail Borden, Father of the Modern Dairy Industry.* New York: Mercer Publishing Company, 1956.

Fielder, Mildred. "Lawrence County," *Lawrence County Dakota Territory Centennial, 1861-1961.* Lead, South Dakota: Suton Publishing Company, 1960.

Gering, John L. "Deadwood," *Lawrence County Dakota Territorial Centennial, 1861-1961.* Lead, South Dakota: Suton Publishing Company, 1960.

Haley, J. Evetts. *F. Reaugh: Man and Artist.* El Paso: Carl Hertzog, 1960.

Henderson, J. S., ed. *100 Years in Montague County, Texas.* Saint Jo, Texas: PTA Printers, 1958.

Long, R. M. *Historic Wichita Cow Town.* Wichita, Kansas: Historic Wichita, Inc., n.d.

Makemson, W. K. *Historical Sketch of First Settlement and Organization of Williamson County.* Georgetown, Texas: Sun Print, 1904.

Meat for America's Millions. Atchison, Topeka & Santa Fe Railway Co., 1940.

Missouri Pacific Lines: The First 112 Years. Company pamphlet, 1963.

Myres, Sandra L. *The Ranch in Spanish Texas, 1691-1800.* Social Science Series, no. 2. El Paso: Texas Western Press, 1969.

New Mexico. *Historical Markers in New Mexico.* Santa Fe: New Mexico State Highway Commission, 1964.

Ogallala Chamber of Commerce Fact Sheet. n.d.

"Old Fort Supply" (Oklahoma). Western State Hospital Fact Sheet.

Old Trail Drivers of Texas Program, 1931.

Proceedings of the First National Convention of Cattlemen and of the First Annual Meeting of the National Cattle and Horse Growers Association of the United States. St. Louis, Missouri: R. P. Studley & Co. (printers and binders), 1884.

Renner, Frederic G. *Charles M. Russell: Paintings, Drawings, and Sculpture in the Amon G. Carter Collection. A descriptive catalogue.* (Brochure on book). Austin: University of Texas Press, 1966.

Santa Fe Railroad's Cyrus K. Holliday. Dedication of the Cyrus K. Holliday Plaque. Topeka: Santa Fe Station, 1949.

Schmidt, Hubert. *Eighty Years of Veterinary Medicine at the Agricultural and Mechanical College of Texas.* College Station: Texas A and M College Archives, 1958.

Spindler, Will H. *Tragedy Strikes at Wounded Knee.* Gordon, Nebraska: Gordon Journal Publishing Company, 1955.

Spring, Agnes Wright. *70 Years Cow Country.* Cheyenne: Wyoming Stock Growers Association, 1942.

————. *The First National Bank of Denver: the Formative Years, 1860-1865.* Bank publication.

Texas Live Stock Association Program, January 15, 1885.

Texas Longhorn Centennial Booklet. San Antonio: Texas Longhorn Breeders Association of America, 1966.

United States Department of the Interior, National Park Service. *Theodore Roosevelt National Memorial Park, North Dakota.* Washington, D.C.: Government Printing Office, 1965.

Utley, Robert M. *Fort Union.* National Park Service Historical Handbook, Series 35. Washington, D.C.: Government Printing Office, 1962.

"Western State Hospital on the Site of old Fort Supply." Fact sheet, n.d.

Whittenburg, Clarice. *Wyoming, Prelude to Statehood.* Cheyenne: Wyoming Travel Commission and Wyoming State Department of Education, 1967.

Wilson, Glenn O. "The Texas County of Trails." *100 Years in Montague County, Texas.* Saint Jo, Texas: PTA Printers, 1958.

Wright, Muriel H., and George H. Shirk. *Mark of*

Heritage. Oklahoma City: Oklahoma Historical Society, 1958.

Interviews and Correspondence

Abbott, Carroll. Kerrville, Texas. *Texas Longhorn* publisher.

Anderson, Dillon. Houston, Texas. Attorney-author.

Ankerson, Mrs. J. Fort Worth, Texas. Secretary of Stockyard Fertilizers Company, 1966.

Armstrong, Pat. San Antonio, Texas. Secretary of Texas Longhorn Breeders Association of America, 1966.

Aston, Mrs. Bert. Roswell, New Mexico. Owner of John Chisum's South Springs Ranch in 1966.

Bailey, Mrs. R. Coleman, Texas. Owner of Coleman County's oldest house, 1966.

Baldridge, Mrs. Lillian Weems. Harlingen, Texas. Writer and history teacher.

Bass, Henry B. Enid, Oklahoma. Historian.

Baughman, J. L. Rockport, Texas. Writer-historian.

Bennet, Val. Gonzales, Texas. Lifelong resident.

Berg, Don. Trinidad, Colorado. Owner of Dick Wootton house, 1965.

Bergquist, Mrs. Betty. Abilene, Texas. Oliver Loving descendant.

Bevinetto, Tony. Cheyenne, Wyoming. Public information director, Wyoming Travel Commission, 1965.

Bobbitt, Robert Lee. San Antonio, Texas. Member, Old Trail Drivers of Texas.

Booth, Mrs. Ross. Gonzales, Texas. Chairman, Gonzales County Historical Survey Committee.

Bracht, Arthur. Fulton and Rockport, Texas. Owner of hide-and-tallow factory painting.

Brown, Mrs. Ray Hyer. Georgetown, Texas. Long-time resident.

Burk, Bill. Chicago, Illinois. Public relations manager, Atchison, Topeka and Santa Fe Railway System, 1965.

Carter, Al. Chicago, Illinois. Trail researcher.

Cassell, L. J. Dallas, Texas. Special representative, Atchison, Topeka and Santa Fe Railway System.

Champion, A. A. Brownsville, Texas. Ranchman-historian.

Clements, William Bishop. Harlingen, Texas. Writer.

Cloud, James. Oklahoma City, Oklahoma. Engineer-historian.

Coker, Mrs. Willie Belle. Austin, Texas. Texana Department, The University of Texas at Austin, 1972.

Colburn, Mrs. Helen. Austin, Texas. Writer.

Conger, Roger. Waco, Texas. Author-historian.

Conner, John E. Kingsville, Texas. Retired history professor, Texas A and I College.

Cook, Mrs. Louise. Oklahoma City, Oklahoma. Newspaper librarian, Oklahoma Historical Society.

Cotten, Fred R. Weatherford, Texas. Former president, Texas State Historical Association.

Cox, Ben F. Coleman, Texas. Member, Coleman County Historical Survey Committee, 1966.

Cring, M. R. St. Louis, Missouri. Vice president, Missouri-Kansas-Texas Railroad Company.

Crouch, Mrs. John. Fredericksburg, Texas. Board member, Pioneer Museum.

Cypher, John A., Jr. Kingsville, Texas. King Ranch public relations director.

Dabney, Taylor. Vernon, Texas. Ranchman-car dealer.

Dameron, Mrs. J. L. Crane, Texas. Long-time resident.

Davis, Jim. Denver, Colorado. Western Collection, Denver Public Library.

Day, James. El Paso, Texas. Former archivist, Texas State Library and Archives, Austin, Texas.

Dow, Edwin. Fort Worth, Texas. Longhorn breeder.

Ekstrom, Mrs. Laura. Denver, Colorado. Research librarian, Historical Society of Colorado Reference Library.

Elmshaeuser, Emil. Ogallala, Nebraska. Director, Trails Museum.

England, Ken. Round Rock and Austin, Texas. Minister-historian.

Fincher, T. P. Fort Griffin, Texas. Lifelong resident.

Fox, Mary Elizabeth. Georgetown, Texas. Professor, Southwestern University.

French, Glen. Abilene, Kansas. Lifelong resident.

Gambrell, Herbert. Dallas, Texas. Historical director, Dallas Historical Society.

Gard, Wayne. Dallas, Texas. Author; former president, Texas State Historical Association.

Girard, Rosell. Austin, Texas. Bureau of Economic Geology.

Goodrich, Harvard. Abilene, Kansas. Manager, Old Abilene Town, 1966.

Grimes, Roy. Victoria, Texas. Newsman-historian.

Grimm, Mrs. Joe. Alice, Texas. Historian.

Haley, J. Evetts. Canyon, Texas. Author-historian.

Halverson, Mrs. Katherine. Cheyenne, Wyoming. Chief, historical division, Wyoming State Archives and Historical Department.

Hammer, Harry E. St. Louis, Missouri. Assistant to the president, Missouri Pacific Lines.

Hansen. Mrs. Peter. Ogallala. Nebraska. Secretary, Chamber of Commerce.

Hastings, Homer. Fort Union, New Mexico. Superintendent, Fort Union National Monument.

Hayes, Mrs. Laura. Cheyenne. Wyoming. Secretary, historical division, Wyoming State Archives and History Department.

Henderson. Mr. and Mrs. Paul. Bridgeport, Nebraska. Historians.

Henrichs. George. Dodge City. Kansas. Manager, Boot Hill and Historic Front Street, 1966.

Herring, Mrs. Charles. Austin, Texas. Owner of an A. H. Pierce bill of sale.

Hertner. Henry. Amarillo. Texas. Chairman, Potter County Historical Survey Committee. 1966.

Hicks. Raymond. Bandera. Texas. Ranchman.

Hightower. Jack. Vernon, Texas. State senator.

Hogarth, Robert. Deadwood, South Dakota. Lifelong resident.

Homsher, Lola. Cheyenne, Wyoming. History department director, Wyoming State Archives and History Department.

Hudson. Mrs. Ernest. Dallas. Texas. Owner of letter from trail driver George T. McGehee.

Hudspeth. Phil K. Pueblo. Colorado. Owner of Rock Cañon Ranch. developed by Charles Goodnight.

Huson. Hobart. Refugio. Texas. Attorney-author-historian.

Inselman, Jake. San Antonio. Texas. City secretary, 1966.

Irving, Ben. Pine Ridge, South Dakota. Long tenure with Indian Service Extension Department.

Isaacks, Mrs. Sam. Carlsbad, Texas. Niece of trail driver James E. Hargis.

James, Judge Otis. Waurika. Oklahoma. Writer-historian.

Jameson, Henry B. Abilene. Kansas. President-editor, *Reflector-Chronicle*; past president, Kansas Historical Society.

Johnson, Bill. Trinidad, Colorado. Professor, Trinidad Junior College.

Johnston, Mrs. Frances. Goliad, Texas. Former curator. Goliad State Park Museum.

Johnston. Mrs. James J. Denver, Colorado. Librarian.

Jones, Robert. Boulder. Colorado. Former ranchman. acquaintance of Charles Goodnight.

Jordan, Mrs. Ben T. Victoria, Texas. Former chairman, Victoria County Historical Survey Committee.

Jordan, R. G. San Antonio, Texas. Former farm and ranch editor, *San Antonio Express*.

Kayser. Ray C. Kermit. Texas. President. Permian Historical Society. 1967-1968.

Kear. V. A. Colby. Kansas. Developer of "Sod Town."

Kelley, Dayton. Brenham. Texas. Director, Washington-on-the-Brazos Museum, 1973.

Kelsey, Harry. Michigan. Former Colorado state historian.

Kielman, Chester. Austin, Texas. Librarian-archivist. Barker Texas History Center, The University of Texas at Austin.

Kilgore. D. E. Clarkwood. Texas. Author-historian.

Laric. Paul H. New York, New York. Public information manager. American Tobacco Company.

Leyendecker, Liston. Denver, Colorado. Assistant editor, *The Colorado Magazine*. 1966.

Long, Walter E. Austin. Texas. Author-historian.

Lorance. Tom. Vernon. Texas. Long-time Waggoner Ranch cowboy.

Lowery. Mrs. Hugh B. Victoria, Texas. Member of pioneer ranch family.

McCaffree. Robert. Sterling, Colorado. Historian.

McCallum. Henry D. and Frances T. Tyler, Texas. Authors and barbed wire collectors.

McCarty, H. A. Vernon. Texas. Waggoner Ranch supply officer.

McClure, Boone. Canyon. Texas. Director, Panhandle-Plains Museum.

McCombs, Holland. Dallas, Texas. Writer-historian.

McCracken. Joe H.. III. Dallas, Texas. Oliver Loving descendant.

McDowell. Catherine. San Antonio, Texas. Librarian, Daughters of the Republic of Texas Library.

McKenna, Mrs. Gerald. Harlingen, Texas. Librarian, Lon C. Hill Memorial Library.

McNeel, Mrs. Jess. San Antonio, Texas. Relative of trail driver John James.

Mauzy. Mrs. Eleanor. Santa Fe, New Mexico. New Mexico State Highway Commission.

Meador. Joe. Lubbock, Texas. Former manager, Vernon Chamber of Commerce.

Mims, Elton T. Water Valley, Texas. Ranchman-historian.

Mitchell, Arthur R. Trinidad, Colorado. Director, Baca House Museum, 1965.

Montgomery, Jack. Weimar, Texas. Postmaster-historian.

Mullen. Frances. Ellsworth, Kansas. Curator, Ellsworth Museum.

Munz, Arthur. Moody. Texas. Ranchman near Stampede Gully.

Munz. Margaret. Moody, Texas. Teacher.

Murray, Robert A. Fort Laramie, Wyoming. Ranger-historian, Fort Laramie National Monument.

Norris, Frank. Las Vegas, New Mexico. Manager, Las Vegas Chamber of Commerce, 1965.

O'Connell, Mrs. Robert. Sterling, Colorado. Life-long resident.

O'Connell, Willis. Miles City, Montana. Curator, Range Riders Museum, 1965.

O'Connor, Dennis. Refugio, Texas. Ranchman.

O'Connor, Mrs. Thomas, Sr. Refugio and Victoria, Texas. Author-historian.

O'Dea, John. Denver, Colorado. Vice president, Denver Union Stockyards.

Osborne, Ray. Austin, Texas. Public relations director, Texas Railroad Association.

Palmer, Mrs. Lee. Goodnight, Texas. Occupant of former Goodnight ranch home.

Patterson, S. M. Cuero, Texas. Manager, Cuero Chamber of Commerce, 1966.

Peck, Ed. Oklahoma City, Oklahoma. Curator of exhibits, Oklahoma Historical Society.

Peeler, Graves. Pleasanton, Texas. Ranchman, Longhorn breeder.

Perenyi, Mrs. Etienne. Denver, Colorado. Owner of castle built by Walter Baron von Richthofen.

Perine, Tom. Buffalo Gap, Texas. Ranchman.

Perrigone, Nell. Deadwood, South Dakota. Secretary, Deadwood Chamber of Commerce, 1966.

Perry, Carmen. San Antonio, Texas. Former archivist, St. Mary's University.

Perryman, Mrs. Sid. Seymour, Texas. Historian and ranch woman.

Pettus, Mrs. William Wheeler. Goliad, Texas. Ranchwife.

Phelps, Mrs. D. L. Victoria, Texas. Wife of trail driver.

Pinckney, Pauline. Austin, Texas. Author-historian.

Prosser, Mrs. Dean, Jr. Cheyenne, Wyoming. Wife of Wyoming Stock Growers Association secretary and ranchman on former J. W. Iliff range.

Raber, Mrs. Jessie M. Littleton, Colorado. Daughter of trail driver Jeff Dillard.

Ragsdale, Mary. Big Spring, Texas. Book collector.

Randow, E. J. Rockport, Texas. Principal, Aransas County Junior High School.

Redfield, Sidney C. Roswell, New Mexico. Artist-historian.

Richardson, Bob. Golden, Colorado. Director, Colorado Railroad Museum.

Rist, Martin. Denver, Colorado. Librarian, Iliff School of Theology.

Roach, Mariana. Dallas, Texas. Oliver Loving descendant.

Rose, Arthur. Fort Dodge, Kansas. Superintendent, Kansas Soldiers' Home (formerly Fort Dodge).

Rosebrock, W. H. Oakville, Texas. Long-time resident.

Ross, Mrs. Bertha Doan. Vernon, Texas. Resident of Doan's Store and daughter of Corwin Doan.

Ross, Charles P. Vernon, Texas. Retired newspaperman.

Rung, A. M. Chicago, Illinois. Pubic relations director, Chicago, Burlington and Quincy Railroad.

Ruth, Kent. Geary, Oklahoma. Author-historian.

Sandhop, Fred. Victoria, Texas. Chairman, Victoria County Historical Survey Committee, 1965.

Sauer, Mr. and Mrs. Oswald. La Coste, Texas. Longhorn breeders.

Saul, Mrs. John. Bandera, Texas. Daughter of J. Marvin Hunter, editor of *The Trail Drivers of Texas*.

Saunders, T. B., III. Fort Worth, Texas. Grand nephew of George W. Saunders, founder of the Old Trail Drivers Association.

Schafer, Edwin C. Omaha, Nebraska. Public relations director, Union Pacific Railroad.

Schreiner, Charles, III. Mountain Home, Texas. Ranchman and founder of Texas Longhorn Breeders Association of America.

Seale, William. Washington, D.C. Author-historian; former professor, Lamar University, Beaumont, Texas.

Shaw, Mrs. Wiley Joe. Austin, Texas. Oliver Loving descendant.

Shay, William J. Fort Laramie, Wyoming. Ranger at Fort Laramie National Monument.

Shinkle, J. D. Roswell, New Mexico. Former school superintendent.

Shrader, C. A. (Heck). Cache, Oklahoma. Inspector, Longhorn Breeders Association, 1966.

Shuffler, R. Henderson, San Antonio, Texas. Director, Institute of Texan Cultures.

Simon, Jim. Cheyenne, Wyoming. Official state photographer, 1965.

Spindler, Will. Gordon, Nebraska. Author; former teacher at Pine Ridge Indian Reservation.

Spoon, J. D. Terral, Oklahoma. Long-time resident.

Stiles, Dowell. Caldwell, Kansas. Editor, *Caldwell Messenger*.

Stone, Judge Sam V. Georgetown, Texas. Chairman, Williamson County Historical Survey Committee, 1966.

Stroder, Charles. Crane, Texas. Teacher-historian.

Stubbs, Mrs. Johnnie. Fort Worth, Texas. Owner of old Tannahill Stage Station.

Taylor, Carl. Trinidad, Colorado. Retired cowman.

Taylor, Ralph C. Pueblo, Colorado. Former president, Historical Society of Colorado.

Teel, Mrs. Lucille. Veterinary librarian, Texas A and M University.

TenEyke, Mrs. James. Denver, Colorado. Realtor.

Thomas, Jim. Amarillo, Texas. Writer-photographer.

Thorne, Sonja. Laramie, Wyoming. Assistant, Western Research Center, University of Wyoming.

Traylor, Mrs. Gene. Point Comfort, Texas. Husband's ancestors drove Chisholm Trail.

Turk, R. D. Bryan, Texas. Former head, Department of Veterinary Parasitology, Texas A and M University.

Turner, Elvie, Jr. Laredo, Texas. Manager of exotic animals, John Mecom Ranch, 1966.

Valine, Delmar E., Sr. East St. Louis, Illinois. Executive secretary, National Museum of Transport.

Vance, James E. Fort Worth, Texas. *Fort Worth Star-Telegram* agricultural writer.

Vivier, P. J., Jr. Brownsville, Texas. Life-long resident and historian.

Weddle, Robert S. Austin, Texas. Author-historian.

Weisiger, Sidney. Victoria, Texas. Former chairman, Victoria County Historical Survey Committee.

Whittenburg, Clarice. Laramie, Wyoming. Author-historian; retired professor, University of Wyoming.

Wilkinson, Fred. Crane, Texas. Crane County agent, 1966.

Williams, J. W. Wichita Falls, Texas. Author-historian.

Williams, Kemper, Sr. Victoria, Texas. Former president, Sons of the Republic of Texas.

Wilson, Glenn O. Nocona, Texas. Attorney-writer-historian.

Wint, George. Darlington, Oklahoma. Superintendent, Oklahoma State Game Farm (site of Cheyenne-Arapaho Agency).

Wood, Corinne. Victoria, Texas. Granddaughter of Mrs. Margaret Heffernan Borland.

Yell, Mr. and Mrs. Curtis B. Oran, Texas.

Index

Page numbers for photograph captions are in italics

formation of, 144; losses of, 158; profits of, 168

Maury, D. A.: 75

Maxwell and Morris: 95

Meat Biscuit: 10–11

Medora, Dakota Territory: cattle starve in, 162; construction of, 146; packing plant in, *148*; Roosevelt near, 149

Mennonites: 90

Mescalero Apache Indians: 25

mesta: defined, 6

Methodist Church: *67*, 185

Mexicans: at Bosque Grande, 26; as cowboys, 4

Mexican War: 11

Mexico: cattle ticks from, 167; railroad to, 145; Western Trail from, 95

Middle Concho River: 21

Miles City, Montana: as cattle market, 136; museum in, 188; ranches around, 126; Texas Trail to, 126

Miles, Nelson: home of, *137*

Miller, James F.: 158

Millett. *See* Ellison, Dewees, Millett, and Mabry

Millett and Mabry: 93

Mineral Wells, Texas: 20, 183

miners: in Black Hills, 92, 95; cattle demanded by, 54, 95

Minnesota: 149

Mission Espíritu Santo: 6, 7

Mission Rosario: 6

missions: cattle at, 37; as origin of cattle industry, 6, 7

Missouri: cattle drives to, 12, 14; Russell from, 142; Mason Brothers from, 91; quarantines in, 14, 55; Shawnee Trail to, 42; Texas fever in, 14

Missouri-Kansas-Texas Railway: 70

Missouri Pacific Railroad. *See* International Railroad Company

Missouri River: 124, *138*

Missouri River, Fort Scott, and Gulf Railroad: 70

Mizpah Creek: 126

Moen. *See* Washburn and Moen

Montague County, Texas: 42

Montana: and cattle industry, 3, 58, 150, 156; Custer in, 95; Indian agencies in, 122; Miles home in, *137*; painters in, 142; Powder River in, *135*; Russell on, 138; Simpson's ranch in, 164; snows in, *131*; in stock growers' association, 149, 153; Texas Trail through, 122, 126; vigilance committees in, 153; XIT holdings in, 161

Monument Hill: 50

Monument Rocks: *45*

Moorcroft, Wyoming: 126

Morecamp, Arthur: 118

Mormon Trail: *130*

Morris. *See* Maxwell and Morris

Motley County, Texas: 144

Mueller, John: home of, 186, *117*

Munday, Seymour: 103

"murrain." *See* Texas fever

Murray, Thomas P.: 19

mustangs: in 1848, 11–12; protection of, 169.

Nail, Hige: 95

National Cattle Trail: advocates of, 154, 155, 158; debates on, 154–157; impediments to, 152; resolution for, 157; support for, 154, 158

Navajo Indians: 25

Nebraska: cattle industry in, 3, 150, 164; Indian removal from, 55; quarantines in, 55, 158; in stock growers' association, 153; railroad through, 66; spring in, *121*

Neches River: 10

Negroes: as cowboys, 4

Neimmela Ranch: 149

Nevada: 3

New Mexico: cattle industry in, 3, 142, 153; Chisum in, 158; Lincoln County War in, 88; military in, 19; ranches in, 25; Scottish investment in, 141; trails through, 19, 24–33 *passim*, 58, 60, 179

New Mexico Stock Grower: 162

New Orleans, Louisiana: beef shipped to, 71, 75; cattle drives to, 9, 11, 16, 21; in 1862, 16

New Orleans Picayune: 80

Newton, Kansas: cattle trade in, 70, 75, 77

New York, New York: and cattle growers' convention, 156; Eastman from, 126; King from, 4; Longhorn cattle in, 14; meat shipped to, 75; Remington from, 142; Roosevelt from, 149

Ninnescah River: 51

Niobrara Cattle Company: 164

North Canadian River: 50

North Concho River: 21

North Dakota: buffalo in, *151*; cattle industry in, 3

Northern Pacific Railroad: 90, 146

North Platte River: *129*; and cattle trails, 118, 124, 126; described, 129; snows along, *131*

Nueces River, *97*; Western Trail near, 97

Oakville, Texas: 97

Ogallala, Nebraska: Boot Hill in, *122*; businesses in, 122; and cattle drives, 118, 124, 158; landscape near, *123*; name of, 118; railroad to, 118; spring near, 187

Ohio: 11, 19

Oklahoma: 4, 111, 158. *See also* Indian Territory

Oklahoma City, Oklahoma: Chisholm Trail near, 50; Cowboy Hall of Fame in, 168–169

Old Trail Drivers of Texas: 16, 53

Old Woman Creek: 126

Oregon Trail: *130, 132*

Osage Indians: 69–70

OX Ranch: 149

Pacific Coast: 12, 33

packing industry: 10

packing plants: activities of, 73; Jones and Company, 10; in Kansas City, 55; in Rockport, Texas, 73; Stabler's, 73

Palo Duro Canyon: *119*; Goodnight's cabin in, 186; JA Ranch in, 118, 119

Palo Pinto, Texas: 20

Panhandle-Plains Museum: 19, 185, *161*

Panic of 1873: and cattle industry, 85, 95; causes of, 85, 88; and hide-and-tallow trade, 85; and railroads, 144, 145; victims of, 118

Panther Creek, *43*

Patterson, James: as cattle contractor, 25; trail opened by, 19

Patterson, Tom: 25

Pecos River: 20, *24*

Pecos Valley: *26*

Peeler, Graves: 178, 183

Pegleg Station, Texas: 97

Pender, Sir John: 149

Pennsylvania: Brisbin from, 142; cattle diseases in, 12; Lytle from, 6; Kenedy from, 4–6; ranch based in, 149

Phantom Hill: 23

Pierce, Abel Head (Shanghai): activities of, 16, 155; breeding practices of, 83; described, 16, 17; and hide-and-tallow trade, 73; quoted, 2; ranch house of, 188; and Santa Fe Railroad, 77; statue of, *17*

Pike's Peak: 31

Pine Bluffs, Wyoming: *131*; and cattle trails, 124, 126, 158

Pine Ridge Agency: church at, *128*. *See also* Red Cloud Agency

Pine Ridge Reservation: 187

Pine Ridge, South Dakota: *124*

Piper, Edward: 11

Plains: cattle trails across, 3; contractors on, 33; development of, 95, 139; and fencing, 85–88; foreign investment in, 126, 141; frontier activities on, 36; immigration to, 88–90; and Indian affairs, 65, 95; international interest in, 126; large-scale ranching on, 56; livestock starve on, 162; Longhorns on, 149–150; near Abilene, 51; settlement of, 55; Texas fever on, 150; windmills on, 88, 166

Platte River: 57; cattle drives near, 58, 70

Polk, M. B.: house of: *100*

Pond Creek: 48, 77

Ponting, Tom Candy: 14, 91

Poole. *See* Allen and Poole

Pope's Crossing: 24

Potter County Historical Park: *87*

Potter, Jack: 146

Powder River: *135*; 126

Powder River Cattle Company: 162

Powder River Valley: *136*

Prairie Cattle Company: demise of, 168; 1883 profits of, 146; investments by, 141; losses of, 158

Promontory Point, Utah: 70

TRAILING THE LONGHORNS

THE SIXTH BOOK PRODUCED BY MADRONA PRESS
HAS BEEN PRINTED ON WARREN'S PATINA
COATED MATTE.
TYPE USED FOR TEXT IS
ELEVEN-POINT WAVERLEY WITH ONE-POINT LEADING
SET ON INTERTYPE BY G&S TYPESETTERS, AUSTIN.
PRINTING BY OFFSET LITHOGRAPHY
WAS DONE BY THE WHITLEY COMPANY OF AUSTIN,
BINDING BY CUSTOM BOOKBINDERY OF AUSTIN.
MAPS BY JOSÉ CISNEROS
DESIGN BY WARD RITCHIE

MADRONA PRESS, INC.
BOX 3750
AUSTIN, TEXAS 78764